Total Customer Service

Also by William H. Davidow

MARKETING HIGH TECHNOLOGY

Total Customer Service

The Ultimate Weapon

WILLIAM H. DAVIDOW

and

BRO UTTAL

1817

HARPER & ROW PUBLISHERS, NEW YORK
GRAND RAPIDS, PHILADELPHIA, ST. LOUIS, SAN FRANCISCO
LONDON, SINGAPORE, SYDNEY, TOKYO, TORONTO

FIRST EDITION

Designer: Barbara DuPree Knowles

LIBRARY OF CONGRESS CATALOGING-IN-PUBLICATION DATA

Davidow, William H.
    Total customer service : the ultimate weapon / by
William H. Davidow and Bro Uttal. — 1st ed.
    p.   cm.
    ISBN 0–06–016180–9
    1. Customer service. I. Uttal, Bro. II. Title.
    HF5415.5.D38   1989
    658.8′12—dc20   89–45033

89 90 91 92 93 CC/HC 10 9 8 7 6 5 4 3 2 1

To my father,
LEONARD S. DAVIDOW,
who taught me that
helping people do their best
is the most satisfying goal
one can pursue.

For my wife,
KATHI PATON UTTAL,
who cheered me on
during months of
research, analysis, and
writing and never doubted
the value of the work.

Contents

_____

Acknowledgments

———

We received generous help from a far greater number of friends, associates, and sources than we can name. At the risk of offending some of them by omission, we would like to thank David Garvin, Chris Hart, Ted Levitt, and Earl Sasser of Harvard Business School for their thoughts on customer service. Several distinguished consultants—Osvald Bjelland, Roland Dumas, George Glaser, John Goodman, Christopher Lovelock, Dick Munn, and Harvey Shycon—also shared their thinking and research with us. Many of the people and companies that appear in these pages—and almost all of those we use as case studies to anchor chapters 3 through 8—gave unstintingly and repeatedly of their time. In addition we are grateful to the editors of *Fortune* magazine. After learning that we were writing this book, they encouraged Bro to produce a feature story on customer service, which appeared in the December 7, 1987 issue of *Fortune*.

Turning our interest in customer service into a book would have been impossible without assistance from a galaxy of collaborators. Our able, persistent reporter/researchers—Julia Martin, Cinda Siler, Lisa Sinclair Smith, Heather Wallace, and, especially, Patty de Llosa—performed much of the fieldwork. Patty also took on the heavy responsibility of checking facts and footnotes and keeping us generally honest; her abilities and dedication never flagged. Stefan Jovanovich and Peter Petre, outstanding business writers, were kind enough to peruse our early manuscripts; their suggestions proved invaluable. Mike Malone also made helpful suggestions. Our original editor, Harriet Rubin, believed in the book strongly enough to bring on board the rest of Harper & Row; Arthur Samuelson, our working editor, did the heavy lifting. We owe Arthur a special debt for his heroic efforts to transform a wayward manuscript into a structured book. Roland Wolfram of McKinsey & Co. assisted in ways that only he should describe. Linda Gray, Bill Davidow's administrative assistant, cheerfully endured the trials of mediating between bicoastal authors (and mastered modems in the process). Finally, thanks to Kathi Paton, our Argus-eyed literary agent, who kept our best interests at heart, protected us from annoying but vital business details—and managed to survive the storm of composition.

The virtues of this book flow largely from others who were kind enough to help; the vices are our own.

Introduction

———

This book grew out of a chance meeting at a hotel in San Francisco. One of the local investment banking firms, a specialist in backing new issues of stock for high-technology companies, was holding its annual conference. It was a frenetic bazaar where entrepreneurs and financiers looked each other over and sniffed out new deals. The presentations shared a common theme: clever exploitation of the latest technology would be a sure formula for success. Everything depended on R&D, product development, manufacturing, marketing, and finance—the business functions needed to exploit a technological edge. With those elements in place, the entrepreneurs crowed, their companies would have unassailable competitive advantages.

But something was missing. The speakers were well aware of the importance of staying close to the customer. Yet not one of them dealt seriously with customer service. At best, they mentioned service operations as an afterthought; more often they simply ignored service in their conviction that pure technology was all that really mattered.

At least two members of the audience noticed the lapse. Bill Davidow had recently left Intel, the world's leading maker of microprocessors, to co-found Mohr, Davidow Ventures, a venture capital partnership. To him, razzle-dazzle technology was simply a prerequisite for success. Companies that possessed it would go nowhere unless they also possessed deep insight about all of their customers' needs, including service.

The other skeptic was Bro Uttal, chief of *Fortune* magazine's West Coast bureau in Menlo Park, California, and author of scores of articles about technology management. His specialty was "explaining how you make money out of technology," and he knew that building close relationships with customers was essential. Yet few of the managers he had been listening to seemed to realize that.

As Bro was calling his office from a booth in the hotel's lofty lobby, Bill walked by and waved hello. The two fell into conversation and quickly zeroed in on the perplexing lack of attention paid to customer service. And soon they discovered a mutual interest that became the foundation for *Total Customer Service.*

Bill's concern with customer service was rooted in his experience at Intel. He had joined the company in 1973 in order to make Intel king of the emerging market for the microprocessor, the famous "computer on a chip." Bill realized the microprocessor business would be radically different from what his competitors were used to. In the semiconductor industry, success came from making very large quantities of high-performance chips at ever lower cost. The key skills were clever design of the chips and the production process, as well as tight control of manufacturing. Not so in microprocessors. Because micros had to be programmed, just like computers, customers would need a lot more help, from software and hardware tools for creating programs to intensive training in programming skills. The name of the game in micros would be customer service, and Bill's strategy for making Intel's micro take off was to provide a level of service never before seen in the semiconductor industry.

One key was to sell a new instrument that could be used for programming Intel's micro, but not the micros made by competitors. Intel called it a microprocessor development system; customers knew it as the "blue box"; today it looks like a primitive personal computer. At first, the "blue box" strategy worked superbly. Customers were so enthusiastic about the devices that within a few years Intel had installed nearly a quarter billion dollars worth, and microprocessor sales had exploded.

Then the sky fell in. The original blue boxes were engineering triumphs, so reliable that Intel never had to learn how to fix them. But they were slow and cumbersome to use. So Bill launched the Series II, exactly the system customers said they wanted.

Within days frustrated customers started clogging Intel's phone lines. The operating manuals for the Series II were so inaccurate that if a customer followed the instructions precisely, the Series II was guaranteed not to work. The new blue box was also plagued by intermittent failures—the kind that come and go unpredictably—and it was vulnerable to static electricity. When a customer touched the Series II, he could electrocute it, eliminating all the programming work stored temporarily in the system.

Thanks to the Series II, Intel went into a downward spiral. Enraged customers spread the bad word. Competitors picked it up, then the press, and finally Intel's employees. The sales force decided to stop selling problems, and Series II revenues collapsed. Intel's service engineers began to give up on fixing the Series II. Soon the company started losing microprocessor orders to its competitors.

Bill's problem was twofold: a product poorly designed for reliability and serviceability, and a near-total lack of service infrastructure for repairing the product. For all the attention he had paid to supporting microprocessors, he had overlooked the need to support blue boxes.

A complete redesign of the Series II produced a more reliable product and one far easier to fix. Developing a system to service the boxes took longer and cost more: it meant producing diagnostic equipment and maintenance manuals, hiring and training a professional service force, stocking depots with more reliable spare parts, and setting up measurement systems to keep track of service performance. Eventually, sales of blue boxes and microprocessors recovered. Yet thanks to Bill's service snafu, Intel permanently lost some of its lead in the microprocessor business.

*   *   *

Bro became concerned with customer service after writing one of his first articles for *Fortune,* an exhaustive profile of Burroughs Corp. In the 1970s, Burroughs was a computer industry phenomenon, just about the only company to compete effectively against IBM. A large part of Burroughs's success was linked to one man: chairman Ray Macdonald. He ran a very tight ship. Burroughs, he declared, would never grow more than 15 percent a year because it couldn't afford to hire and train enough salesmen and service engineers to support higher growth. Macdonald was a demon on product costs, constantly pressing designers to scale back their ambitions so manufacturing costs would be low. And he saw customer service as a skirmish between Burroughs, which strove to keep a lid on its service and support costs, and customers, who wanted, he thought, as much free support as they could get. Macdonald's motto was that the service level was right when customers were "sullen but not rebellious."

While Macdonald's miserliness had given Burroughs several competitive advantages, it also undermined one of the company's most promising families of computers, the mid-range 1700 series. Striving to please their chief by eliminating frills, the designers of the 1700 had omitted certain hardware for diagnosing failures. When the machine failed, a service engineer would show up and tell the customer that without this hardware, repair would be almost impossible. Then he would sell the missing equipment for a fat price. Essentially, Burroughs was pulling a bait and switch maneuver with customer service, promising what it couldn't deliver.

But the problem went far beyond the 1700. By the early 1980s, Burroughs was reaping a bitter harvest from the doctrine of "sullen but not rebellious." Hundreds of buyers of Burroughs's smallest machines were suing the company, alleging that they had been promised software and support that never materialized, rendering their computers useless. The damage to Burroughs's pocketbook ran into the millions; the damage to its reputation was incalculable.

The more Bro learned about the computer and allied industries, the more he saw that customer service often spelled the difference between success and failure. IBM's competitors marveled to him about that company's dedication to service and admitted that customer confidence in IBM's responsiveness gave Big Blue a nearly insurmountable advantage. In the personal computer industry, he saw both hardware and software companies go down the tubes because of lousy service. In the notoriously cyclical semiconductor business, he learned that one of the few bulwarks U.S. producers had against their Japanese rivals was superior service, which helped keep customers loyal during downturns. Studying makers of semiconductor manufacturing equipment— exotic machines used to etch chips with lines thinner than a human hair—he saw that the major barrier keeping them out of the Japanese market was not technology, where they had a clear lead, but the exquisite service Japanese suppliers offered their customers. And when he examined dozens of companies that had been destroyed by technological change, Bro noticed that the last part to die—the most vital part—was almost always the customer service operation.

We were convinced that customer service was becoming the make or break factor for the industries we knew. We saw that most technology companies were unaware of this shift in the source of their competitive advantage. But how important was customer service in other businesses? To find out, we spent nearly a year talking with managers outside the technology industries and digging deeply into the literature on service.

Customer service, we discovered, is a potent competitive weapon in *every* business. Service leaders almost always seem to dominate their industries, both in sales growth and profitability; service laggards end up at the bottom of the heap. The pattern holds true across the board, with minor variations. Producing superior service is as important for coal companies as it is for IBM, as crucial for McDonald's as it is for management consultants.

When service starts slipping, it's often because of the same factors that knocked Bill's business into a loop and that undermined Burroughs. For example:

√ Products poorly designed for reliability and serviceability, like Intel's Series II blue box and Burroughs's 1700 series, make satisfactory service impossible, while products that eliminate the need for service allow their makers to render the best possible service. In the early days of plain paper copying, Xerox built a sterling reputation by creating a vast force of service technicians. Xerox repairmen would show up quickly to fix broken copiers, and they could do the job in just a few hours. But then competitors started selling machines that hardly broke at all. Quickly, Xerox's good service became inferior in the eyes of customers.

√ A weak service infrastructure, like the one that kept Bill from fixing his blue boxes, isn't just a high-tech problem. Both General Motors and BMW have suffered because their dealers' technicians haven't received enough training and can't get spare parts quickly enough.

√ The downward service spiral that plagued Intel and Burroughs can trap any business. When employees feel they can't win service wars, they give up, and customers get more disgruntled. In a self-reinforcing way, unhappy customers create unhappy employees who create more unhappy customers. Just try to get an Eastern Airlines worker to smile when customers are on the verge of rioting because of a canceled flight.

Several other discoveries galvanized us to write *Total Customer Service*. The more we explored customer service, the more convinced we became that a service crisis is brewing. More sophisticated customers are demanding better service in order to cope with more complex services and products. Thanks to booming global competition, they have little loyalty and plenty of alternatives. Yet all but a few managers are blind to the growing demand for service and to the victories they might achieve by learning to wield the ultimate weapon. The result is a ground swell of dissatisfaction. Customers, we found, are searching for opportunities to get even. They don't tell the retailers, manufacturers, and service providers that have served them poorly—they tell their friends and colleagues. As the bad word passes along, it creates a time bomb.

We also found that even managers who hear the bomb ticking seldom succeed in defusing it. They come up with nifty service slogans, take out advertisements proclaiming their "rededication to service," send their front-line employees off to "smile school." Either through ignorance or insincerity, they fail to make the basic changes needed to gain control of their service problems. The programs they put in place are too little, too late. Their market shares erode. Their customers come to see them as suppliers of last resort. The downward spiral of service becomes a death spiral.

Finally, we came to realize that providing outstanding service is incredibly difficult, a far greater challenge than achieving leadership in technology, cost, or quality. You can't begin tackling the problem until your business is doing everything else right, from R&D through distribution. Becoming a service leader takes more than good general management. It calls for making profound changes in the way you operate. It often requires building a new, service-oriented culture. The task is daunting for effective companies and impossible for ones that are foundering.

THE ELEMENTS OF SERVICE

Most companies don't become service leaders through blind evolution. They have to try hard and keep trying. They labor under the burden of past mistakes.

They also have an opportunity. Pursuing outstanding service in a conscious, rational way can be far more efficient than developing service willy-nilly. There's a close analogy in the history of quality control. Before Deming, Juran, and Crosby became household names, many businesses were able to make high-quality products. Sheer leadership and dedication drove them to develop excellent quality control systems. Yet they lacked today's methods of quality control, both statistical and organizational. These early leaders spent inordinate amounts of time and money to achieve quality levels that were less than perfect. Companies that started chasing quality later on, with a deeper and more formal understanding of what the pursuit would take, had a leg-up.

Our goal is to provide a set of principles for improving customer service. After examining scores of service leaders and laggards, we found a number of amply-proven principles. They fell into six closely linked categories, and we have devoted a chapter to each category. Each of chapters 3 through 8 begins with a case study that highlights the importance of a category, then reviews empirical and theoretical research in order to develop a small set of principles for achieving great service. Though we feel these principles are paramount, we don't feel they're exhaustive.

Strategy comes first because it is the framework that organizes all the other elements of service. Successful strategies clearly segment customers by their service needs in order to concentrate on just a few, closely related segments. Tight focus is imperative because you can't provide great service unless your business system is optimized to the needs of certain segments.

Customers themselves prefer sharp focus because they like to do business with companies that serve customers just like themselves. Blue jeans and pin-striped suits don't mix well in restaurants. Small companies frequently eschew suppliers who concentrate on serving big companies because the small fry know they'll come second whenever the big customer makes a demand.

Successful strategies also match a business's service abilities with the expectations of its target customers, modifying those expectations when necessary through price, advertising, and other tools.

Leadership makes strategy an everyday reality. We have yet to find a company that can provide superior service without top managers who are fanatically committed to service. Leadership matters because employees must exercise broad discretion when serving customers. Instead of rules and regulations, they have to rely on a strong service culture to guide them in making decisions. That culture takes its tone and its values from its leaders. Moreover, providing great service almost always entails tough financial decisions. Companies that aspire to excel in service have to spend heavily with little prospect of short-term rewards, and they have to turn down customers they can't serve well. "Rational" financial analysis discourages both kinds of decisions. Strong leadership ensures that service to the customer doesn't lose out to the bean counters.

Leaders are nothing without effective followers, so chapter 5 focuses on *personnel.* How employees behave is a make-or-break factor because so much customer service is delivered in face-to-face encounters between employees and customers. While many cynical managers see front-line employees as cannon fodder, companies that shine in service take pains to hire people capable of providing good service and to train and motivate them. Realizing that "customer relations mirror employee relations," they invest heavily in their people and provide believable career paths.[1] They make heroes of their front-line workers and reap the rewards of low turnover and enviably high performance.

Design constrains customer service nearly as much as strategy does. Products and services that have not been designed from the ground up to permit easy, effective maintenance and repair destroy a company's ability to satisfy customers at a reasonable price. Automobiles designed without a thought for the mechanic can never be repaired as quickly, reliably, and inexpensively as customers would wish; bank services that are overly complex confuse both customers and bank employees, ensuring a flood of inappropriate decisions and basic errors.

To avoid these problems, companies that produce great service make sure that employees who deliver service sit in on the design process from day one. They press designers to pay attention to service equivalents, such as self-diagnostic hardware and operating manuals. By scaling the complexity of a design to the competence of the target customer, they increase the customer's ability to derive full value from a core product or service.

Service after the sale usually depends on *infrastructures*—training departments and curriculums, far-flung armies of service technicians, dispersed stocks of spare parts, and computerized banks of information about customers and products. Though essential, infrastructures tend to be hugely expensive. The service leaders we studied charged compensatory prices for the services their infrastructures delivered, grew their infrastructures in line

[1]See Robert L. Desatnick, *Managing to Keep the Customer* (Josey-Bass, 1987), pp. 15–33.

with sales growth, and used advanced technology to cut infrastructure costs and improve performance. Their infrastructures often became bristling barriers to competition.

Measurements of service quality close the loop that began with strategy, showing managers how well their strategies are working and underlining weaknesses in the other elements of service. Companies that take customer service seriously constantly assess their own performance with three types of measures. Process measures compare the actual work employees perform with standards for quality and quantity. Product measures show whether that work has produced the desired result, such as delivering packages when customers want them delivered. Satisfaction measures look at the extent to which customers are satisfied with the service they have received. As customer service constantly changes, so do systems for assessing its quality.

Attacking all six of these areas at once is a tall order. Fortunately, taking some of the basic steps can improve customer service dramatically. When customers see the change, they give positive feedback, and momentum for further improvement builds.

Service standards keep rising. As competitors render better and better service, customers become more demanding. Their expectations grow. When every company's service is shoddy, doing a few things well can earn you a reputation as the customer's savior. But when a competitor emerges from the pack as a service leader, you have to do a lot more things right. Suddenly, achieving service leadership costs more and takes longer. It may even be impossible if the competition has too much of a head start.

The longer you wait, the harder it is to produce outstanding service. If you want to benefit from the service crisis instead of being overwhelmed by it, there's no time to waste.

Total Customer Service

1

The Service Crisis

———

A customer service crisis is building throughout the business world, and most managers don't know it. Even those who do seldom understand how to cope. The price of their ignorance will be high: by the 1990s, thousands of businesses will be shaken and even shattered by their inability to render effective customer service. The spoils will go to those few companies that both perceive the crisis and learn how to out-service their competitors.

"Crisis" is a strong word but no exaggeration. Most customer service is poor, much of it is awful, and service quality generally appears to be falling. At the same time, the penalty is growing for companies that render inferior service. Customers, both retail and industrial buyers, are getting smarter about the value of service. They're increasingly frustrated and more willing than ever to take their business elsewhere.

Consumer loyalty to many brands of durable goods, from automobiles to household appliances, has been eroding for years, in large part because of shoddy service. Industrial companies have been slashing the numbers of their parts and materials suppliers to concentrate on just a few, mainly for the sake of getting better service from the survivors.[1] Corporate customers are pressuring

[1] See Donald B. Thompson, "Customer Service Nears Center Stage," *Industry Week,* September 5, 1983, pp. 59–61; "PM's Inch Toward More Sole Sourcing," *Purchasing,*

1

leviathans like AT&T and IBM, which have difficulty achieving consistently good service. By carving out large chunks of business for relative upstarts—MCI for long-distance telecommunications, Amdahl for mainframe computers—these customers are driving to extract the best possible service from both the giant suppliers and the midgets.[2]

Paradoxically, managers seem to know customer service is essential to the health of their businesses, yet service keeps getting worse. In 1987 the Gallup Organization, working for the American Society for Quality Control, asked 615 senior executives of U.S. companies to select the most critical factor for their businesses in the 1986–89 period, from the cost of materials and labor to the availability of capital. The clear winner was service quality, ranked first by nearly half the sample.[3] European managers have similar views, says a survey conducted jointly by Management Centre Europe, a consulting firm, and the business magazine *Profile*. When asked whether service would be essential in the future to successful companies, three fourths of the 322 European executives polled expressed strong agreement.[4]

Customer service gets great lip service. Dedication to customers is the featured message of corporate image advertisements, the keynote of annual reports, the revealed wisdom of consul-

---

October 22, 1987, p. 41; "Ford Makes Some Changes," *American Shipping* (August 1986), p. 8; and "New Operational Philosophy Means Smart Supplier Selection Is a Must," *Marketing News*, November 7, 1986, p. 31.

[2]Computer manufacturers used to count heavily on making and selling all the equipment a customer might need, and they devised ingenious pricing and service schemes to enforce brand loyalty, particularly the de facto policy of refusing to service any "foreign" equipment hooked up to their own.

Now computer buyers have become more sophisticated and multi-vendor shops are the norm. To cope with this change, IBM, Unisys (the merged Burroughs-Sperry company), Digital Equipment Corp., and others have shifted focus from selling and supporting only their own equipment to integrating equipment made by themselves and others into single systems for which they take broad responsibility.

This shift to "systems integration" has cranked up the pressure on customer service in two related ways: computer users expect more comprehensive service, and computer manufacturers, forced to support equipment they did not design or manufacture, have a tougher time meeting that expectation.

[3]*'87 Gallup Survey: Executives' Perceptions Concerning the Quality of American Products and Services,* American Society for Quality Control, 1987.

[4]Arild Lillebo, "Serving Tomorrow's Needs," *Profile* (August 1983).

tants. Asked whether serving customers well is a crucial weapon for winning in business, most managers will nod sagely in agreement and utter some variation on the timeless theme that the customer is "king," "key," "number one," or "the person who signs our paychecks."

Yet for all their awareness and good words, managers rarely succeed in delivering outstanding service. Is the customer king? Ask almost any consumer who has recently endured the abominations of air travel in the United States, or tried to get an automobile repaired promptly and reliably, or attempted to figure out a personal computer, or vainly searched for a sales clerk in a major department store.

Do most suppliers act as though the customer signs their paychecks? Ask the industrial buyer who has tried to get all the items in a parts order delivered at the same time, or struggled to get a new robot to work the day it arrives, or pleaded with a software company to update a program, or tried to reduce the paperwork needed to purchase almost anything. Despite the veneration business people express for their customers, horror stories about customer service have become a conversational staple, right up there with sex and real estate.

THE SERVICE CONUNDRUM

Why the gap between managerial awareness and performance? Why do so many companies appear to be at a loss in dealing with the service crisis? It's not that they lack evidence about consumer sentiment, or about the business consequences of rendering lousy service. A host of polls have shown that consumers find most service is mediocre to atrocious, and that they believe service quality is getting worse.[5] Extensive research by Technical Assist-

[5]Some examples: In 1985–86 the Gallup Organization asked 2,575 consumers to rate the quality of service provided by different institutions, from "1" for very poor to "10" for very high. Roughly half the respondents gave scores of "7" or lower to supermarkets, banks, airlines, restaurants, hospitals, and hotels. About three fourths of them awarded such middling scores to department stores and real estate firms, while half felt that auto repair shops and insurance companies provided service deserving a "5" or worse. The biggest gripes: failure to get work done properly; indifferent, unqualified,

ance Research Programs, Inc., on behalf of the U.S. Office of Consumer Affairs reveals that at some two hundred giant companies, customer service departments are fielding over twice as many complaints today as they did seven years ago (and that people who complain represent *less than 5 percent* of all dissatisfied customers).[6] *Time* magazine was concerned enough by the decline of customer service to ask, in a 1987 cover story, "Why Is Service So Bad?"[7]

The impact of this service slump on corporate performance should be equally clear. For example, Management Horizons, a division of the Price Waterhouse accounting firm that consults to retailers, cautioned in a 1986 report that rotten service was undermining customer satisfaction. "Despite an industry-wide 'customer-first' philosophy in retailing," the report concluded, "the level of customer satisfaction appears to have deteriorated substantially over the past decade" as a result of extreme pressures on profits, overexpansion, understaffing, and an obsession with short-term cash flow.[8] Bad service—in this case, failure to deliver goods on time—was a major reason that the U.S. machine tool industry lost over half its domestic market to Japanese suppliers between

---

or rude personnel; slowness; and high cost (*The Gallup Poll,* March 9, 1986 [Princeton, New Jersey]).

The Yankelovich Monitor, an annual survey of 2,500 consumers that tracks social change, includes questions about the perceived quality of service in many industries. Only the quality of service in supermarkets seems to have improved in recent years. Perceived service levels of restaurants, hotels, and department stores haven't changed much, while those of airlines, banks, and cable TV operators have plunged. Moreover, four years of polls conducted by Gallup for the American Society for Quality Control show U.S. consumers largely believe that service quality has fallen and will continue to fall.

[6]Technical Assistance Research Programs, Inc., *Consumer Complaint Handling in America: An Update Study, Part II* (Washington, D.C., 1986), p. ES-4. Although one reason for the upsurge in complaints is an increase in the ease of complaining—more corporate consumer affairs departments, tougher consumer protection rules—customer satisfaction still seems to be falling.

[7]*Time,* February 2, 1987. The question isn't new, but the urgency is. More than fifteen years ago, *U.S. News and World Report* asked, in a three-page story, "Whatever Happened to Service with a Smile?" (October 15, 1973, pp. 40–42). The answer then: difficulty in finding conscientious employees, and "lackadaisical behavior" among the young people that low-paying service operations were able to hire. Those problems in fact lie more with managers than with employees, as we explain in chapter 4.

[8]"Customer Service and Satisfaction as a Differential Advantage," *Management Horizons Retail Focus/Critical Issues Series,* November 1986.

1975 and 1985, according to James L. Koontz, a director of the National Machine Tool Builder's Association. "It killed us," he says. "This lack of service was the single most important contributor to the Japanese success."[9] A specially poignant plaint recently came from the president of the American Management Association:

> Sales persons at many department stores appear ignorant of both their merchandise and the rudiments of customer service. Flight attendants often seem more interested in socializing with one another than in attending to their passengers. Bank employees are confused by any but the most simple transactions and seem interested in none. Merchandise ordered by mail arrives in the wrong size or color, and the formidable challenge of getting the order corrected falls to the customer. . . . Sadly, we are not moving toward a service economy, but a no service economy.[10]

The gap between perception and performance, we believe, can be traced to three factors. For one thing, most managers don't seem to understand the roots of the service crisis. They may see that their businesses are threatened by a tidal wave of customer dissatisfaction, but they don't comprehend its seriousness. They fail to appreciate the deep and abiding forces that drive the wave. Moreover, the measures of customer service and satisfaction that managers normally look at are misleading. Such figures can easily lead them to think the problem is less severe than it actually is. Third, and most important, very few managers appear to understand what customer service is. Most of them are locked into old, dangerously limited ways of thinking about service. And those outmoded frameworks render managers incapable of dealing effectively with the service crisis.

ROOTS OF THE NO-SERVICE ECONOMY

Like any failure, the no-service economy has many unacknowledged fathers, from government policy to economics, technology,

[9]James L. Koontz, "Taking a Lesson from McDonald's," *Production* (August 1985), p. 29.

[10]Thomas R. Horton, "Our No-Service Economy," speech delivered to the Commonwealth Club of California, San Francisco, January 11, 1988.

and demographics. Changes in the rules of competition have thrown entire industries into disarray. As companies scramble to master new sets of basic skills and to find new formulas for success, customers often suffer.

THE CHAOS OF DEREGULATION

Recently deregulated businesses are prime offenders. Ever since 1978, when the federal government started to remove ceilings on the interest rates savings banks could pay their depositors, retail bankers have been rocked by reforms that have cracked open their once protected markets. Now savings banks, commercial banks, brokerage houses, insurance companies, and even retailers like Sears, Roebuck are battling for the same business, squeezing each other's prices. Cost pressures are driving bank managers to keep a lid on salaries, cut staff, and demand for greater productivity.

These actions often sabotage service, as anyone can attest who has waited for fifteen minutes to reach a teller, only to be treated as an annoying obstacle in the teller's race to push paper. Charging fees for services that formerly were "free," and cutting out expected services such as returning canceled checks, tend to darken customers' perceptions of service, especially when banks fail to explain such actions clearly and honestly, as they usually fail to do. No wonder that banking ranks second only to insurance in lack of perceived responsiveness to consumers.[11]

Banks are not alone. Deregulation of domestic airlines has created one of the great customer service disasters of the late twentieth century. Thanks to cost cutting brought on by fare wars, an uncontrolled explosion in the number of flights, and an orgy of mergers, the number of air passenger complaints made to DOT—the U.S. Department of Transportation—more than quadrupled between 1985 and 1987.[12]

It isn't just that deregulation is sapping service by setting off

[11]See John A. Goodman, Ted Marra, and Liz Brigham, "Customer Service: Costly Nuisance or Low-Cost Strategy?" *Journal of Retail Banking,* vol. VIII, no. 3 (Fall 1986).

[12]U.S. Department of Transportation, Office of Consumer Affairs, *Air Travel Consumer Complaint Report,* January 1986 and January 1988.

competitive firestorms; it also is confusing inward-looking, traditional managers. Before AT&T agreed to break up the Bell system
in January 1982, the company's basic telephone service was outstanding. Now, years after the break-up, managers at AT&T and
at some of the seven regional "Baby Bells" that provide local
telephone service have let customer service reach new lows. Billing errors are more common, getting or changing telephone service
is harder, and finding the right telephone company person to solve
a problem literally can take days.[13]

SHORT-TERM ECONOMICS

Business economics over the last two decades have forced a
change in managerial thinking that is undermining customer service in subtle, pernicious ways. Battered by high inflation in the
late 1970s, fierce competition from foreign companies in the 1980s,
and the continuing threat of being taken over by raiders, many
managers have accepted a new, some would say myopic, philosophy. More than ever before, they want to cut costs and turn out
strong short-term financial results. They've been advised to view
their businesses as a raider would, always sizing up the stock
market value of their companies and looking for underperforming
assets to sell or inefficient operations to restructure.[14]

The result: many managers have developed an involuntary re-
flex of trimming any business activity whose impact on profits
isn't immediately obvious to a first-year accounting student—or
an institutional investor. Customer service is a favorite victim
because many of the activities that produce service seem extrane-
ous, and returns to spending on service tend to accrue over the
long term. Indeed, Stanley Marcus, the retailer who made Neiman-

---

[13]The irony is that when banks, airlines, and telephone companies were regulated,
their strategies were based on customer service. They were allowed to use no other
competitive weapon. Once deregulated, however, they lost their focus on service and
naively turned to competing on price. Their margins eroded. They began to disassem-
ble service infrastructures that had taken years to build. They disenfranchised or got
rid of employees who still believed in service. In short, they contributed heavily to the
service crisis.

[14]See Walter Kiechel III, "Corporate Strategy for the 1990's," *Fortune*, February 29,
1988.

Marcus department stores legendary for service, once observed that publicly owned companies, constantly scrutinized by stockholders, have more difficulty giving good service than private firms that can spend money as they see fit. Public ownership, Marcus said, has a way of "turning corporations into commodities that are traded like pork bellies and soybeans," destroying managers' understanding of how important service is and their motivation to provide it.[15]

THE TYRANNY OF TECHNOLOGY

A major cause of the service crisis is technological change. Technology is a two-edged sword. Much of the cost of serving customers is labor cost. Managers are desperate to contain labor costs by investing in technology that improves productivity—hand-held computer terminals, for example, that allow restaurant waiters to send orders directly to the kitchen—and that substitutes for labor, as do automated teller machines and telephone answering systems. The miraculous fact that the cost of electronic components keeps dropping about 20 percent a year ensures ever greater opportunities for applying technology to customer service problems.[16]

But using more technology to serve customers also carries the danger of alienating them and tarnishing their perceptions of service quality. As trend-watcher John Naisbitt has noted, the more high tech the world becomes, the more people crave high touch.[17]

[15]Joe Agnew, "Marcus on Marketing: Profits Are By-Product of Rendering Satisfactory Customer Service," *Marketing News,* April 10, 1987, pp. 1, 30.

[16]See James Bryan Quinn, Jordan J. Baruch, and Penny Cushman Paquette, "Technology in Services," *Scientific American* (December 1987), pp. 50–58, for an excellent review of the impact of technology investments on productivity in service industries. This paper focuses on the broad range of economic sectors lumped together as services, from professional baby-sitters to electric utilities. Yet many of the authors' conclusions apply to customer service activities, e.g., their findings that service industries are quite capital-intensive and buy some three fourths of all computer and telecommunications equipment sold in the United States and the United Kingdom.

[17]See John Naisbitt, *Megatrends: Ten New Directions Transforming Our Lives* (Warner Books, 1982).

The fast-growing use of technology in medical care, for instance, has gone hand in hand with a resurgence of demand for personalized service from the family doctor. As automation has come to supermarkets, so have more personalized "boutique" departments, like cheese and pasta counters. Brokerages that allow customers to trade securities using personal computers, and any business that uses voice mail, have learned there's no way to eliminate the need for human contact.

Consider automated teller machines. In some ways, ATMs give far better service than tellers do: they are open for business around the clock, don't have long queues, seldom make mistakes, and are never nasty at the end of a long day. Banks in large metropolitan areas, where the population is dense enough to support the networks, see ATM technology as an excellent way to cut costs and improve service too. As one officer at Citibank told *Fortune* magazine, "You can't [afford to] deliver service in the old way, but new systems can actually deliver it better. People tell us: don't be polite—be efficient, fast, and knowledgeable."[18]

If that's so, why do some customers see ATMs as a scourge? For people accustomed to courteous, efficient teller service, the machines are cold substitutes for the warmth of human interactions.[19] Even people who laud the convenience of ATMs chafe under their limitations. When a customer wants to apply for a loan or adjust an error, he or she still has to grab the attention of somebody inside the bank. The benefits of using an ATM are so

[18]Jeremy Main, "Toward Service Without a Snarl," *Fortune,* March 23, 1981, p. 58.

[19]ATMs have done nothing to improve the general impression that banks are heartless and mechanistic. In a series of focus groups that the American Bankers Association held in 1986, consumers in large cities "kept bringing the discussion back to service. . . . What they meant was . . . a quality of caring, of being sensitive to their needs and even their feelings. They used words like 'cold' and 'impersonal' and some of them said they're taking their business elsewhere as a result." Owners of small businesses complained about "lack of understanding or caring," and twenty-five- to forty-four-year-old consumers in small towns expressed "anger about what they call an arbitrary system. They feel left out . . . they kept mentioning a lack of personal service and a cold attitude as being the roots of the problem." Donald G. Ogilvie, "Customer Sensitivity—The Challenge That Can't Be Ignored," *Bank Marketing* (November 1986), p. 8.

obscure to many customers that some banks have had to mount
hard-sell campaigns to build up machine usage to the breakeven
point.[20]

Technology also undermines customer service by pumping up
demand for service faster than businesses can meet it. Almost
unnoticed, the microprocessor has become pervasive. Electronic
intelligence lurks not only within personal computers, watches,
and calculators, but inside washing machines, cars, and toys. It
gives clerks at McDonald's the ability to total a bill just by pressing keys marked with names from the menu; enables packaged
food salesmen to take inventory in supermarkets by passing a
wand across the shelves; and keeps track of how much credit is
left in a credit card. Because the tiny computer-on-a-chip can be
programmed, it is a wonder of flexibility: adding new features to
a microprocessor-based product is basically a matter of rewriting
some software. The same kind of flexibility characterizes services
based on the ever cheaper power of big computer networks, such
as banking and brokerage. Technology gives designers enor-
mously greater scope for adding new features, and they exploit
that freedom to the hilt.

New features sound attractive, but often the net effect for customers is confusion and frustration. Who can tell the differences
anymore among the complex, ever-changing offerings of financial
services companies? Short of spending thousands of dollars on
tests and studies, how can a manufacturer choose between one

[20]See, for example, Catherine L. Bond, "Making Your ATM Programs Come Alive,"
Bank Marketing (August 1987), pp. 10–14. Despite the seeming prevalence of ATMs,
banks have a spotty record in using technology to cut service costs and improve
service quality. Citibank lost money on ATMs for years because usage remained low.
Many banks have had difficulty in using "platform automation"—giving officers computers to help answer customer questions—and in getting customers themselves to use
computer "inquiry terminals" installed in bank lobbies. See Jan Bone, "Platform Automation: Beyond the Glitz," *Bank Administration* (March 1987), pp. 38–42, and Charlene
M. Brewis, "Customer Self-Service Terminals: Will They Survive?" *The Magazine of
Bank Administration* (April 1986), pp. 12 and 16.

supplier's microprocessor and another's? When it comes to consumer electronics and household appliances, the most discerning buyer can feel defeated by the richness and duplication of features. Even *Consumer Reports* magazine, which tests products exhaustively in order to rate them, finds few salient differences among the best models of automated cameras, video cassette recorders, and microwave ovens.[21] Increasingly, the only way to distinguish among products and services is by the customer service that comes along with them.[22] Thus technology feeds demand for service.

At the same time, technology can make it more difficult for companies to supply effective service. Electronics have made automobiles so complicated that home mechanics give up in despair. Professional mechanics need constant retraining, along with costly diagnostic computers. Nonetheless they're frequently stumped.[23] The problem, says Steven Brobeck, executive director of the Consumer Federation of America, is that "The complexity of technology has increased much more rapidly than the ability of

[21]See *Consumer Reports* for January 1988 (microwave ovens), March 1988 (video cassette recorders), and September 1986 (auto-focus cameras).

[22]Of course, the distinction is most important for products and services that may require significant after-sales service: " . . . many products are now so complicated that they are undifferentiated regarding quality. Consumers cannot decide that the quality of one service is better than that of another until they encounter problems. Then this product becomes differentiated from other products on the basis of service. Industries in which this situation now exists include consumer electronic products, banking, insurance, air travel, major appliances, and automobiles." John A. Goodman and Ronald W. Stampfl, "The Consumer Affairs Department in Business: Expanding Its Functions and Identifying Its Bottom-Line Contributions," Wisconsin Working Paper #10-83-19 (October 1983, Graduate School of Business, University of Wisconsin-Madison).

[23]To solve the problem, both General Motors and Ford are testing "expert systems," computer programs that guide mechanics through repairs according to rules of thumb developed by the most experienced technicians (see Lawrence M. Fisher, "A Tool to Track That Odd Noise," *New York Times,* February 10, 1988, p. D8). Although forcing experienced mechanics to work through every step in an expert system in order to diagnose faults could slow down the mechanic, Fisher notes that "the inclusion of rapidly changing sophisticated technology in automobiles is ending that. An intermittent circuit in a computerized ignition system is less easily deduced by intuition than a set of burned ignition points in a distributor. Similarly, problems caused by emission controls have been largely cured by such advances as programmed fuel injection, but trouble-shooting such a system calls upon far different skills than adjusting a carburetor."

service personnel to keep track of it."[24] Whether the broken product is a microwave oven or a machine tool, the owner wouldn't think of trying to repair it himself, and he feels lucky to find anyone who can do the job right.

Note that complexity affects not just repair service but also the customer's need for less traditional types of service. Marketing professor Ted Levitt has stressed for years that customers do not buy products or services so much as they buy expectations.[25] Nobody buys a quarter-inch drill, a car stereo, or a cash management account; they buy the expectation of a quarter-inch hole, beautiful sound, or convenient money management. But the more complex the product or service, the more help the buyer needs to realize his or her expectations. Getting the most out of a state-of-the-art car stereo is difficult without clear directions and even some training. Hooking up a printer to a personal computer is impossible without well-written manuals and, usually, expert help.

RISING EXPECTATIONS

Even if the absolute quality of customer service had not dropped, customer dissatisfaction would still have grown. The culprit is rising expectations. The consumerist movement that began in the 1960s, personified by Ralph Nader and his epic attacks on federal regulators who had failed to protect consumers, radically revised America's expectations of business. Government at all levels responded with new consumer protection laws and new agencies like the Consumer Product Safety Commission and the White House Office of Consumer Affairs. These political responses in turn raised expectations even higher. Product liability suits mushroomed. Hundreds of corporations sought to defend themselves by setting up their own consumer affairs departments, and a new

[24]As quoted in *Time* magazine, February 2, 1987, p. 52.

[25]Among Levitt's many writings, see chapters 4 and 5 of *The Marketing Imagination* (Free Press, 1983).

profession was born along with its own association, the Society of Consumer Affairs Professionals, founded in 1973.

Rising expectations of service are an economic and social phenomenon, as well as a political one. Consumers are richer and better educated than ever before, and thus more demanding about the service they receive. As one demographer observes: "The quality of people who serve is fast becoming the critical factor in business competition. This is because the enormous baby-boom generation is beginning to make money. Households headed by 35-to-50-year-olds will control 42 percent of household income by 2000. More than half of these households will have incomes of $35,000 and over (in 1985 dollars). They will demand good service, and they will be able to pay for it. If they don't get it from your company, they'll get it from your competitor."[26]

Service expectations are higher today, and will continue growing, because customers are becoming more sophisticated. With greater sophistication comes less willingness to believe that a product by itself, bereft of service and support, can do the job it's supposed to. That's why the public is increasingly skeptical of product claims and increasingly inclined to rate service as more important than product cost and features, according to John J. Franco, president of Xerox Learning Systems: "In fact, of the top nine reasons consumers give for buying a specific product, eight pertain to the abilities of the customer service system (e.g., responsiveness, technical skill, professional attitude)."[27]

Industrial customers also expect higher levels of service. They too are more sophisticated, thanks to the globalization of business and hotter competition among suppliers. For example, when U.S. semiconductor companies learned that Japanese suppliers of chipmaking machines offered much more effective maintenance

[26]Cheryl Russell, "Editor's Note: Bad Service," *American Demographics* (November 1987), p. 7. Of course, outstanding customer service depends not just on the quality of people who serve but on a host of other business factors, from strategy to measurement systems.

[27]John J. Franco, "Why Customer Service Matters," *International Executive* (Spring 1985), pp. 16–17.

than U.S. suppliers did, the chipmakers drastically increased their service expectations. In the world market for jet engines used in commercial aircraft, Pratt & Whitney dominated for fifteen years, even though it had trouble supplying spare parts for its sixty different types of engines. But after General Electric entered the business in 1968 with superior technology and service, Pratt & Whitney's share of this multi-billion-dollar market slipped from a near monopoly to less than 40 percent. GE had revolutionized customers' expectations of service.[28]

The main reason business buyers expect more service is their growing interdependence with suppliers, a result of the trend toward more flexible and efficient manufacturing of goods with higher quality. Key to that trend is "just-in-time manufacturing." In essence, "JIT" calls for factories virtually to eliminate their inventories, as well as their inspections of incoming parts, and to rely instead on suppliers that will ship parts of guaranteed quality within days, sometimes hours, of receiving an order. JIT has marched through all sorts of industries that manufacture goods and services; even companies like GM and IBM, once strong believers in vertical integration, have decided to liberate their assets by getting outsiders to supply greater portions of their needs. Thanks to JIT, many business buyers and sellers have embraced the idea of "co-destiny." They're planning future products and future capacity together. And co-destiny is impossible without impeccable service.

Not surprisingly, industrial customers tend to value good service more than retail customers do. They depend on getting good service to serve their own customers, and they can measure the impact of poor service by lost sales and profits. Moreover, the costs of bad service tend to swell as they cascade through an industrial system. Late delivery of contaminated iron ore cripples the steelmaker's ability to serve the rolling mill, and hence the rolling mill's efforts to serve the maker of refrigerators. Then the

[28]"GE's Military Engines Take Off," *Fortune,* December 24, 1984, p. 128, and William M. Carley, "Reverse Thrust: How Pratt & Whitney Lost Jet-Engine Lead to GE After 30 Years," *Wall Street Journal,* January 27, 1988, pp. 1, 10.

refrigerator maker fails to serve the appliance dealer. Ultimately the appliance dealer is forced to frustrate the consumer.

BLINDED BY STATISTICS

The roots of the service crisis are deep, widespread, and durable. The crisis isn't going to vanish. Yet managers often fail to see their predicament because they don't know how fed up customers actually are. The information that companies normally collect about customer satisfaction is grossly misleading.

The most visible, popular indicator is the rate of complaints. While complaints are useful in all sorts of ways, from pinpointing performance problems to selling collateral products, they're a remarkably feeble index of satisfaction levels. John Goodman of Technical Assistance Research Programs, Inc., who has studied the complaint process at over three hundred companies and government agencies, concludes that customers who complain to headquarters about routine problems represent a tiny fraction of all dissatisfied customers, somewhere between 2 and 4 percent.[29] The majority of the dissatisfied keep mum because they don't think grousing will be worthwhile; others tell their problems in passing to friends or to sales and service people, but not to the customer service department, the only place that tallies complaints.

Yet thousands of managers think customers generally are satisfied because few complaints bubble to the surface. In late 1987, any U.S. airline executive had to worry because the number of air travel complaints made to the U.S. Department of Transportation had increased sixfold over the previous year. But if the absolute rate of complaints was his main measure of customer satisfaction, he wasn't likely to worry much. Even the airline with the worst record, Northwest, could contend that it was a paragon of customer service because only eighteen of every 100,000 passengers,

[29]Technical Assistance Research Programs Institute, *Consumer Complaint Handling in America: An Update Study for the U.S. Office of Consumer Affairs* (Washington, D.C., 1986), Part II, chapter 3.

or less than one tenth of 1 percent, squawked to the Transportation Department.[30] Such blindness can be fatal, as the saga of People Express shows. Several months before the airline was forced to merge with Texas Air because its abominable service had alienated customers, People Express chairman Donald Barr was proclaiming that his outfit gave excellent service.[31]

Customer surveys, the other popular index of satisfaction, can paint a much sharper picture than complaint rates. But surveys usually deceive because their designs are naive. Look at the "guest comment cards" that are a staple of hotels and chain restaurants. The only people motivated to fill them out are the extremely satisfied and the extremely dissatisfied, that is, an extremely unrepresentative sample. Questions on the cards—e.g., "How satisfied were you with the check-in procedure?"—seldom are related to a guest's overall satisfaction and intention to return, and none of the answers can tell managers how much weight different types of guests place on different aspects of a hotel or restaurant experience.[32] True, guest comment cards can flag areas where customer service is disastrous, but that's all.

Most other customer surveys have the same faults; their designs tend to mask service failures. Because of flaws in survey design, for example, half the customers who told a major communications retailer that they were "fairly satisfied" with the service they received also said they wouldn't do business with the retailer again—and so did 7 percent of the customers who termed the

---

[30]U.S. Department of Transportation, *1987 Air Travel Consumer Report.*

[31]On March 23, 1986, Leslie Stahl interviewed Barr for the TV program "Face the Nation." The following colloquy took place before millions of viewers:

Barr: And so . . . you've got to have far and away the best service. . . .
Stahl: You have the best service?
Barr: Absolutely.
Stahl: Come on. It's called People Distress. That's the joke about your airline. . . . You are always overbooked. . . . Now you can't start claiming you have the best service.
Barr: We do, absolutely have the best service.

See William M. Carley, "Bumpy Flights: Many Travelers Gripe About People Express, Citing Overbooking," *Wall Street Journal,* May 19, 1986, pp. 1, 12.

[32]For more on measuring satisfaction, see chapter 8 of this book, and Robert C. Lewis and Abraham Pizan, "Guest Surveys: A Missed Opportunity," *The Cornell H.R.A. Quarterly* (November 1981), pp. 37–44.

service "good."[33] Obviously, the survey had failed to find and measure the aspects of service that customers cared about, that produced actual satisfaction.

TUNNEL VISION

The most important reason for the gap between managerial awareness of the service crisis and managerial performance in dealing with the problem, we believe, is tunnel vision. The majority of managers tend to take a narrow view of service and hence a narrow view of how to produce it. They design and run their organizations more to insulate themselves from customers than to serve them. Instead of dealing with customer service as a top strategic issue and making service quality everybody's business, they shuffle those responsibilities off onto a customer service or consumer affairs department. Within these corporate ghettos, small, impotent groups of people struggle to field complaints. Their training is superficial, stressing politeness on the telephone and coolness under fire. They have almost no power actually to do their jobs: solving customers' problems. Their status is low—many are part-timers—and they know full well that no one ever rose through their ranks to become a chief executive.

Even their pay is an insult. Middle managers in customer service make only $38,000, on average; top managers pull down a paltry $53,000.[34] Front-line workers may be called "customer service representatives" or "consumer affairs professionals," but their primary mission is to protect a company from angry customers. The true measures of their success are how few complaints they receive and how cheaply they can deal with them. The more problems they hear about and pass on, the less heed their bosses

[33]John A. Goodman and Arlene R. Malech, "Issues in the Development of Valid, Actionable Satisfaction Measurement and Incentives Systems," TARP Working Paper, Washington, D.C., 1985, p. 2.

[34]International Customer Service Association, *Compensation Survey Special Report*, January 1988.

pay, creating a vicious circle that leads to ever more customer service problems.[35] Find a company that shunts customers' problems to a customer service department, and you probably have found a company that provides poor service.

Tunnel vision is obvious in the definitions different companies use for customer service. Consumer-oriented businesses think service means handling complaints and fixing broken products. Companies that sell capital equipment focus on repairs and preventative maintenance.[36] Financial service companies such as banks say customer service means error-free transactions. Most companies that sell industrial goods identify service with filling orders and distributing products,[37] and they measure service levels by looking at the breadth and depth of inventory they carry and the credit terms they provide.[38]

None of these definitions encompasses the entire complex of services that customers expect and that managers can use to build customer satisfaction. For example, the definitions listed above don't address the need to design a product or service for ease of use and, if it's something that breaks down, for ease of repair.

[35]See Claes Fornell and Robert A. Westbrook, "The Vicious Circle of Consumer Complaints," *Journal of Marketing* (Summer 1984), pp. 68–78. The authors examined 268 companies to test the hypotheses that "(1) the more consumer complaints relative to other communications a firm receives, the more isolated its consumer affairs function becomes from marketing decision making; and (2) as the isolation of the consumer affairs function increases, so does the relative amount of consumer complaints." Having proved these hypotheses, they dismally concluded: "Contrary to what may be in the best interest of both the firm and consumers, an organization's willingness to listen to and act upon its customers' complaints is *negatively* related to the proportion of consumer problems voiced. This contributes to a process that can be described as a vicious circle: high proportions of consumer complaints contribute to isolation of the consumer affairs function and to a limitation of its activities to individual case-by-case complaint handling, which precludes marketing actions to reduce future complaints. The complaint proportion thus remains high, which further isolates consumer affairs, and the cycle is perpetuated. . . ."

[36]See, for example, Milind M. Lele and Uday S. Karmarkar, "Good Product Support Is Smart Marketing," *Harvard Business Review* (November–December 1983), pp. 124–132.

[37]See, for example, Herbert W. Davis, "Save Consulting Fees: Do-It-Yourself Measures of Customer-Service Effectiveness," *S.A.M. Advanced Management Journal* (Spring 1984), p. 41ff.

[38]When economists of the firm speak of customer service, they usually mean product availability and credit terms, as in Yoram C. Peles and Meir I. Schneller, "Financial Ratios and the Analysis of Marketing Policy," *European Journal of Marketing*, vol. 16, no. 5 (1982), pp. 12–21.

Neither do they cover the need to provide effective operating manuals and training for complex products and services, or to mold the behavior of every employee who contacts the customer. The narrowness of these definitions deludes managers into thinking they have customer service under control.

DIGGING FOR A DEFINITION

In order to deal with the service crisis, managers need a more useful definition of customer service. But if customer service means more than taking orders, distributing products, handling complaints, and fixing things, then what does it mean?

In the broadest sense, customer service is whatever enhances customer satisfaction. Satisfaction, or lack of it, is the difference between how a customer *expects* to be treated and how he or she *perceives* being treated. Both expectations and perceptions are shaped by factors that can be hard to control, from advertised prices to product design to the behavior of employees. So the sources of satisfaction—the elements of customer service—are diverse and sometimes subtle or surprising.

Digging into management books and business journals, we found three schools of thought about service. First, a small but invaluable literature on service management deals with organizations whose principal business is service, such as hotels and banks.[39] These writings are key to understanding how to "manufacture" and market service in general. They make clear distinctions between the traditional services that people perform and "service equivalents," things like operating manuals, self-diagnostic computers, and videotaped training, all of which can substitute effectively for people-to-people service. Yet this school of thought tends to ignore the customer service rendered by manufacturers

[39]See, especially, W. Earl Sasser, R. Paul Olsen, and D. Daryl Wycoff, *Management of Service Operations* (Allyn & Bacon, 1978); Christopher H. Lovelock, *Services Marketing* (Prentice-Hall, 1984); Richard A. Normann, *Service Management* (John Wiley & Sons, 1984); John A. Czepiel, Michael A. Solomon, and Carol F. Surprenant, eds., *The Service Encounter* (Lexington Books, 1985); and James L. Heskett, *Managing in the Service Economy* (Harvard Business School Press, 1986).

of products. And it doesn't distinguish between what we call "core services"—such as air transportation—and customer services like issuing boarding passes along with tickets.

At the opposite pole are the customer service traditionalists. They focus on a few activities native to classical manufacturing companies—optimizing physical distribution, designing credit policies, smoothing the cycle of order, shipment, and invoicing—and on training people assigned to handle complaints.[40] While these are important activities, they're just fragments of the total task. The traditionalists use such narrow definitions of customer service that anybody who followed their thinking and advice could achieve, say, the world's most efficient distribution system—and at the same time a disastrously low level of customer satisfaction.

Thirdly, there's a fast-growing body of thought and opinion on the subjects of "customer focus" and "customer sensitivity."[41] In the wake of *In Search of Excellence,* the best-selling management book ever, thousands of executives have concluded that "keeping close to the customer" is the source of higher customer satisfaction and thus higher sales and earnings—and even the elusive quality of "excellence." For them, cozying up to customers means changing a company's culture so that every employee puts the customer first.

A customer-oriented culture is a big and necessary factor in producing superior service. But it's glaringly insufficient without appropriate strategies, systems, and designs of products or services. The gurus of customer focus seem to look exclusively at human behavior and to assume that producing customer service means having the right mind-set. Yet in dozens of cases, employ-

---

[40]See, for example, Warren Blanding, *Practical Handbook of Distribution/Customer Service* (The Traffic Service Corporation, 1985); E. Patricia Birsner and Ronald D. Balsley, *How to Improve Customer Service* (American Management Association, 1980); and William B. Martin, *Quality Customer Service* (Crisp Publications, 1987).

[41]See, for example, Karl Albrecht and Ron Zemke, *Service America!* (Dow Jones-Irwin, 1985); Robert L. Desatnick, *Managing to Keep the Customer* (Josey-Bass, 1987); and Milind M. Lele with Jagdish N. Sheth, *The Customer Is Key* (John Wiley & Sons, 1987).

ees with the "right" mind-set can't deliver good service because they lack training, or have to handle unreliable products, or can't count on getting spare parts quickly.

CREATING A NEW DEFINITION

Without an existing definition of customer service that seems workable, we were forced to develop a new one. Important help in that effort came from Ted Levitt, the sachem of marketing. In his view, every product—or service—has four incarnations: *generic, expected, augmented,* and *potential.* The *generic* product is the "fundamental, but rudimentary, substantive 'thing.' . . . It is, for the steel producer, the steel itself. . . . For a bank, it's loanable funds."[42]

The *expected* product adds to the generic one all the traditional services customers expect, like convenient delivery, attractive terms and conditions of sale, and adequate after-sale support.

In turn, the *augmented* product adds to the expected one a bundle of benefits the customer doesn't expect, like training for his employees or a bank statement that analyzes sources and uses of funds. Since the augmented product exceeds the customer's expectations, it can produce lots of customer satisfaction.

As customers experience augmented products, of course, they come to expect augmentation. Once augmentation has lost its power to increase satisfaction, suppliers must focus on the *potential* product, which includes everything that might be done to attract and hold customers and that can be added to the augmented product in the future. As Levitt explains: "To the potential buyer, a product is a complex cluster of value satisfactions. The generic thing is not itself the product; it is merely, as in poker, table stakes—the minimum that is necessary at the outset to give its producer the chance to play the game. It is the playing that gets

[42]Theodore Levitt, "Marketing Success Through Differentiation—of Anything," *Harvard Business Review* (January–February 1980), p. 85.

the results, and in business this means getting and keeping customers."[43]

Applying Levitt's ideas to customer service produced a new definition, one that seems specific enough to help managers improve service, yet broad enough to embrace everything customers mean when they think of service. For our purposes,

> Customer service means all features, acts, and information that augment the customer's ability to realize the potential value of a core product or service.

This definition appears to offer several advantages. It covers traditional customer service activities, such as handling complaints, but it also embraces many newer types of service, such as the microprocessor that tracks the performance of a car and informs the owner when service is needed. It covers the spectrum of customer service from designing a product for easy maintenance to offering attractive salvage terms for products that are past their useful lives.

At the same time, this definition excludes many aspects of a product or service that are unrelated to customer service. The wheels on a car, for example, belong to the core product. They're part of what the customer expects ("table stakes," in Levitt's language). Though the car is useless without wheels, the wheels in no way augment the customer's ability to use the car, even if they're particularly fancy wheels. But special valve stems that indicate tire pressure may fall under the heading of customer service if they help the customer achieve value from the car by maintaining proper tire pressures, and if they exceed what the customer expects.

It's the same with core services, such as a savings account. Customers expect banks to protect their savings, keep accurate records, and offer adequate interest rates. Those are table stakes. When banks talk about reducing inaccuracies, they're really talking about improving the quality of their core service, not about

[43]Levitt, "Marketing Success Through Differentiation—of Anything," p. 84.

offering better customer service. To do that, they would have to cut the time customers spend waiting in line or supply pre-paid envelopes for mailing in deposits, both actions that help customers realize the value of a savings account.

Another advantage of this definition is that it underlines an important trait of customer service: It's a moving target. Once all car manufacturers offer special valve stems and all banks have cut waiting lines, such features and acts cease to be customer services. They have become part of the core product or service, what customers now expect. A company seeking to win through superior customer service constantly has to create new and different ways of enabling customers to realize value.

Finally, this definition concentrates on the value of products and services *as they are used.* All too many companies, when developing customer services, never bother asking customers what they expect. Not surprisingly, the services they provide often do nothing to raise customer satisfaction and may even undermine it. For instance, walk-in repair service for personal computers sounds just great—until you have to disconnect your PC and lug the darn thing into a dealer. By concentrating on the customer's ability to realize potential value, this new definition directs attention to what really matters, rather than addressing what's convenient for corporations to provide.

The first steps toward dealing with the customer service crisis are to see its roots, to forget what conventional measures of service and satisfaction indicate, and to understand how broad customer service really is—how many aspects of a business it affects. But that change of mind isn't enough to galvanize a company to pursue excellence in service. Performing that arduous task calls for yet another change of mind, in this case an understanding of how potent customer service can be as a competitive weapon.

The Ultimate Weapon

The war of business has shifted onto a new battleground. In the 1960s, marketing was the watchword for achieving competitive advantage. In the 1970s, manufacturing became the hot topic, and in the 1980s, quality. Now competition has arrived at the fourth battlefield—customer service.

In the evolution of most markets, competition appears to progress from *features* to *cost* to *quality* to *service.* With new products and services, competitors focus on features such as horsepower or direct dialing of long-distance calls. Companies battle each other with "specsmanship," particularly in industrial markets, where product specifications matter most.

But as competitors swarm in, generally matching each other feature for feature, the skirmishing shifts to price and cost. Constant innovation can fend off cost-based competition temporarily, but not forever. Few companies reap all the rewards of innovation before competitors catch up, and technological barriers to competition are getting harder to sustain as technology becomes more widely and easily available. In banking, for example, trying to sustain competitive advantage through technology is a myth, according to William Giles, a British consultant in marketing planning and strategy: "One day we will all have the technology, plagiarized from each other. By then there will be as little differentiation between competitors' technology and delivery systems as there is today between competing products and services. Competitively, back to square one. . . . The net outcome is that technology represents a massive investment just to stay and play in the game."[1]

In the course of price-based competition, high-cost producers drop out or reposition themselves, and the survivors roughly match each other's prices and costs. Then the battleground changes again. In this third phase customers realize that the true cost to them of a product or service depends on its quality. Producers respond by scrambling to differentiate themselves through product or service quality. That's what car companies, chipmakers, banks, airlines, and firms in scores of other industries are doing today.

In time, though, customers get "spoiled." They come to expect competitive features, prices, and quality. Those attributes become table stakes, not effective methods of differentiation. When competition is generally mature, as it is in consumer packaged goods and automobiles, even the most artful advertising fails to convince customers that real differences exist. Video Storyboard Tests, Inc., which polls consumers to select the most popular television commercials, finds that recall of commercials is dropping. It's not because the ads are any worse than they used to be, says David Vadehra, president of the company, but because consumers are more indifferent: "People believe more and more that all brands are basically the same, so they figure, 'Why watch commercials?' "[2]

The fourth battleground, onto which most companies have moved without knowing it, is service to the customer. Lacking meaningful ways to distinguish among core products and services, people decide to do business based on how they expect to be treated. They start scrutinizing the efforts that competing sellers make to ensure buyers will get all the value a purchase promises.

[1]William Giles, "Marketing Planning and Customer Policy," *Management Decision* (May 1986), p. 19.

[2]As quoted in Ronald Alsop, "In TV Viewers' Favorite 1987 Ads, Offbeat Characters Were the Stars," *Wall Street Journal,* March 3, 1988, p. 19.

Has the selling company paid close attention to making a product or service easy to use, and effective from the customer's standpoint? How difficult is it to do business with the company? What happens when something goes wrong? Do people who come into contact with the buyer behave as if they're working mainly for the company, or for the customer? These questions have become critical, but too many managers, fighting the old battles of features, cost, and quality, think of service issues as secondary, akin to window dressing.

SERVICE WINNERS

As a competitive weapon, customer service may be less effective during the early phases of highly innovative industries like consumer electronics. But when the sparkle of new products, low prices, and high quality dims, as it quickly does, the company that has built a reputation for service retains a nearly insurmountable lead. The garment trade, for example, is notoriously innovative. Yet Liz Claiborne, Inc., doesn't try to hit every fashion trend with its women's sportswear. Instead, it concentrates on service to retailers and consumers. Claiborne salespeople make sure that store buyers order only what they're likely to sell. To make up for the declining number and quality of department store clerks, the company sends its own salespeople to staff certain stores, and it pays for a group of fifteen traveling trainers who show retailers how to sell the Claiborne line. The result: Claiborne has posted faster and more stable sales growth than its peers, and its earnings have grown at an annually compounded rate of better than 50 percent since 1982, reaching $114 million in 1987.[3]

Even in the most routine, commonplace businesses, outstanding service offers great leverage. Take pest control. A $2.8 billion industry with few barriers to entry, it swarms with small, shaky operators who do a shoddy job. Exterminators typically "control"

[3]Ann Hagedorn, "Apparel Makers Play Bigger Part on Sales Floor," *The Wall Street Journal*, March 2, 1988.

roaches and rodents but never really eliminate them, so customers are hardened to mediocre performance and tend to buy on price, shaving exterminators' margins.

But one company stands out. The only excellent exterminator in the United States, say competitors and customers, is "Bugs" Burger Bug Killers, a Miami-based company that Johnson Wax recently bought. BBBK charges at least four times what competitors do and brings 9 to 12 cents of each sales dollar to the bottom line, a remarkably healthy performance for its industry.

The main reason for BBBK's success is the extra value customers get in the form of service guarantees. They don't have to pay fees for initial clean-out and monthly service until they agree that BBBK's swat team has destroyed all nesting and breeding places on their premises. If the bug killers can't keep up the good work, customers get a refund for their last twelve months of service, plus free service from another exterminator for a year. If a hotel or restaurant guest spots a roach, BBBK takes the rap. It pays the guest for his meal or room, writes a letter of apology, and issues a gift certificate for a future meal or room, a policy that costs some $2,000 a month.[4]

Or consider Shelby Williams Industries, which dominates the $600 million business of contract seating (making chairs for hotels and restaurants). In this low-technology, commodity market, where nearly anyone can jump in and the customers keep a sharp eye on price, Shelby Williams claims the largest share, about 20 percent. Sales have grown at 17 percent a year since 1981, and profit margins hover around 7 percent, among the best in the business.

The essence of Shelby Williams's success is that all operations "take a back seat to customer service," chairman Manfred Steinfeld says. If a last-minute production glitch threatens to delay shipment of chairs to a customer who needs them badly, the company will air-express loaners. It sends last-minute loaners even if

[4]Christopher W. L. Hart, assistant professor at Harvard Business School, brought "Bugs" Burger Bug Killers to our attention; see Hart's paper, "The Power of Unconditional Service Guarantees," *Harvard Business Review* (July–August 1988), pp. 54–62, and Tom Richman, "Getting the Bugs Out," *Inc.* (June 1984), pp. 61–64.

the customer has caused the delay by, say, failing to send custom upholstery fabrics to the factory. According to Steinfeld:

> [Shelby Williams] has established itself as a service company, without the internal, product focus that limits many manufacturers. . . . [T]he value the customer is most willing to pay for is not necessarily the product itself. Often, the greatest value is provided by giving the customer peace of mind—the assurance that his hotel or restaurant won't open without chairs, that the chairs will be properly manufactured, and that the supplier will stand behind them. . . . The key has been to emphasize the items that the customer values most. . . .[5]

For a perfect illustration of the uncanny power of service, look at IBM's experience in the market for personal computers. When IBM entered the business in August 1981, it seemed to be courting catastrophe. The original IBM PC offered no exciting technology and almost no proprietary features: Some four fifths of the system's components came straight off the shelves of outside suppliers: Compared with other machines, the PC looked overpriced. And to sell it, IBM had to go through retail channels that viewed Big Blue as a threatening stranger. Apple Computer, the market leader at the time, was so far from being frightened that it ran cocky advertisements welcoming IBM to the world of personal computing.

By 1983, of course, the IBM PC had become a smash hit, outselling Apple's computers, raking in nearly $2 billion in revenue for IBM, and entrenching itself as an industry standard. By launching a plain vanilla machine, IBM made it easy for outsiders to design hardware and software to work with the PC, and thousands of companies flocked to do so, vastly enhancing the PC's value to users.

But the biggest reason for IBM's success was its name. Decades of superior service had convinced business buyers, who were leery of personal computers and the upstart companies that sold them, that IBM was the safe choice. They knew that if the machines failed to perform as advertised, IBM would stand behind

[5]Manfred Steinfeld, "The Shelby Williams Approach to Building a Unique Identity in a Low-Technology Market," *Journal of Business Strategy* (Spring 1987), pp. 87–89.

them. Thus Apple and others ruefully discovered what mainframe computer companies had known all along: IBM often wins because of the "FUD" factor—the fear, uncertainty, and doubt that assail corporate customers when they think of buying any gear that isn't blue.[6] As those customers have been saying for nearly a quarter of a century, "Nobody ever got fired for buying IBM."

In fact, many corporations that bought IBM PCs later complained that they couldn't get good service and support because IBM had shuffled off those burdens onto the dealers who sold the machines. But the facts of the case were irrelevant. IBM had the "unfair" advantage of its reputation.

The same is true for Delta Airlines. Delta's records for arriving late, losing baggage, and provoking customers to complain to the Department of Transportation are about average for its industry today, and some of its flights have been involved in well-publicized near accidents. Yet fliers continue to rank Delta as either the best major domestic airline or the second best, behind American. For Delta, as for IBM, word of mouth and customers' past experiences have created an invisible cocoon that keeps competitors at bay. Trying to combat that advantage is like wrestling with fog.

THE PHONY CONFLICT

What do customer service winners like "Bugs" Burger Bug Killers and IBM know that other companies don't? Why are they willing to invest significant effort and money in producing outstanding service? The short answer is they know that service pays.

Most managers don't invest heavily in service because they can't see the bottom-line effects. In fact, the seeming conflict between good financial performance and good service is so clear to

---

[6]The term "FUD" appears to have been coined by Gene Amdahl, a designer of big IBM machines who founded Amdahl Corp. in 1976 to compete with his former employer. By the second half of the 1980s, corporations were sufficiently comfortable with personal computers that followed IBM's standard—so-called clone computers—that the power of FUD in the personal computer market waned, and clonemakers as a group outsold IBM.

certain management writers that they classify all companies into one of two categories: the small group of service leaders that never count the cost of satisfying customers, and the huge majority of businesses that seek to maximize profits by minimizing costs, which means they can't produce superior service.[7] The implication is that managers can focus *either* on customer service *or* on profits but not on both.

Yet outstanding customer service is essential to long-term profits. Its benefits come both in "soft dollars"—or cost avoidance—and in the "hard dollars" of higher margins and larger market shares.

SAVING MONEY

The most obvious benefits of superior service, like those of total quality control, come in terms of money saved. Just as doing things right the first time on the factory floor saves the costs of rework and scrap, so providing good customer service avoids the heavy costs of alienating buyers. For proof, look at any complex machine that comes with instructions so abstruse that ordinary users can't figure them out, or at toys supposedly designed so that even a child can assemble them, when putting them together in fact takes so much persistence that *only* a child can do it. Such indifference to documentation and design annoys and frustrates customers. Fail to provide those kinds of service, and customers will think twice before buying your products again. Getting them to take the plunge a second time can cost dearly.

By far the largest costs that outstanding service saves are those of replacing lost customers. There is no proven method for measuring these savings, but a common rule of thumb is that the marketing costs of landing a new customer run three to five times the marketing costs of retaining an old one.[8]

---

[7]See, for example, Tom Peters, *Thriving on Chaos* (Alfred A. Knopf, 1987) and Milind M. Lele with Jagdish N. Sheth, *The Customer Is Key* (John Wiley & Sons, 1987).

[8]Robert L. Desatnick, *Managing to Keep the Customer* (Jossey-Bass, 1987), p. 3.

This disparity is most important in markets where repeat purchases come slowly, where the price of a good or service is high, and where customers bear heavy costs for switching brands or suppliers. In markets like these—computer systems, automobiles, independent auditing—customers lost to a competitor often are lost forever.

On the other hand, the fact that retaining customers is cheaper than acquiring new ones may not seem to matter much in mass markets for low-priced goods such as laundry soap. There the apparent costs of acquiring a customer are relatively low, buyers switch brands pretty freely, and most competent suppliers can expect a share of the business over time. Even in those markets, however, customer service can pay off. By building brand loyalty, it dramatically improves the returns to advertising and promotion.[9]

Loyal customers—the ones not lost because of bad service—are worth thousands of dollars in sales over the life of their relationship with a company. According to Tom Peters, one of Federal Express's smaller accounts may represent ten-year revenues of $180,000, while the patron of an upscale grocery spends $50,000 over a decade.[10] Over the lifetime of a loyal customer, an automobile dealer can count on some $150,000 in revenues, estimates John Goodman of Technical Assistance Research Programs. Even appliance makers can expect roughly $3,000 in sales to a loyal customer over twenty years.[11]

Exactly how much can lousy service cost a company, or even an industry? In the case of retail banks, surveys by Raddon Financial Group, a consulting firm, indicated that in 1987, 42 percent of

[9]For a comparison of "always-a-share" and "lost-for-good" markets, see Barbara Bund Jackson, *Winning and Keeping Industrial Customers* (Lexington Books, 1985), chapter 2.

[10]Peters, *Thriving on Chaos*, p. 98.

[11]"Making Service a Potent Marketing Tool," *Business Week,* June 11, 1984, pp. 165 and 167. Using his findings about the purchasing behavior of customers who complain, Goodman has gone on to calculate some awesome figures for the returns on "investments" made to answer complaints, mainly the costs of setting up telephone complaint departments using 800 numbers. The projected returns range from 15% to 400%.

the consumers who switched banks did so because of service problems. The switchers, on average, had used three bank "products"—checking accounts, savings accounts, and so forth—and had total deposit balances of more than $23,000 apiece. In total, Raddon estimates, banks that lost customers because of service problems saw earnings worth hundreds of millions of dollars walk out of their vaults.[12]

By contrast, loyal customers offer their suppliers a triple payoff. They buy instead of being sold, so the marketing and sales costs of reaching them are lower than those of prospecting for new customers. Second, a company that deals with loyal customers knows a good deal about them and about how to get in touch with them, so the firm doesn't have to spend as much for transactions and communications—credit checking, or setting up new records for ordering, shipment, and returns. And a very loyal customer buys more than the moderately loyal or the new customer. In short, loyal customers are valuable not only because they represent lush streams of future revenues, but also because the costs of those revenues are relatively small and the profits commensurately larger. Companies that score higher than their competitors in customer satisfaction and repeat business have the upper hand in financial performance.

Some of the most suggestive evidence about the money companies can save by providing superior service and building customer satisfaction comes from studies of consumer complaint behavior. For several years A. C. Nielsen Co. surveyed customers of one large food processor to find out how often they complained when they were dissatisfied and what they were likely to do about their lack of satisfaction. Nielsen's findings: only 2 percent of unhappy customers complained, while 34 percent of all the dissatisfied penalized the manufacturer by quietly switching brands. Another

---

[12]Gary H. Raddon, "Quality Service—A Low-Cost Profit Strategy," *Bank Marketing* (September 1987), pp. 10–11. It is important to note that Raddon didn't disclose the size or structure of his sample or his survey methods, and that other studies show the main cause of bank switching is the quest for a more convenient location, probably due to customers' changing houses or jobs.

4 percent stopped buying any manufacturer's brand of the offending product type.

Nielsen's figures make for scary arithmetic. Given that 40,000 customers had complained to the manufacturer, it's likely that some 2 million customers were dissatisfied, and that 760,000 switched brands or stopped buying the product altogether.[13] The annual revenue loss to this manufacturer must have run into the millions. Though Nielsen didn't isolate the contribution bad service made to customer dissatisfaction, there's reason to think it's high. One study of why customers switch car dealers, for example, has shown that 68 percent do so because of "indifference shown them by a dealer's sales or service persons." Only 14 percent switch because of dissatisfaction with the actual car.[14]

In distribution businesses, where the essence of customer service is having goods in stock, a pile of academic research demonstrates the costs that good service can avoid. When customers at state liquor stores can't get a particular size and brand, 14 percent will go to another store instead of picking another size or brand of liquor; the second time a stock-out happens, 40 percent will desert.[15] Apparently business customers are even touchier. Studies of the distribution of drugs, dry goods, plumbing supplies and fixtures, and various other industrial products show that business buyers "tend to exaggerate the importance of relatively poor service which may be provided them. However, customers tend to be extremely perceptive in evaluating alternate levels of service provided by different suppliers. [This ability] can result in customers' segmenting suppliers into distinct categories of acceptable and unacceptable levels of service."[16]

In short, when it comes to distribution service, business buyers

[13]C. L. Kendall and Frederick A. Russ, "Warranty and Complaint Policies: An Opportunity for Marketing Management," *Journal of Marketing* (April 1975), p. 37.

[14]Tom Peters, "More Expensive, But Worth It," *U.S. News and World Report,* February 3, 1986, p. 54.

[15]Clyde K. Walter and Bernard J. LaLonde, "Development and Test of Two Stockout Cost Models," *International Journal of Physical Distribution,* vol. 5, no. 3 (1975), p. 121.

[16]Paul H. Zinszer, "Customer Service as an Element of the Marketing Mix" (doctoral dissertation, Ohio State University, 1976), pp. 21–23.

are hypersensitive, quite smart, and prone to see their suppliers in black and white. As manufacturers sell more through distributors and less through their own sales forces,[17] they likely will find that customers are less loyal and more critical, and that the penalties for bad service are higher.

ON THE TRACK OF HARD-DOLLAR BENEFITS

Besides "negative" or "soft-dollar" benefits like cost avoidance, superior service has positive, hard-dollar returns. They tend to accrue over the long term, as a company builds its reputation. Positive customer expectations are among the richest of these payoffs. What has given IBM dominant market share in nearly every industrialized nation is customers' beliefs that Big Blue will solve their problems. Similar expectations are the most valuable assets of American Express, Daimler Benz, L. L. Bean, Caterpillar, and scores of other legendary enterprises.

Generally, customers' expectations are shaped by the way a company has treated them. But for new customers, and for those whose experience is second-hand or infrequent, the biggest shaper of expectations is word of mouth, what people hear about a company from their friends and associates. Word of mouth can influence purchasing decisions more than advertising. General Electric, for instance, has found that word of mouth has twice the effect on a consumer's repurchase decision that corporate advertising does.[18]

Negative word of mouth is a heavy curse. Seriously dissatisfied customers tend to be far more vocal than the satisfied. Depending on the industry and the nature of their bad experience, the dissat-

---

[17]In 1986, when the Conference Board surveyed 214 large manufacturers, half of the companies said they reached most of their customers through distribution channels other than their own salesmen. *Rethinking the Company's Selling and Distribution Channels* (Conference Board Report 885, 1986).

[18]*The Information Challenge*, General Electric Company, Louisville, Kentucky, 1982. Other research indicates that word of mouth is most powerful in determining the purchase of services, a type of decision consumers feel is highly risky because services are intangible and therefore hard to size up before the sale.

isfied will complain to between ten and twenty friends and acquaintances, about three times more than the number of people
who will hear tales of service triumph from a delighted customer.[19]
And negative word of mouth is especially influential. Consumers
generally place more weight on negative information than on the
positive when deciding to buy;[20] some research has shown that
bad word of mouth depresses sales of packaged foods twice as
much as good word of mouth elevates sales.[21]

Unhappily for take-charge managers, word of mouth eludes
direct manipulation. You can't go out and buy so many pounds of
good reputation or invest so many millions in a word-of-mouth
machine. All we know for certain about the creation of word of
mouth is that very satisfied and very dissatisfied customers tend
to tell other people—*lots* of other people—about their experiences. And the only action a company can take to create positive
word of mouth is to offer service that makes every customer extraordinarily satisfied.

Though pinning down the hard-dollar benefits of superior service is difficult, a growing stack of evidence suggests the payoffs
are quite tangible. Much of this proof focuses narrowly on a few
aspects of customer service, or on certain industries. One rigorous
study of twenty-three manufacturing industries in Great Britain
found that suppliers that offered higher levels of inventory and
more liberal credit terms tended to have fatter profits, an association supported by other research as well.[22] In 1982, Shycon Associates, an American management consulting firm, surveyed the customer service activities and financial results of 185 U.S. industrial
companies with annual sales ranging from $50 million to $8 billion.

[19]Technical Assistance Research Programs, "Measuring the Grapevine, Consumer
Response and Word of Mouth" (Coca-Cola USA, Atlanta, Ga., 1981).

[20]Richard J. Lutz, "Changing Brand Attitudes Through Modification of Cognitive
Structure," *Journal of Consumer Research* (March 1975), pp. 49–59.

[21]Johan Arndt, "Role of Product Related Conversations in the Diffusion of a New
Product," *Journal of Marketing Research* (August 1967), pp. 291–295.

[22]Yoram C. Peles and Meir I. Schneller, "Financial Ratios and the Analysis of
Marketing Policy," *European Journal of Marketing,* vol. 16, no. 5 (1982), pp. 12–21. See
also Paul S. Bender, *Design and Operation of Customer Service Systems* (AMACOM,
1976).

The study's main finding: The difference between very good and very bad service can make a difference in absolute sales of 6 percent or more.

According to Shycon, a company with revenues of $250 million can attribute $12.5–15 million of sales to its customer service performance, and some $4–5 million of profits. Within limits, a 1 percent increase in service levels (such as lead time for orders or percentage of on-time deliveries) ultimately will boost sales 1 percent, Shycon estimated, while a 1 percent decrease in service depresses sales by more than 1 percent (just as studies of consumer complaint behavior would suggest). Most important, Shycon found that the "typical" company in the survey could have improved service levels by up to one third before the costs of better service would have overwhelmed the benefits of higher sales and profits.[23] In other words, these companies could have boosted sales up to 33 percent just by improving service.

Or look at supermarkets. At first glance you might think that grocers aren't interested in competing on service. Most stores today are based on the idea of self-service, and price competition is so intense that the typical profit margin for supermarkets is less than 2 percent. Moreover, surveys show that when consumers decide where to shop for food, more of them care about convenient location, wide selection, quality of produce and meat, and low prices than about courteous, friendly service and fast checkout.[24]

[23]"Quality of Customer Service Affects Share of Market," *Sales and Marketing Executive Report,* February 1983, p. 5; "Does Your Customer Service Program Stack Up?" *Traffic Management* magazine (September 1982), pp. 54–58; Shycon Associates, *Survey of Customer Service Requirements of American Industry* (Waltham, Mass., September 1982). The Shycon survey is especially provocative because it used a restricted, traditional definition of customer service, examining ten activities such as order cycle time, emergency deliveries, and order accuracy, and because it examined the impact of service only on distributors and retailers, not on consumers. With a broader definition that included consumers and looked at, say, customer training and after-sale support as well, the results likely would have been even more dramatic.

[24]See Douglas J. Tigert, "Does Your Store Have the Winning Formula?" *Progressive Grocer Executive Report—Loyalty* (August 1986), pp. 45–48. A professor of retail marketing at Babson College, Tigert studies the reasons consumers pick stores. Twenty years worth of surveys with over 40,000 food shoppers in some 40 European, Canadian, and U.S. cities show that "friendly, courteous service and fast checkout" rank sixth in importance, right behind "overall shopping environment and cleanliness."

Yet some of the biggest, most competitive supermarket chains have been adding personal service departments as fast as they can. Among stores with more than $12 million in annual sales, over 85 percent now have delicatessens where a human being waits on customers, two thirds have "service centers" to answer shoppers' questions and cash their checks, and more than half offer fish and cheese departments staffed by living, breathing fish- and cheesemongers.[25]

The more competitive a supermarket's selling area, the more benefit the grocer can expect from customer service. In a fascinating study of independent Texas grocers, researchers first obtained from 379 owner-managers their rankings of the importance of six retailing strategies: store location, product assortment, advertising and promotion, competitive pricing, quality of store personnel, and customer service. The respondents also ranked their local competition as weak, moderate, or strong. Finally they reported their sales, profits, and inventory levels.

When the researchers correlated the grocers' rankings of retail strategies with the financial results of the stores, they found that regardless of the degree of competition, grocers who emphasized price and advertising/promotion tended to be the least successful. By contrast, the winning stores in markets with weak competition tended to stress location (reasonable enough if the local market won't support more than a few stores). Most important, when competition was either moderate or strong, the managers who put customer service first tended to come out ahead.[26]

BIG BUCKS FOR CAR DEALERS

Nowhere is the link between customer service and success in the marketplace clearer than among car dealers. Study after study has

[25]"Customer Service Expands Across the Board," *Progressive Grocer 54th Annual Report,* April 1987, p. 25.

[26]L. Lynn Judd and Bobby C. Vaught, "An Analysis of Market Strategy and Store Profitability by Area Competition," *An Assessment of Marketing Thought and Practice: Educators Conference Proceedings, Series 48* (American Marketing Association, 1982), pp. 220–223.

shown a very strong relationship between a customer's experience when getting his car repaired and his intention to buy another car from the dealer who's doing the work.[27] The single best way to drive away a customer is to make him keep coming back to get the same problem fixed.[28] And it's not just the offended car owner who will stay away, but most of his friends and acquaintances as well: "Owners who experience mechanical difficulties with their new car that are not fixed with dispatch, and stay fixed, are quick to broadcast their woes to anyone who will listen."[29]

The hard-dollar benefits of customer service for car dealers are enormous. Ivyl Lee Gilbert, a veteran of a quarter century in the automobile business, measured the benefits of service by looking at customer satisfaction ratings for the more than 5,000 dealers of one U.S. car maker. Then he correlated certain important service ratings with market penetration. Among Gilbert's findings: dealers that excel at preparing new cars for delivery, cheerfully honoring warranties, and fixing things right the first time can expect roughly *twice* as much market share as dealers that flub those jobs.[30]

Ford recently stacked up the business performance of its 850 largest U.S. dealers against the satisfaction of customers during their first year of ownership. On average, dealers in the top 10 percent of the satisfaction ratings had car market shares 3 percentage points greater than the mean share for all Ford dealers, and truck market shares 4.5 percentage points greater. Dealers who did the best job of satisfying customers sported returns on

[27]J. L. Braden, "Measuring Consumer Satisfaction with Automobile Repairs (Summary)," *Proceedings of the Second Annual Conference on Consumer Satisfaction, Dissatisfaction and Complaining Behavior, 2* (1977), p. 172, cited in Ivyl Lee Gilbert, "Service Begets Sales: An Investigation into the Relationship of Automotive Dealership Customer Service Satisfaction with Sales Success" (doctoral thesis, Western Michigan University, 1986).

[28]See almost any issue of *The Power Newsletter,* as well as M. D. Bernacchi, K. Kono, and G. L. Willette, "An Analysis of Automobile Warranty Service Dissatisfaction (Summary)," *Proceedings of the Fourth Annual Conference on Consumer Satisfaction, Dissatisfaction and Complaining Behavior, 4* (1979), pp. 141–143, cited in Gilbert, "Service Begets Sales. . . ."

[29]J. D. Power, "Recurring Repair Problems Undermine Customer Loyalty," *The Power Newsletter* (March 1982), pp. 4–5.

[30]Gilbert, "Service Begets Sales. . . ."

investment nearly 30 percent higher than average. One major reason for that superior performance: people who had bought cars from these star dealers were three times more likely to repurchase than were the "very dissatisfied" customers of other dealers.[31]

A sterling example of the impact of service is Tasca Lincoln-Mercury of Seekonk, Massachusetts. As *Fortune* magazine observed, the Tasca dealership "ought to be dying. It is a single-line car dealer in an era of hungry multiline megadealers. Its cramped showroom-garage is 17 years old. The salesmen look like sharks. The mechanics are scruffy. And Seekonk . . . is hardly a go-go growth area." Yet in 1986 and 1987, Tasca sold more cars than any other Lincoln-Mercury dealer in America. Why? Because an unusually high percentage of Tasca's customers were delighted with the service they'd received.[32]

WHERE SERVICE MATTERS MOST

The impact of outstanding customer service is almost always positive, but it does vary. Service may not be crucial for monopolies, or in dictatorships, or when poverty forces customers to buy strictly on price.[33] Even in those cases, though, indifference to service is dangerous. When customer dissatisfaction gets bad enough, monopolies can be broken. Dictatorships can be forced to admit competition, as the Soviet Union has done by condoning private enterprises that have taken up the slack left by incompetent state-managed businesses. Lacking adequate service, impoverished price buyers will switch brands at the first opportunity.

The payoffs to service seem to be greatest in:

mature markets, like those for cars, farm equipment, and certain chemicals;

[31]Joseph A. Kordick, vice president and general manager, Ford Parts and Service Division, speech to the 32nd Annual Conference of Service Managers, Dearborn, Michigan, October 12, 1987.

[32]Thomas Moore, "Would You Buy a Car from This Man?" *Fortune,* April 11, 1988, pp. 72–74.

[33]See Milind M. Lele with Jagdish N. Sheth, *The Customer Is Key,* pp. 12–13.

highly competitive industries, like air transport, office equipment, and packaged foods;

so-called *commodity businesses* like banking and primary steelmaking, where customer service is the only means of differentiation; and

any business based on products that cost a lot, last for a while, and need after-sale support and maintenance to be useful, all characteristics that lead customers to pay extra attention to the service that comes with a product.

THE FINAL SCORE

Though nobody has developed a general model of service costs and benefits and applied it to different industries, we can confidently make one assertion: *In all industries, when competitors are roughly matched, those that stress customer service will win.*

For supporting evidence look at the largest, longest analysis of corporate strategy and financial performance ever undertaken, the Profit Impact of Marketing Strategy—or PIMS—study conducted by the Strategic Planning Institute (SPI), of Cambridge, Massachusetts. Beginning in 1972, SPI has collected data about the market characteristics, competitive positions, and financial and operating performance of some 2,600 "business units"—freestanding companies or divisions of large corporations, four fifths of them manufacturers. Since SPI's goal was to discover the broadest range of strategic principles that affect financial performance, it analyzed any element of strategy that seemed likely to work, might apply across all business units, and could be measured, such as capital intensity.

The PIMS study found at least a dozen elements of strategy that strongly influenced performance, but the most effective was quality as customers perceive it: *"In the long run, the most important single factor affecting a business unit's performance is the quality of its products and services, relative to those of competitors"* (italics in the original).[34] Companies that ranked among the top

[34]Robert D. Buzzell and Bradley T. Gale, *The PIMS Principles: Linking Strategy to Performance* (Free Press, 1987), p. 7.

one fifth in perceived quality had an average return on investment of 32 percent and an average return on sales of 14 percent, versus 17 percent and 7 percent, respectively, for companies in the lowest quintile of perceived quality. And though many quality leaders succeeded by making better quality products, the PIMS study noted that "better performance on product attributes is not the only way to win. By our definition, relative perceived quality covers all the non-price attributes that count in the purchase decision. Businesses frequently achieve a superior overall quality position by developing a better *image* than competitors or providing better *customer services* than competitors."[35] For example, PIMS data about chemical businesses in very similar markets showed that the winners in market share and production volume characteristically offered "superior *service* to immediate customers and continued to upgrade it."[36] True, the PIMS study didn't measure exactly what factors shaped perceptions of quality. But since service has an overwhelming impact on those perceptions, it's clearly a prime competitive weapon. And because it tends to be less tangible, more durable, and harder to create than product quality, high-quality customer service is the ultimate weapon.

NO LEAPFROGGING

The service winners know that customer service is both a potent competitive advantage and a peculiarly defensible one. Because customers perceive service in relative terms, a competitor who wants to beat a company that offers relatively superior service can't play catch up. He has to leapfrog, to outdistance the competition. But since providing great service tends to be expensive, leapfrogging can break the bank.

Leapfrogging is difficult because good service tends to be self-reinforcing. In a phenomenon some researchers call the "virtuous circle," customers that are well served tend to cooperate more in

[35]Buzzell and Gale, *The PIMS Principles: Linking Strategy to Performance,* p. 115.
[36]*Ibid.,* p. 133.

service processes, making it easier and less expensive to satisfy them and to increase their levels of satisfaction.[37] Thanks to the virtuous circle, companies that provide better service have lower service costs and higher service productivity.

They also can achieve significant economies of scale and of scope. Providing good service usually means investing in infrastructures—branch offices, training centers, repair vehicles, spare parts, and, especially, computer systems that collect data about customers in order to improve responses to customer needs. Once those infrastructures are in place, the unit costs of customer service keep falling with increased volume, up to the point where infrastructure capacity has to be increased. A competitor who comes late to the customer service game is almost certain to have higher unit costs for a long time.

Moreover, with an infrastructure in place, the cost of adding additional services is incremental and relatively low. A maintenance operation designed to keep office copiers running can take on the added task of repairing typewriters fairly easily; customer information collected mainly to answer questions about bills can also be used to plan a shipping schedule that matches the customer's historic consumption pattern. While a competitor struggles to build customer service infrastructures, the company that already has them in place keeps upping the stakes by adding new services.

WHEN THE ULTIMATE WEAPON BACKFIRES

How to create the ultimate weapon is by no means obvious. Contrary to the opinions of many management writers, simply declaring your company will do anything to please customers and following up to make sure it does may lead to disaster. As Christopher Lovelock, a specialist in service operations, has noted, "a purely marketing mind set that only desires to satisfy the

[37]See, for example, Richard Normann, *Service Management: Strategy and Leadership in Service Businesses* (John Wiley & Sons, 1984), Chapter 12, pp. 117–127.

needs of the customer" is a prescription for bankruptcy. Efforts to improve service have to be balanced against a company's operational needs, like standardizing the production of service, managing capacity, and controlling quality.[38]

It's possible to go too far. Companies that don't pay attention to the mechanics of producing service end up making questionable sacrifices in their search for service stardom. Service Supply Corp., for example, is an Indianapolis-based, family-owned distributor of industrial fasteners—nuts, bolts, screws—that *Industrial Distribution* magazine named "Distributor of the Century," based on the opinions of competitors and suppliers.[39] Fastener distributors, on average, can ship from stock about sixty-five of every one hundred items that a customer orders; excellent ones have "fill rates" of 80 to 85 percent. The fill rate for Service Supply, which calls itself the "House of a Million Screws," is an astounding 95 percent, thanks to an inventory that includes over 74,000 items. With its own fleet of trucks, the company delivers most orders overnight, and its manager-owners delight in filling emergency orders.

Not surprisingly, the company's 15,000 customers are very pleased. Service Supply charges about 5 percent more than the competition, but its sales, some $75 million in 1988, have grown faster than industry sales. Yet earnings are substandard. Carrying all that inventory takes about 3 percent out of profit margins; other special services gobble up at least that much. "The return doesn't necessarily come to the bottom line," explains president Mel Seitz, Jr. "But we feel our reputation—and the increased business we get through reputation—are worth it." Outsized increases in sales and market share may eventually lead to lower costs and higher profits for Service Supply, as the PIMS data suggest they will. But until those superior profits materialize, Seitz sounds a little like the foolish retailer who keeps cutting price in hopes of making it up in volume.

[38]See C. Lovelock, "Services Marketers Must Balance Customer Satisfaction Against Their Operational Needs," *Marketing News,* October 10, 1986, pp. 1 and 14.
[39]See *Industrial Distribution* (December 1986).

Phil Bressler also is famous for his dedication to customers. The owner of eighteen Domino's Pizza outlets in the Baltimore area, Bressler strictly enforces a Domino's policy of taking $3 off any pizza that's delivered more than thirty minutes after it's ordered. During one snowstorm, Bressler's chain delivered 330 pizzas free.

The results? Among Domino's roughly 4,000 outlets, Bressler's have the highest percentage of customers who return, 98.2 percent. But his operations also have some of Domino's lowest profit margins. Bressler reasons that extraordinary service will protect his company from competitors and help him grab share in an immature regional market.[40] Like Seitz, he seems to count on recovering foregone profits in the long run by building volume today. But what if costs don't decline continuously as volume rises? Then the only way for Bressler and Seitz to improve profitability will be to raise prices and/or lower service. Either course threatens to offend the customers they have pampered so well.

It's also possible to put the cart before the horse, trying to capitalize on customer service when your core product or service is grossly inferior in design, performance, or cost. Just as controlling quality at the end of a production line is ineffective and ruinously expensive, so is trying to repair a poorly designed and manufactured product once it's in customers' hands. Repair and maintenance costs will eat you alive. The same holds true for service industries. The current drive by airlines to please customers with better meals, more convenient check-in, and nicer cabin crews will backfire unless the airlines can reliably produce their core service—getting passengers from point A to point B on time and with their luggage.

A leading cause of service mishaps is aiming at the wrong target. Definitions of good service vary by industry, by channel of distribution, by type of product, by class of customer, and by the service levels your competitors offer. Many aspiring service leaders have come to grief because they didn't take time to figure out exactly how customers defined outstanding service.

[40]We thank Chris Hart for bringing Bressler to our attention. See John Hillkirk, "Domino's Service No Game," *USA Today,* July 21, 1987, p. 7b, and Peters, *Thriving on Chaos,* pp. 95 and 186–190.

In the prescription drug industry, for example, different classes of retailers see service differently. Retailers with low growth and low sales want wholesalers to supply services that save time and money and help pull drugs through the distribution channel. But high-growth, high-sales retailers want far fewer services. They tend to view wholesalers simply as conduits from manufacturers and as back-ups for the retailers' own distribution centers.[41] In other industries, suppliers regularly give customers more than they want of some kinds of service, and too little of others.[42] And even when sellers offer exactly the services buyers require, the buyers don't necessarily know it.[43]

Sticking to your own definition of service, without asking customers what they want and expect, is always a mistake. Intel, for example, believed for years that it was serving customers well by shipping chips within one week of the promised shipment date. Yet the company discovered that major customers viewed Intel's service as unacceptable because their criterion for timely shipment was plus or minus a few days. Xerox used to define good service as repairing copiers quickly and effectively when they broke down. Customers seemed to agree. But then Japanese companies entered the market with new, more reliable machines.

[41]Frances Gaither Tucker, "Customer Service in a Channel of Distribution: The Case of the Manufacturer-Wholesaler-Chain Drug Retailer Channel in the Prescription Drug Industry" (doctoral thesis, Ohio State University, 1980), pp. 160–161. Tucker suggests (p. 165) that concepts of customer service vary so much that they must be defined by industry and even by company. Other studies concur, especially Bernard J. LaLonde and Paul H. Zinszer, *Customer Service: Meaning and Measurement* (National Council of Physical Distribution Managers, 1976).

[42]"Over-servicing" and giving the wrong kind of service appear to be common when service is defined narrowly as physical distribution: "In most cases, firms that have conducted surveys of customer expectations of services have found that the firm was attempting to provide higher levels of services than the customers required. Furthermore, customers' interests have shifted from a focus on speed of delivery to a focus on constancy of delivery. In some industries, primarily in the food industry, it is considered as bad a practice for a shipment to arrive early as for it to arrive late because of unloading or warehousing constraints." James F. Robeson and Robert G. House, *The Distribution Handbook* (Free Press, 1985), p. 245.

[43]See Rammohan Pisharodi, "A Behavioral Process Model of Customer Service Evaluation Based on Supplier-Customer Differences in Perception" (doctoral thesis, University of Tennessee, Knoxville, 1985). Pisharodi found that most grocery wholesalers in his sample didn't know about the customer service policies of their suppliers, even when those policies were clearly stated and handed out to the wholesalers.

They triumphed over Xerox by discovering that what customers really meant by good service was machines that didn't break down.

By now it should be obvious that customer service is indeed the ultimate weapon. Companies that enjoy a service advantage are essentially unstoppable.

What may be less obvious is that achieving outstanding service isn't simple. Much customer service has attributes that make it hard to manage. It's intangible, so it eludes clear-cut measures of productivity. It's often produced, delivered, and consumed all at once, and by a human being, so it's hard to break down and control with any consistency. It can't be stockpiled or kept in inventory, so service capacity and service demand have to be matched with great precision. And the company that offers customer service has less than complete control over producing it. In almost every case, the customer, who is difficult to manage, helps produce the service—by picking items off a supermarket shelf, reading a computer manual, or describing a broken appliance over the telephone.

For those and other reasons, producing great service is an enormous challenge. But there's really no choice. We hope the next chapters will give you some valuable ideas about how to do it.

Setting the Stage:
Strategy

The first and most important step toward outstanding service is developing a service strategy. Strategy sets the stage and defines the constraints for all the other steps. Overlooking strategy and rushing headlong to improve service is always a mistake.

The elements of strategy sound simple to achieve. Developing a strategy means nothing more than segmenting customers according to their service expectations, finding out exactly what those expectations are, and adjusting customer expectations to match your ability to deliver service. With those three elements in place, high levels of customer satisfaction are much more likely.

But as this chapter shows, creating a service strategy is a subtle and demanding task. Only a few lucky organizations manage to get it right without continual effort.

Shouldice Hospital, near Toronto, Canada, is an institution beloved by students of customer service.[1] For one thing, it is a model

[1]Professor James L. Heskett of the Harvard Business School made Shouldice famous by describing it in an HBS case ("Shouldice Hospital Limited," 1983, revised 1988, ICCH #9-683-068) and in *Managing in the Service Economy* (Harvard Business School

of productivity in an industry bedeviled by rising costs. Surgery patients stay at Shouldice for three and a half days, on average, compared with five to eight days at most hospitals. With only eighty-nine beds, Shouldice performs some 7,500 operations a year. Doctors get paid less than they would in private practice; nurses attend to several times as many patients as they would elsewhere. Patients care for themselves, getting to the operating room on their own steam, walking to the recovery room, taking their meals in a common dining room.

The bottom line: Shouldice charges about $1,200 for a hospital stay that usually costs at least $3,500 in the United States, and it reliably turns a profit. Between 1982 and 1986, while many hospitals showed deficits despite their rising prices, Shouldice's profits increased 6 percent a year.

Does this sound like a low-quality, uncaring production line? It's just the opposite. Measured by how often patients need to be treated again for the same problem, Shouldice is over ten times as effective as other hospitals. Nurses spend an inordinate amount of time counseling patients. The patients are so delighted with the Shouldice experience that they hold an annual reunion to commemorate it. The January 1988 jamboree at the Royal York Hotel in Toronto attracted 1,500 alumni. Shouldice doesn't advertise, and it gets relatively few referrals from private doctors. Yet the hospital draws patients from all over the United States and Canada, and even a few from Europe, because delighted customers keep spreading the good word.

There's only one thing wrong with this picture of great service: most sick people can't get admitted to Shouldice. If you have a broken bone, clogged arteries, or even a mole that needs removing, you had better apply elsewhere. Shouldice accepts just one type of patient, those whose only complaint is a hernia. The hospital will reject even hernia victims if they have a history of heart trouble or have undergone surgery within the last

---

Press, 1986), pp. 27–29. Alan O'Dell, the administrator of Shouldice, was kind enough to update and expand on Heskett's material for us.

twelve months, or if they show up weighing more than Shouldice recommends.

SHOULDICE'S SECRET

A tightly focused strategy is the key to Shouldice's performance. By segmenting the market of sick people according to their complaint, then concentrating on a single segment, Shouldice has gained the ability to optimize its operations far more than general hospitals can. Its doctors have become highly proficient after doing hundreds of hernia repairs a year using Shouldice's special technique. They rarely use general anesthesia because local anesthesia, which is safer and less expensive, will do for hernia repairs. Patients are able to walk after their operations, and they recover from surgery faster if they're up and about, so Shouldice doesn't have to pay for wheelchairs and gurneys, or attendants to push them, or banks of wide elevators. Instead, it gives patients hallways with comfortable carpeting, staircases that have especially low risers, and acres of well-groomed grounds on which to stroll. Television sets and toilets are located centrally, which encourages patients to walk around even as it saves the hospital money.

Homing in on hernias enables Shouldice to produce a highly competitive core service: a hernia repair that works better and costs less. But that's not the main reason for Shouldice's success. Other organizations, notably the Lichtenstein Hernia Institute of Los Angeles, do low-cost repairs that work at least as well.

No, people flock to Shouldice because they hear from former patients that being there is a great experience. The hospital earns this enthusiastic word of mouth because it augments the ability of patients to derive value from its core service. Of course, few people can evaluate the quality of a hospital's core service, medical care. What they can and do appraise is the experience of hospitalization, from the welcome they receive at check-in to the behavior of their fellow patients to the attentiveness and perceived competence of doctors and nurses.

Shouldice ensures a first-rate experience by stressing camaraderie among patients and by giving them a sizable role in producing hospital services. It tries to assign roommates with similar backgrounds and interests, and it arranges for patients to get together frequently, at check-in, at mealtimes, and at evening socials. To minimize the feelings of impotence and frustration that come with waiting to be served, Shouldice has its customers fill out pre-registration forms that streamline check-in and diagnosis. Instead of counting the minutes until nurses show up, patients shave their own abdomens and groins before the operation and move around the hospital with little help. They conduct their own physical therapy by walking and climbing stairs instead of depending on a staff of therapists.

Do-it-yourself service cuts costs, of course. But it also counteracts a major anxiety that preys on basically well people in hospitals—the feeling that they have lost control of their daily lives. "By the way they act, you'd think our patients own this place," Shouldice administrator Alan O'Dell told one researcher. "And while they're here, in a way they do."[2]

Moreover, by reducing dependence on the hospital staff, self-service reduces the chances that a nurse or doctor will appear to have treated a patient with indifference. While most patients who have recovered from surgery can't wait to go home, Shouldice's customers often are so satisfied that they ask to stay an extra day.

Could Shouldice produce outstanding customer service absent its clear strategy? Probably not without redesigning its physical and social systems and sending its rates sky high. Shouldice is ill-suited for treating people with broken legs or weak hearts, who can't walk much, or those who have had major surgery and need intravenous feeding, or patients recovering from plastic surgery, who seldom want to socialize. Shouldice managers have thought about doing minor eye surgery and repairing varicose veins and hemorrhoids, procedures fairly similar to hernia repair in terms of

[2]Heskett, "Shouldice Hospital Limited."

their demands on the hospital's systems. But "fairly similar" isn't close enough. Shouldice has rejected those ideas in order to stick with the segment it knows best and serves most effectively.

THE COST OF FUZZY FOCUS

By contrast, fuzzy or conflicting strategies make good customer service impossible. Look at People Express. Jumping into the airline business in 1981, it targeted budget travelers—students, backpackers, vacationers, and others who were willing to sacrifice convenient schedules and airport gates for low prices. People Express customers seemed to enjoy the airline's widely advertised "no frills" service, which gave them the options of bringing their own food or paying extra for a snack in flight, of carrying their luggage or paying $3 a bag to check it, and of buying a ticket on board instead of purchasing one in advance. The People Express fleet grew from three airplanes to 117 in five years, and the company's revenues soared from $38 million to nearly $1 billion.

But People soon discovered it had overexpanded. The airline had thousands of seats available each day, but its traditional customers flew mainly on weekends and during the summer and other vacation times. The glut of empty seats produced a $3.7 million loss in 1984, People's first deficit ever.

So People scrambled to get more revenue from its fleet. It scheduled each plane for as many flights as possible, and it grossly overbooked to compensate for passengers who made reservations but didn't show up. The linchpin of the new strategy was to broaden, in effect to blur, People's original strategy by going after business travelers, whose demand for flights is heaviest during the week and nicely complements the demand pattern of budget fliers. The airline started pitching businessmen to try its luxurious first-class service, complete with leather seats.[3]

[3]Douglas B. Feaver, "Will Success Dampen People Express' Spirit?" *San Jose Mercury News,* November 3, 1985, and William M. Carley, "Bumpy Ride: Many Travelers Gripe About People Express, Citing Overbooking," *Wall Street Journal,* May 19, 1986.

Nearly everything People Express had done to serve the budget-minded conflicted with this strategy. Among the aspects of travel that business people most dislike are inconvenient schedules and gates, paying extra for checked baggage and meals, and waiting until the last minute to buy tickets. People's tight scheduling meant that many flights were late, and overbooking meant that it often turned away passengers who had reserved seats, earning itself a new name, "People Distress."

Budget travelers might have put up with these annoyances, but not the kind of flier who has to be on time for a meeting. Ironically, in-flight service in first class often was excellent—if you were smart enough to fly during the troughs of People's demand. Nonetheless, business travelers stayed away. The airline racked up a net loss of $300 million for 1986 and was taken over by Texas Air. People Express might still be around if it had continued to focus tightly on budget fliers and had sold off or leased planes to cut capacity.

WHO NEEDS A STRATEGY?

Developing a strategy for customer service may sound like a waste of time. How much strategy do you need to send out a repairman or to adjust an erroneous bill? Yet even those simple activities won't do much for customer satisfaction or corporate profits unless they are part of a considered strategy. Without a strategy, you don't know exactly who your customers are, how much they value different aspects of service, how much you will have to spend to satisfy them, and how big the payoffs are likely to be. Without a strategy, you can't develop a concept of service to rally around, or catch conflicts between corporate strategy and customer service, or come up with effective ways to measure service performance and perceived quality. In short, without a strategy you can't get to first base.

Companies without clear service strategies have a hard time perceiving conflicts among different types of customers. Pan Am, for example, uses flights from Europe to New York to feed flights it runs out of New York to the West Coast. As the European flights often are delayed because of congestion and bad weather, Pan Am holds its coast-to-coast flights so travelers from Europe can make connections. The result: Pan Am's coast-to-coast service frequently starts late, sometimes hours late. So while travelers from Europe get good service, bi-coastal regulars don't, and they tend to steer away from Pan Am. A coherent strategy for customer service would show the airline that it can't provide outstanding service to both segments and force it to concentrate on one or the other.

A clear strategy also helps flush out product, marketing, and distribution decisions that undermine good service. After a computer maker launches a new operating system—a suite of housekeeping programs that control a computer's basic operations—it has to spend heavily on modifying that software to suit customers' needs and on keeping it up to date. Since the fixed costs of producing these software services totally overwhelm the variable costs, the sensible strategy is to support just one operating system that will suit many market segments. In the early 1960s, however, General Electric introduced three computer systems with three different operating systems. Daisy Systems tried the same thing in the mid-1980s. Both companies saw profits dwindle because they didn't have enough users for each system to cover the fixed costs of customer service, a result they could have foreseen if they had done some strategic thinking.[4]

Perhaps the most important reason for developing a service strategy is that it's the only effective way to choose the optimum mix and level of service for different customer sets. Provide too little service, and of the wrong kind, and customers will leave; provide too much, even of the right kind, and your company will either go broke or price itself out of the market.

[4]At one point Digital Equipment Corp. supported nearly two dozen operating systems because it refused to follow the industry practice of dropping support for old systems as new ones took hold. DEC could afford this singularly high level of customer service because most of the operating systems it supported were quite mature, and it had loyal, free-spending customers for each one. IBM can support several operating systems because each one serves a large market segment. Today, both companies are trying to concentrate on just one operating system.

Proof of that truism comes from a General Electric experiment that varied the levels of repair service for out-of-warranty appliances over a two-year period. GE discovered that repair service is very much subject to the law of diminishing returns.[5] There's a certain point where each incremental investment in service yields lower returns than the previous investment. And the only way to find that point is to segment customers, find out how much they value different levels of service, and calculate the costs and benefits of serving them well.

Simply charging ahead with extraordinary service doesn't guarantee high profits, as Service Supply Corp., the "House of a Million Screws," should know. If Service Supply had a cogent strategy for customer service, it would stratify its 15,000 customers according to their sensitivity to stock-outs of different classes of fasteners, then adjust its inventory levels and prices to address those tiers with the highest potential profits. As it is, Service Supply gives outstanding service to *all* its customers, regardless of their different needs for service and willingness to pay, and it can't charge enough on average to bring profits up to industry norms.

DIVIDE AND CONQUER

The essence of any customer service strategy is to segment the customers to be served. As James L. Heskett of the Harvard Business School puts it when discussing services in general:

> A service cannot be all things to all people. Unlike product manufacturers, service organizations can have considerable difficulty delivering more than one "product," more than one type or level of service, at one time. Groups or "segments" of customers must be singled out for a particular service, their needs determined, and a service concept developed that provides a competitive advantage for the server in the eyes of those to be served. . . . *Segmentation is the process of identifying groups of customers with enough characteristics in common to make*

[5]Cited in "Customer Service and Satisfaction as a Differential Advantage," *Management Horizons Retail Focus/Critical Issues Series,* November 1986.

*possible the design and presentation of a product or service each group
needs.* (emphasis added)[6]

In practice, marketing segmentation focuses on what various people and organizations need, while customer service segmentation focuses on what they expect. Marketers tend to use immediate sales to judge whether a segment is valid. Since purchasing decisions look binary—the sale is made or it isn't—the validity of marketing segments seems easy to assess.

Customer service expectations, and the satisfaction levels that go with meeting or exceeding them, are more diverse than sale/no sale. All sorts of business customers will buy parts from a distributor; yet their expectations for service vary by industry, geographical region, company size, and nature of the production process. First-time buyers of Ferrari cars are easy to target for sales purposes: they tend to be extroverted males in their mid-forties with very high disposable incomes, some leisure time, and a number of cars in the garage already. But segmenting them for the purposes of customer service is more complex. Some enjoy working on the cars themselves, some expect the dealer to give perfect, fix-it-the-first-time service, and others don't care much about repairs because they intend to replace the car quickly.

Occasionally, marketing segments and customer service segments are the same, especially for service companies that have well-focused, comprehensive marketing strategies. Those strategies can meet a broad range of expectations for service. Federal Express's strategy, for example, is to meet expectations for all the actions and reactions that customers perceive they have purchased, including not only pick up and delivery but also documentation and information about shipments. More often, though, defining customer service segments means rethinking overly broad market segments and the ways in which they impede superior service.

Intelligent segmentation can transform the productivity and profitability of customer service operations, as Shouldice's strat-

[6]Heskett, *Managing in the Service Economy*, pp. 8–9.

egy shows. Much customer service consists of employees interacting with customers in high-touch environments like hotel lobbies. It's hard to control service quality in those settings because human behavior is so unpredictable. It's also hard to get big productivity gains by substituting capital and technology for labor since high-touch customer service means, by definition, lots of flexible, warm, human interaction. So managers often seek to substitute low-touch service for the high-touch kind, offering, for instance, automatic check-out from the hotel instead of the usual front-desk check-out.

The problem is that some customers welcome low-touch substitutes while others view them as cost-cutting measures that reduce the quality of service. Compared with business travelers, tourists staying at a grand hotel have far less expectation of fast checkout. They may see automatic check-out as a jarring, impersonal note in their hotel experience. Veteran users of home appliances may prefer getting repair instructions over the telephone, while novices expect a human repairman to show up. Only after a company has segmented its customers and chosen which ones to serve can it figure out where to substitute low touch for high, thus improving productivity without imperiling customer satisfaction.

THE CONUNDRUM OF SERVICE CAPACITY

Segmentation also is key to solving one of the thorniest problems in customer service—matching supply and demand. When manufacturers of physical goods find they have too much capacity, they produce for inventory or shut down machines and lay off workers. When they have too much demand, they draw down inventory, run factories continuously, hire extra shifts, and call on the capacity of other suppliers.

Companies trying to give good customer service have fewer options. Service can't be stored in inventory. Seldom can you substitute another company's service for your own and keep meeting customer expectations, since those expectations refer to a unique experience, not an interchangeable product. Suddenly increasing or decreasing service capacity—people, mainly—ensures shoddy quality, or even a breakdown of the service "factory," as anyone can attest who has stayed at a large hotel when it's hosting a convention. Since demand for customer service isn't homogeneous—every segment demands somewhat different versions of excellent service—service organizations need slack capacity for adapting their product to mixed demand. By some estimates, the quality of service drops off sharply when demand exceeds as little as 75 percent of theoretical capacity.[7]

Until it segments, a hotel or a field force of computer engineers may see huge and apparently random fluctuations in demand. But segmenting usually shows that the overall pattern is made up of several smaller, more predictable patterns that are more manageable.[8] For instance, convention visitors, ordinary business travelers, foreign tourists, and vacationing families all contribute to variations in demand for service in hotels. With any luck, the distinctive patterns of their demands can be forecast. Then the hotel can adjust capacity accordingly by, say, shifting employees from the front desk to banquet service, or by cutting prices during slack periods in order to boost demand. Similarly, though the general demand for field service may appear to vary randomly, computer users in banks and universities demand different kinds of service and at different times. The smart manager schedules field engineers to shift from one segment to another as bank users shut down for the day and academic users rev up, and he varies prices to reflect the cost and value of different levels of service. Segmenting may even reveal that some kinds of demand are undesirable and should be finessed, such as the demand on a bank to make change for non-customers and the demand on a fire department to rescue cats from trees.[9]

[7]Heskett, *Managing in the Service Economy*, p. 38.

[8]Christopher H. Lovelock, *Services Marketing* (Prentice-Hall, 1984), p. 280.

[9]The cats come courtesy of Lovelock, *ibid.* Simply ignoring demand is nearly always dangerous. Disgruntled non-customers, like the grandmother whose cat is up a tree, can spread just as much bad word about a company as customers can. Better than ignoring inappropriate demand is lowering the expectations of non-customers—making sure cat owners know that the fire department is always busy fighting fires—or creating disincentives, like a $20 charge for restoring arboreal cats to earth.

Among the most powerful ways to vary service capacity with demand is to expand the role of customers in producing service, to make them more effective co-producers. The customer always helps produce service to some degree, by reading a manual, returning an appliance for repair, filling out an airbill, or participating in the service ritual at a fancy restaurant. Finding opportunities to expand his role, to move toward self-service, often depends on savvy segmentation.

Automated teller machines, for example, increase the role of customers in producing some banking services and thus represent highly flexible capacity. The greater the demand on the machines, the greater the capacity customers provide (at least until the waiting line gets too long).

But targeting the right kinds of customers for ATMs is crucial. Retirees and other older people tend to resist the machines, especially in smaller towns. So do the very wealthy, who expect the attention and service of human beings in return for their lucrative business. Even the prime targets for ATMs—computer-literate professionals in big cities—won't be satisfied unless the bank segments out those customers, studies their expectations, and designs the ATM system to meet or exceed expectations.

Large corporations that use personal computers may prefer to do as much repair in house as possible, and they can afford technicians to handle the job; individual users expect some degree of outside help, depending on whether they're seasoned hobbyists or technophobic novices. A personal computer maker, having segmented its customers according to their service expectations, will know to offer diagnostic software to large corporations that can serve themselves, telephone consultation to hobbyists who would like to serve themselves, and full-blown repair service to novices who have no interest in self-service.

SALVATION BY SEGMENTATION

For some companies, carving out segments is a matter of life and death. The best examples come from banking, where core services are close to being pure commodities. Pundits have forecast the death of the small town bank ever since the early 1980s, when deregulation started opening local markets to efficient regional and money center banks. Many local banks in fact have closed their doors or disappeared into the maws of acquisition-hungry super-regionals, big chains that serve contiguous states.

Surprisingly often, though, local banks have prospered despite the competition by focusing on certain customer segments whose service expectations the big boys don't satisfy. University National Bank & Trust (UNBT) of Palo Alto, California, which Tom Peters eulogizes for its service, has just one office. The bank discourages small depositors by setting a high monthly fee for checking accounts—$20—and waiving it only for average monthly balances of at least $3,000. Deadbeats need not apply: new customers are accepted only with a referral or after a credit check, and bouncing two checks will close your account.

Yet UNBT keeps gaining market share and consistently earns a return on assets more than twice the average for California banks. Like its mammoth competitors, Wells Fargo, First Interstate, and Bank of America, UNBT has targeted individuals with high net worth, generally over $500,000. Unlike its competitors, UNBT serves *only* those customers, and it serves them with a specialized array of services that includes free travelers checks, cashier's checks, and stop payment orders, streamlined approval of large loans, free shoeshines when they visit the bank, and a free sack of sweet onions every July. More important than any of these features, says Carl J. Schmitt, chairman, "was the concept that we would keep the ½ of 1% of [customers who are] bad guys out of the bank's customer base. It is that ½ of 1% that causes the large banks to create the arbitrary rules that in turn create the 'hassle' experienced in the large bank."[10]

Countless other small banks have prospered by following UNBT's strategy, from the Bank of Darien in Darien, Connecticut, which brags that it was founded "of, by, and for the rich," to the

[10]Letter from Carl J. Schmitt, chairman and chief executive officer, University National Bank & Trust Company, June 30, 1988.

tiny Bank of San Francisco, with less than $300 million in assets. As Don Stephens, chairman of Bank of San Francisco, describes his strategy: "There are two main things rich people want. It's important to customers that the people they bank with don't change—when they get to know someone, that person should continue to be their banker virtually forever. That's the single most important thing in banking. We provide that and the big banks don't. Second, they want a bank to make a decision with reasonable swiftness and make a decision outside of normal banking habits. And we have those abilities."[11]

Significantly, it's the segmenting that counts, not whether the customers are particularly rich. For sixty-eight years, the only bank on Catalina Island, off Los Angeles, was a branch of California's giant Security Pacific. In 1982, the National Bank of Catalina Island (NBCI), a rank upstart, entered the market. Realizing that most Catalina residents were more than fifty-five years old, NBCI focused on that segment, offering several augmented services: chatty tellers, Saturday hours, and, especially valuable, a car that would come to elderly customers' homes to accept deposits. In less than two years NBCI had more accounts than Security Pacific; in less than three years it had driven Security Pacific off the island.[12]

In Florida, small, independent banks have been popping up everywhere and taking business from the super-regionals that hold over half the market. The independents, styling themselves "community bankers," focus on individuals and small businesses that resent the impersonal service big banks offer. Their success has forced some big banks to see the error of standardizing service across very different segments. For example, Stephen Hansell, chief operating officer of Barnett Banks, Florida's biggest super-regional, now notes that retired people "are less time-sensitive or credit-sensitive [than most customers], but . . . very service-sensitive."[13]

[11]Quoted in Mard Naman, "Competitive Banking," *San Francisco Business Magazine,* April 1, 1986, p. 16.

[12]We learned of National Bank of Catalina Island from Richard Whiteley, president of Forum North America, which trains sales and service forces.

[13]John Helyar, "Multistate Banks Rile Many Customers," *Wall Street Journal,* April 20, 1988, p. 25.

CHOICE CUTS

In reality, most companies can't segment their customers as sharply as Shouldice Hospital and National Bank of Catalina Island do. The set of existing customers is usually too diverse to be stuffed into one clearly labeled pigeonhole. That's especially true for manufacturing companies. They have special problems segmenting because they sell to a wide range of buyers and use distribution channels that insulate them from direct knowledge about their customers.

Nonetheless, any company can carve out useful segments, rank their attractiveness, and develop a service strategy simply by examining a few key characteristics of its customers and its business. The traits to look at first are obvious financial ones. How do the typical size of a sale and the likelihood of repeat sales vary across customers? What are the costs of giving superior service to different types of customers? Approximating the answers to these questions produces a rough segmentation and a working notion of the benefits and costs of different service strategies.

In any well-run business, service levels correlate closely with size of sale. Buy a $150 suit off the rack at a discount store, and you won't get free alterations, let alone any advice from a salesman about fashion trends, the fit of the suit, or appropriate accessories. Full price men's retailers and department stores, where suits go for $250 to $600 and customers tend to come back, will throw in minor alterations and, if you're lucky, a fair amount of personal attention. Make an appointment with Bijan, which sells $1,500 suits behind barred storefronts on Hollywood's Rodeo Drive and New York's Fifth Avenue, and you can expect head-to-toe fashion advice, any alteration you care to name, and a call after the sale to make sure that everything fits as well as you thought it would. Note that people who buy suits at discount don't necessarily get worse service. They do get less of it, but whether they perceive that consequence as low-quality service depends on what they expected.

It's the same with cars. When Martin Stein, president of the Society of Automotive Analysts and a consultant with Abt Associates, agreed to develop a service program for Hyundai, he analyzed twenty-six other automotive service programs and their impact on customer satisfaction. Naturally, he found that the more expensive the car, the more elaborate the service. Manufacturers like Mercedes and Acura take the "open pocketbook" approach: whatever service the customer wants, he gets, including twenty-four-hour roadside assistance in the case of Mercedes, Volvo, and a few other pricey, low-volume brands.

Manufacturers of cars that sell for less and in greater numbers have to be more discriminating. The most successful ones manage service by exception, relying on sophisticated information systems to tell them where they are lacking and to suggest the most cost-effective ways of compensating.

The companies with the worst service quality and the least customer satisfaction weren't those that make the lowest-priced cars or offer the lowest absolute levels of service, but those that lack a service strategy and fail to match service levels with size of sale. Except in the case of Cadillac, General Motors takes a "cosmetic" approach to service. It sends service managers through a training program—or charm school—where they learn to refuse customer requests for service politely, and it uses 800 numbers to field complaints. "This approach backfires," says Stein. "Customers say that General Motors is 'supercilious' and that 'they are overly courteous but don't want to fix your car.' Polite evasion antagonizes people more than if you just say you can't do it. Tactically, there's nothing wrong with 800 numbers, but given GM's lack of a service strategy, they don't see any positive change in customer satisfaction. A five-point drop in market share in 1987 is not a good sign that people want to buy your cars."[14]

SERVICE COSTS AND SERVICE VALUE

When analyzing the costs of providing outstanding service to different types of customers, sophisticated companies look for

[14]Interview with Martin Stein, April 27, 1988.

segments that are inherently less costly to serve. Part of Shouldice's secret is that basically well people cost less to serve than the seriously ill. Older, more conservative car owners who live in the suburbs are less costly to serve than people in their twenties who live in urban and rural areas, a fact that automobile dealers and insurance companies both realize. Companies with strong central purchasing offices usually are less expensive to serve than those that let each branch or division make its own buying decisions.

Besides inherent traits like health, age, and geographical location, some segments have behavioral traits that cut the costs of serving them. Certain types of customers are happy to share the burdens of service, like shoppers at self-service stores and industrial buyers who order parts and supplies through computers linked directly to their suppliers. Other types of customers are willing to modify their demand for service to accommodate the supplier, like people who make—and keep—reservations at restaurants and automobile repair shops, owners of copying machines who are willing to accept slower service for non-critical equipment, and utility customers who agree to limit their electrical usage during peak demand hours.[15]

In many cases you can classify customers quite precisely by the economic values they place on service. Milind Lele and his colleagues have developed an intriguing way of doing this for customers with equipment that is liable to break, from farm machinery and airplanes to automatic coffee makers.[16] When equipment breaks, the customer incurs a number of fixed and variable costs. The fixed costs usually are those of repairing or replacing the machine; the variable costs include both out-of-pocket expenses, like the wages an airline has to pay the flight crew when an airplane is grounded, and opportunity costs, like the passenger

[15]Heskett, *Managing in the Service Economy*, p. 48.

[16]Milind M. Lele and Uday S. Karmarkar, "Good Product Support Is Smart Marketing," *Harvard Business Review* (November–December 1983), pp. 124–132; Milind M. Lele, "How Service Needs Influence Product Strategy," *Sloan Management Review* (Fall 1986), pp. 63–70; and Milind M. Lele with Jagdish N. Sheth, *The Customer Is Key* (John Wiley & Sons, 1987), pp. 200–207.

revenue the airline loses. Fixed costs of machine failure don't change with the length of time the machine is down; variable costs do. When the coffee maker breaks, it costs so much to repair or replace, plus certain other costs—out-of-pocket expenses for buying coffee from a delicatessen, opportunity costs for taking time to use a manual coffee maker—that increase the longer the coffee maker is down.

Using fixed and variable costs as the two dimensions of a matrix, Lele roughly groups equipment users into four categories of fix-it type service:[17]

When failure imposes *low fixed and low variable costs* on the customer, as in the case of a broken coffee maker, an attractive strategy is not to repair the appliance at all but to make it inexpensive enough to replace easily, and reliable enough so the customer isn't buying a new one too often. That's exactly what Timex does by selling inexpensive watches with a full-replacement warranty and making them impossible to repair.

When *fixed costs are high relative to variable costs,* as they are for cars, where repair bills loom larger than the costs of arranging for transportation while the car is in the shop, reliability and cost of repair become crucial.

Conversely, for earth-moving equipment and personal computers used in business, *where variable costs exceed fixed costs,* customers demand very fast fix-it service. Manufacturers in those cases have to concentrate on infrastructures—repair teams in the field, spare parts, communications and transportation systems—and on designing products to be repaired quickly, often by making them modular and swapping out bad modules for good ones. This is the strategy Toshiba and other companies use for laptop computers: if a laptop under warranty breaks, Toshiba will swap it for one that works within 24 hours.

Finally, when the customer can't tolerate breakdowns because *both fixed and variable costs are enormous,* as they are for banks that base their operations on sophisticated communications net-

---

[17]Lele with Sheth, *The Customer Is Key,* pp. 206–207.

works, the most effective support strategy is to design fail-safe gear that includes redundant or back-up components and to monitor and maintain the equipment continuously (see chapter 7).

THE COST AND VALUE OF CUSTOMERS

Segmenting customers by the value they place on service and the kinds of service they expect says a lot about how much service should cost. Satisfying the expectations of people who buy Timex watches should be less costly than keeping owners of copiers happy.

But the cost of service also is affected by how knowledgeable customers are, and by their ability and willingness to cooperate in producing service. The most sophisticated users of mainframe computers know enough about the systems that they seldom need the cradle-to-grave service IBM traditionally has offered. Unless IBM offers such users steep discounts that reflect the lower cost of satisfying them, they are quite willing to buy from lower-service competitors.

Segmenting customers by their abilities to cooperate can transform your ideas about the cost of service. All buyers of semiconductor chips expect products that meet their specifications, and living up to specs is a crucial aspect of the service chipmakers offer. But unless the buyer adjusts his automated test equipment to perform the same way the chipmaker's does, he will constantly reject batches of chips for being out of spec, even though the chipmaker's test equipment showed that the parts were fine when they left the factory. By contrast, customers that correlate their testing gear with the chipmaker's will reject fewer components and are a lot less expensive to serve.

Industrial buyers that are good at predicting their demand cost less to serve than those whose forecasts are always haywire. Consumers who cooperate by making hotel, airplane, and rental-car reservations are less expensive to serve well than those who show up out of the blue expecting immediate service. The costs of serving unsophisticated, individual users of personal computers drop when those customers form user's groups that in effect distribute technical assistance from the computer maker to the naive user.

The process of segmenting customers by their service expectations often generates a rough idea of how much it will cost to satisfy the different segments. But which ones are the best targets? That depends on how valuable they are compared with the likely costs of serving them. As we suggested above, size and frequency of purchase make good indicators of value. A customer's total value, however, is multidimensional. Customers whose demand for a product or service is likely to grow faster than average (young families, industrial buyers at the beginning of a boom) have extra worth; so do particularly influential customers, who will generate powerful word of mouth, and particularly loyal ones, whose future value is relatively certain. Customers that are especially demanding, sophisticated, or technologically advanced often go to the top of the list because serving them gives a supplier insight into the future needs of more ordinary customers.

Even the manner in which customers buy a product affects their value. One $300 million paper manufacturer couldn't understand why its profits by customer varied until it interviewed customers about the ways in which they purchased paper products. Modes of purchase accounted for two thirds of the profit variance and showed that customers fell into five "value" categories:

1 / small, fast-growing companies that needed technical assistance in developing new products;

2 / established customers that used the paper company as a sole source;

3 / companies that took competitive bids from two or three very skilled suppliers;

4 / customers that bought from four or five pre-selected suppliers; and

5 / companies that bought purely on price, regardless of other values the supplier might offer.

By paying more attention to the high-value customers at the top of the list, and less to the low-value customers at the bottom, the paper company achieved profit margins well above average for its industry.[18]

Ranking customers by their value—assigning them to tiers—is essential for any service operation that faces big swings in aggregate demand and can't adjust capacity quickly to meet those swings. Ranks or tiers allow allocation. When capacity is short, smart suppliers give top-tier customers first claim on service and cut back on service to lower-value customers. That's what popular restaurants do at peak dining times by finding tables for regulars and keeping newcomers waiting, and it's what Japanese semiconductor makers do when capacity is short and they fill the orders of long-term customers first. Without assigning its customers to tiers, a company that serves numbers of segments has difficulty getting the most out of its service capacity. Stretching and straining to satisfy every segment, it frequently ends up giving low-quality service to all customers, not just the less desirable ones in lower tiers.

NEVER MIX, NEVER WORRY

Companies whose main business is service have discovered through bitter experience that using the same organization to serve different market segments, or to provide very different services to the same segment, seldom works. People Express's inability to please both budget and business travelers is only one example of many. Richard Normann, head of the Service Management Group, a European consulting firm, cites three other cases: Jacques Borel, a French company that specialized in institutional food service and came a cropper trying to run the Sofitel hotel chain; Booz, Allen & Hamilton, the U.S.-based consulting firm,

[18]See Gordon Canning, Jr., "Do a Value Analysis of Your Customer Base," *Industrial Marketing Management,* 11 (1982), pp. 89–93.

which tried and failed to add executive recruiting to its service offerings; and International Service System, a Danish company that thought security guard services looked like a natural extension of contract cleaning, its main business, but found out the two operations had to be run separately.[19] In the United States it's obvious that diversified financial services companies have difficulty melding their operations and excelling in all the segments they address—Citicorp rules consumer banking with its ATM and credit card operations but trails in "private" banking for the wealthy, and no large commercial bank has succeeded in taking much underwriting business from investment banks and brokerage houses.

The problem with diversification isn't that the companies involved are ignorant about their new businesses or lack relevant skills. It's that service is more an experience than a product. Different customer segments have different expectations about the experience, and minute deviations from their expectations have powerful effects on their satisfaction. Look at Swissair: after starting to fly new planes between Geneva and Stockholm, it had to completely redesign its food-loading system, its galleys, and its crew training to accommodate both Scandinavian passengers, who accept cold sandwiches for dinner but insist on getting drinks before their food, and Swiss passengers, who demand hot meals even on short flights but don't care if drinks arrive before or with their meals.[20] Some hotels refuse to accept convention business because the presence of convention visitors changes the experience of other customers and violates their expectations.

Experience, of course, is intangible, and intangibility is another reason segments don't mix. Customers, lacking a physical product to inspect, tend to view a service "product" and its delivery sys-

---

[19]Richard Normann, *Service Management: Strategy and Leadership in Service Businesses* (John Wiley & Sons, 1984), pp. 97–98. Normann comments: "The moral of these and many other examples is clear: it is difficult to mix service management systems, which represent delicate formulas for poised success, without destroying or disturbing something valuable in the process. . . . Even mixing images can lead to great confusion in the external market and among the present or potential employees of a company. . . . [W]here the service on offer may be abstract and intangible, clean and concrete images are vital to success."

[20]Lele with Sheth, *The Customer Is Key,* pp. 133–134.

tem as one. How the repairman is dressed and what his truck looks like have nearly as much to do with perceptions of what a service is as whether he can fix the broken machine. By the same token, delivery systems have to be different for customers to perceive a difference in the service "product." American Express knows this well: when holders of American Express Gold cards contact the company, they deal with a totally different service organization than do holders of the super-premium Platinum card.

Mixing segments also is dangerous because highly efficient customer service is highly specialized. Shouldice Hospital proves the point. So does Frito-Lay, the Pepsico subsidiary that leads the potato chip business. Frito-Lay is indomitable among smaller grocers because of its customer service. A corps of 10,000 route drivers visits most stores two to three times weekly to ensure that their stock is fresh—and prominently displayed. Since Frito-Lay has done well by using the same network to distribute other salty snacks like corn chips, it decided to try pushing cookies, a packaged snack that would seem quite similar to chips and such. The attempt failed. Frito-Lay's service infrastructure, while very efficient for potato chips, was too specialized to handle cookies well. As W. Leo Kiely III, senior vice president for sales and marketing, explains it: "On the surface it looked easy, but there were underlying problems. . . . Our other products turn in about seven days— that's very rapid. Cookies have a much slower turn, with sixty- to ninety-day shelf life. That is a different inventory problem for our drivers, so our regular visit two to three times a week turned out to be inefficient for cookies."[21]

As customer service looms larger for other types of manufacturers, they too will find that it's hard to amortize the costs of specialized service infrastructures across more than one segment or one class of product. Many will discover they have less flexibility in addressing new and different markets than they once thought.

In practice, few companies can afford the luxury of addressing just one segment. The challenge of exploiting service capacity forces them to diversify at least a little, as airlines do by targeting

[21]Interview with W. Leo Kiely III, October 23, 1987.

both business and vacation travelers. Moreover, the same customer is often a different type of customer at different times. Businessmen go on vacation. New bank customers, who value location and convenience most, quickly become established bank customers and start giving the highest rankings to operational accuracy, dependability, and friendliness.[22] Compared with most service companies, manufacturers face greater problems because they have less control over which types of customers buy their products, yet they must try to give those diverse customers outstanding service.

The main solutions are to pick segments that are as similar as possible and to keep your priorities straight. No airline can give outstanding service to very frequent fliers and to penny-pinchers who go for deeply discounted charter flights; some airlines succeed in giving good service to businessmen and in selling off unfilled seats at reduced rates to the budget-conscious.

Segmenting by customer expectations, rather than by customer, often reveals that it's possible to give great service to a wide range of people who share a narrowly defined set of expectations. Automated teller machines can serve several sorts of customers well, even though some of those customers also want personal contact when applying for loans or setting up trusts.[23] Gourmets may disdain McDonald's cooking, but they're happy to go there when they expect and receive fast service, standardized food, and low prices.

Finally, expectations can be adjusted through advertising, guarantees, and other clues that indicate the type and level of service a customer will get. Price can be a potent clue: few people who buy a $99 air ticket from New York to Los Angeles expect the same kind of service as people who pay $500 for the same flight, and anyone who pays an independent auto mechanic half the labor rate that authorized dealers charge expects a lower level of service.

[22]Biff Motley, "Developing a Customer Service Index," *Bank Marketing* (May 1985), pp. 6 and 57.

[23]Osvald Bjelland of Bjelland, Dahl & Partners, Ltd., calls this an "island" strategy because it focuses on islands of expectations in the sea of customers.

FINDING OUT WHAT CUSTOMERS EXPECT

Since most companies see customer service as a necessary evil, it's no wonder they don't research customers' service expectations. Since such research is key to a workable service strategy, this failure is a scandal. "One thing is crucial to success in service," notes Osvald Bjelland of Bjelland, Dahl & Partners, Ltd., a Scandinavian management consulting firm: "Finding out who your customers are and what they expect."[24] Segmentation takes care of the first requirement, research of the second one.

Pinpointing customers' service expectations is more difficult than finding out what they want in, say, a breakfast cereal. Crunch, sweetness, and toasty flavor are easier to specify than the experiential traits of a service, which range from hard, easily measurable quantities like speed of repair, to soft, elusive qualities like feelings of security or of being respected. As one British scholar has noted, services are fuzzy and ambiguous. Research is stymied because services are intangible; because they're hard to standardize; because customers' judgments of service are colored by who performs the service and by their own involvement in producing it; and because a service is hard to distinguish from the manner in which it's produced and delivered.[25]

But the payoffs to research are tangible sales and profits. In Norway, where customers are particularly sensitive to service, Toyota used to think of cars simply as products. Then the company began looking into the total car experience and asking what kinds of service customers expected. Discovering that they were concerned not just with reliability and performance but with the ease of buying cars and car insurance and with the anxieties of repair, Toyota used its large customer base to bargain for very competitive financing and insurance services, and it started offering free diagnostic service. Between 1985 and 1986, Toyota's sales

---

[24]Interview with Osvald Bjelland, October 28, 1987.

[25]Donald Cowell, *The Marketing of Services* (William Heinemann, London, 1984), pp. 90–91. Cowell is concerned mainly with market-testing new services such as income tax preparation, but his observations about research difficulties apply equally well to the problem of discovering expectations of customer service.

in Norway rose more than 30 percent, from 20,200 vehicles to 27,500, and its profits exploded from the equivalent of $12 million to $22 million. Because of this strategy, Toyota became the best-selling foreign nameplate in Norway, knocking off Ford, which had held that place for fifteen years. Volvo, which makes relatively expensive cars, is nonetheless the best-selling nameplate in all of Scandinavia. After analyzing its customers' expectations, Volvo arranged for certain gas stations to bill Volvo owners through the car company, made it easy to order spare parts by mail, and propped up the value of used Volvos so that customers wouldn't fear massive depreciation when buying new ones.[26]

Useful research depends on three factors: concentrating on the most important customers; flushing out the differences between your company's definition of service and theirs; and using research methods that reflect qualitative reality even at the expense of quantitative precision. No matter how well you have segmented, focusing on the most important customers is seldom simple. Consumers gobble up millions of Frito-Lay's packaged snacks, but that company's crucial customers, in terms of the service they expect, are grocers that stock snacks. It's the same for most companies that rely on outside distributors for their competitive advantage, from clothing manufacturer Liz Claiborne to Johnson & Johnson.

Who's the most important customer when the user of a product or service isn't the buyer? For companies that sell to other businesses, the answer can be tricky. Purchasing agents are always important, but so are users, particularly when a product is so complex that it calls for lots of service before and after the sale. Confusingly, the two groups have different sets of expectations, and any supplier who wants to be number one must satisfy both sets.

Retailers have an easier time playing who's who. F. A. O. Schwarz, the chain of luxury toy stores, knows that parents make the final decisions. Near the holidays kids get the run of the store while adults sip coffee in quiet, living-room-like lounges where

[26]Interview with Osvald Bjelland, October 28, 1987.

salesmen demonstrate the latest gadgets. The grown-ups can pick up pre-wrapped gifts from Schwarz's One Minute Shop, and they secretly leave lists of toys their children like with salesmen, who select and wrap the gifts and see to their delivery.

The temptation to assume you know what customers expect is enormous, and so is the importance of resisting temptation. As service gurus Karl Albrecht and Ron Zemke note, "There is often a great deal of assuming or guessing going on in service organizations about the customer's attitudes and habits. It is common for those who run service organizations to form their views of the customer through long years of experience but with little actual data. Each manager has a theory about what is important to the customer, but in relatively few cases is this theory actually grounded in reasonably sophisticated research."[27]

Guessing doesn't make for effective customer service strategies. Inward-looking companies that are guided just by industry norms and their own past practices end up with inappropriate strategies, lower market shares, and anemic profits.[28] Time after time, studies have shown large differences between the ways that customers define service and rank the importance of different service activities and the ways suppliers do.[29]

GOLD IN THE GAP

Numbers of companies have triumphed mainly by filling the gap between what customers see as good service and what competitors think it is. Federal Express understood that customers valued reliable overnight delivery, pick-ups from their offices, and the ability to allay anxiety by tracking critical shipments en route. The U.S. Postal Service, a potentially formidable competitor to

[27]Karl Albrecht and Ron Zemke, *Service America!* (Dow Jones-Irwin, 1985), p. 59.

[28]D. M. Lambert and M. C. Lewis, "Managing Customer Service to Build Market Share and Increase Profits," *Business Quarterly,* vol. 48, no. 3 (Autumn 1983), pp. 50–57.

[29]See, for example, Norman Marr, "Do Managers Really Know What Service Their Customers Require?" *International Journal of Physical Distribution and Materials Management,* vol. 10, no. 7 (1980), pp. 433–444.

Fed Ex, has not yet caught on. Honda understands that customers expect minimum difficulty in having their cars serviced and repaired, a research finding that has only now begun to impress General Motors. The trends of sales and profits at the two companies speak for themselves.

Jan Carlzon's turnaround of Scandinavian Airlines System (SAS) is an outstanding example of the importance of seeing service as your customers see it. In 1981, when Carlzon took over at SAS, the airline recorded an $8 million loss, having lost $20 million the year before. But in 1982, Carlzon showed a profit of $72 million, even though international airlines as a group lost $2 billion.

Carlzon achieved the turnaround not mainly by cost cutting—the net decrease in costs for 1982 was only some $5 million—but by making heavy investments of money and people to improve service to business travelers going to and from Scandinavia. Carlzon's reward was an upsurge of demand. Over the three years from 1982 through 1984, while the market for air travel stagnated, the number of full-fare passengers traveling on SAS rose 23 percent, and the number of discount fare passengers increased 7 percent.[30]

Carlzon did many things right, from segmenting his service target quite precisely, to exercising charismatic leadership, to redesigning his fleet of planes to suit business travelers. His most effective action, though, was to see that how SAS defined service for its own purposes had little to do with customers' perceptions of service. As Carlzon explains, "Last year [1985], each of our 10 million customers came in contact with approximately five SAS employees, and this contact lasted an average of 15 seconds each time. Thus, SAS is 'created' in the minds of our customers 50 million times a year, 15 seconds at a time. These 50 million 'moments of truth' are the moments that ultimately determine whether SAS will succeed or fail as a company. They are the moments when we must prove to our customers that SAS is their best alternative."[31] Seeing that the quality of those moments

[30]Jan Carlzon, *Moments of Truth* (Ballinger, 1987), pp. 21–29.
[31]*Ibid.*, p. 3.

of truth was largely determined by front-line SAS employees, Carlzon delegated to them the responsibility of figuring out what customers expected. He even shifted most of the airline's forty-person market survey department to the field.

Carlzon's idea of abolishing market research is too extreme for most companies that need to develop a service strategy. But it dramatizes the facts that customers care intensely about the inter-personal aspects of service, and that they sometimes care more about those moments of truth than about more obvious, controllable traits like the speed of checking in at the airport. Russell E. Christiansen, chairman and chief executive of Midwest Energy Corp, an Iowa-based gas and electric utility, is a follower of Carlzon's who underlines the difference:

> ... service means different things to customers and to utility managers. To illustrate his point during an interview, Christiansen switched a reading lamp on and off. "At the precise moment a customer creates demand, we create the supply, and at the precise location you demand it—not three feet away. But a customer equates service with some kind of contact with the company. So each contact is a 'moment of truth,' an opportunity for the company to make a positive or negative impression. It's never neutral."[32]

The point is that it's dangerous to assume that the way a company views service has much to do with the views of its customers.

ASKING THE RIGHT QUESTIONS

That's especially true when researching customers' expectations and what customers value. A sure way to get misleading, useless results is to call a staff meeting, brainstorm a list of service attributes, make them into a questionnaire, administer the questionnaire to hundreds of customers, and precisely tabulate the answers. The result is a very persuasive argument for adopting a service strategy that perpetuates both the vices and virtues of the existing strategy.

[32]John Morrissey, "Gas Service Expands Iowa Strategy," *Business Record* (Des Moines, Iowa), September 29, 1986, Section 1, p. 2.

Masters of customer service know that research begins with open-ended questions, focus groups, and other non-directive methods that flush out what customers really care about. The results are almost always a surprise to managers. When British Airways decided to transform itself into a service leader, it asked incoming passengers open-ended questions about what they expect of an airline. Four qualities led the list. Two were expected— the care and concern demonstrated by airline personnel, and the ability of front-line employees to solve problems. But the other two were eye-openers. Contrary to what British Airways managers had imagined, customers were also quite concerned with how spontaneous and flexible BA employees were in applying company policies, and with their ability to recover from mistakes by making things right for the passenger.[33]

Open-ended questions can have major impact on customer service strategies. For example, Travelers Express Corp., which provides banking services to credit unions, had been spending heavily on training its customers to use TE's systems. But research that looked at what customers really valued surprised the company. Credit unions cared a lot less about training than they did about the speed and accuracy of problem solving. Travelers Express shifted spending away from training and invested instead in better copying machines to speed paperwork, a new phone system with a hot line to guide callers to the right contact person, and a new organization that placed customer service representatives closer to customers. The result, says TE, is better profit margins, more loyal customers, and less expensive sales.[34]

Open-ended questions are the prelude to more formal research. An excellent model of how to combine these research methods comes from American Express. To stay on top of customer expectations, the company's Travel Related Services operation, which manages all charge card activities, conducts frequent focus groups and follows them up with hundreds of interviews that take up to

[33]Leigh Bruce, "British Airways Jolts Staff with a Cultural Revolution," *International Management*, March 1987, pp. 36–38.

[34]Kevin S. Lytle and Linda J. McAleer, "Intangible Customer Service Will Help to Bolster the Bottom Line," *Marketing News*, April 24, 1987, pp. 13 ff.

two hours apiece. The point is to uncover what aspects of AMEX's service customers value most. The company uses this information to develop surveys of customer satisfaction that are extraordinarily specific and thorough: the four-page survey forms, which take ten to fifteen minutes to complete, are mailed to some 12,000 AMEX customers a year, just after they have had some contact or transaction with the company.

Such elaborate research may seem like overkill, but American Express doesn't think so. The research has revealed, for example, that card customers place very high value on getting their purchases authorized quickly and on getting replacements for lost cards almost instantaneously. As a result, AMEX has invested over $7 million in computer systems that help its authorizers make swift decisions, and in systems for replacing cards within twenty-four hours, if necessary. Every aspect of the service American Express offers is shaped by this research. Says MaryAnne Rasmussen, vice president for worldwide quality assurance: "We do transaction surveys for all kinds of experiences, not just card replacement. For example, nobody likes being dunned, but we try to discover whether customers' feelings about American Express are at least as positive after dunning as they were before. We hope they feel like members of a club, that they have been treated with courtesy and respect. . . . Whatever they talk with us about, we want them to feel better about American Express than they did before picking up the phone."[35]

HONING THE STRATEGY

Careful segmentation and perceptive research will make a workable strategy obvious. But the optimum strategy, the one that will be most devastating to competitors, is a product of further refinement. Ideally, it is a defensible strategy, and it leads customers to perceive that your company is out-servicing competitors.

[35]Interview with MaryAnne Rasmussen, vice president, quality assurance, American Express Travel Related Services Company, February 27, 1988.

How much service competitors offer, and the kinds of service they give customers, strongly determine the effectiveness of a service strategy. Tom Ford, founder and chief executive of the Ford Land Company of Menlo Park, California, perceived that most developers of office buildings see their businesses entirely as financial plays where return on assets is paramount. Most commercial tenants, he found, think their landlords are trying to squeeze the last penny of return from their properties.

So Ford decided to stress tenant service. He doesn't charge for extras like putting in electrical outlets, laying computer cable, or changing names on doors and building directories. When remodeling creates a racket that disturbs neighboring tenants, Ford brings the neighbors wine and flowers to show he's at least aware of the problem.

The results? Ford has built and now operates thirty-four office and industrial buildings on the peninsula south of San Francisco. Since 1977, his properties have been 100 percent leased, a remarkable record in an area where vacancy rates have been running at between 10 and 30 percent. A competitor who opened an office building next to Ford's flagship property in Menlo Park tried to draw away Ford's tenants by offering months of free or reduced rent. None of the tenants would bite, and the new building had only 50 percent occupancy more than fifteen months after it opened.

Competitors often force companies to revise their service strategies. When Xerox stood alone in the copier business, it shipped machines with engineering bugs that undermined reliability, and customers accepted Xerox's practice of improving copiers in the field. Once competitors entered the fray and changed the norm by shipping machines that broke down less often, Xerox had to change its own service strategy. Now that Nordstrom department stores are famous for the personal service they give customers, the chain's direct competitors have been forced to try to match or surpass Nordstrom. When TGI Friday's, Inc., the fast food chain, found sales and profits slipping, it couldn't cut costs. Instead, it had to increase the numbers of employees in its stores in order to bring service closer to the levels its upscale competitors offered.[36]

Far better than reacting to competitors is analyzing their service strategies and executing a preemptive strike that will be hard for them to counter. Many customer service operations seem to go through life cycles.[37] A basic service like repair starts out being performed by hand. Repair service is personal, customized, and time-consuming. Since a human being produces the service with little mechanical, managerial, or informational assistance, repairs are costly. There are few economies of scale: costs rise almost directly with the volume of repairs.

As a company's volume of repairs grows, it strives to contain costs by making greater investments in diagnostic equipment, setting up central repair offices, and giving repair people easily accessible information about likely causes of failure and likely cures. Thus as repair service matures, it becomes increasingly mechanized, impersonal, standardized, and efficient. Economies of scale become more and more significant; costs tend to fall with volume.

Eventually the market for repair service nears saturation, the drive to improve efficiency weakens, and stagnation sets in. Then it's time to begin the cycle again by finding new forms of service to offer customers, or by trying to extend repair service to other kinds of equipment.

Understanding where competitors are in the life cycles of their customer service operations leads to more intelligent strategic choices. The analysis should steer your company away from copycat strategies, which are hard to defend and do little either to differentiate a company or to inspire employees. When competitors lag in the customer service life cycle, it's possible to estimate with surprising precision how much it will cost to stay just ahead

[36]Karen Blumenthal, "TGI Friday's Sees 3rd Qtr Net Off 20% from Year-Ago Level," *Wall Street Journal,* October 18, 1985.

[37]See Donald Cowell, *The Marketing of Services,* pp. 115–146, and Theodore H. Levitt, "The Industrialization of Service," *Harvard Business Review,* September–October 1976, pp. 63–74.

of them. When they lead, however, the cost of leapfrogging them is often so high that the smartest strategy may be to farm out more mature services to third-party service companies like Team Xerox and to concentrate new investments in less mature fields where competitors have less formidable advantages.

Life cycle analysis is especially useful for revealing the downward service spiral. The spiral victimizes companies that are behind in the cycle. Giving less effective service, they have to charge lower prices for their core products or services; giving less efficient service, they must spend more to come up to speed. So they are caught in a cost/price squeeze that gets tighter with every increase in the competition's level of service. Being sucked into a downward service spiral is a disaster. Pushing competitors into one by outspending and out-organizing them can be a triumph.

REINING IN EXPECTATIONS

The third and last step in creating a world-beating service strategy is to find ways of influencing customer expectations. The importance of setting expectations should be obvious: when expectations exceed perceived levels of service, customers are dissatisfied; but when service exceeds expectations, customers are pleasantly surprised and highly satisfied. It's a waste of time to segment customers, research their expectations, and develop a strategy unless you also consider how to control levels of expectation.[38] All of the fifteen companies Milind Lele studied because they had a knack for satisfying customers concentrated on this task by controlling communications such as advertising and sales-

[38]In one study of 348 "critical incidents" in which hotel, restaurant, and airline employees recalled difficult and uncomfortable communications with customers, fully 75% of the incidents could be attributed to the fact that customer expectations exceeded the ability of the service system to perform—e.g., customers made unreasonable demands, demands against policies, and so forth. The remaining 25% of the incidents arose because a firm or its employees produced substandard service or simply failed to produce a promised service. See Jody D. Nyquist, Mary J. Bittner, and Bernard H. Booms, "Identifying Communication Difficulties in the Service Encounter: A Critical Incident Approach," in John A. Czepiel, Michael R. Solomon, and Carol F. Surprenant, eds., *The Service Encounter* (Lexington Books, 1985), pp. 196–212.

men's promises and by staying on top of their distribution channels to ensure that they too communicated appropriate expectations. The common goal of these service leaders was to under-promise and over-deliver.[39]

There are limits, of course, to any company's ability to set expectations. The strictest one is reality. Few patrons of a high-priced hotel can be led to expect anything other than luxury service, and few people who have experienced bad service can be persuaded to expect anything else. As Martin Stein of Abt Associates observes, "General Motors' advertising campaign for Mr. Goodwrench, the GM dealer's mythical service expert, doesn't work because people doubt the quality of service being advertised will be available. They may be looking for Mr. Goodwrench, but they aren't finding him."[40] Trying to set expectations that vary widely from the realities that customers perceive is futile.

Expectations are formed by many uncontrollable factors, from the experience of customers with other companies and their advertising to a customer's psychological state at the time he or she receives service.[41] Strictly speaking, what customers expect is as diverse as their backgrounds, education, values, and experiences. The same advertisement that shouts "personal service" to one person tells another that the advertiser has promised more than he possibly can deliver.

Yet some straightforward tactics can help bring expectations into line with the service strategy. The job is basically the same as positioning a company or product in the marketplace. Positioning starts with four givens: the segments targeted, the expectations of those segments, the strategy for exceeding those expectations, and the positions of competitors, i.e., the images they have created for their companies in customers' minds.

A winning position meets two criteria. It uniquely distinguishes a company from the competition, and it leads customers to expect slightly less service than a company can deliver. That's what Avis

[39]Lele with Sheth, *The Customer Is Key,* pp. 64–67.

[40]Interview with Martin Stein, April 26, 1988.

[41]Robert A. Westbrook, "Intrapersonal Affective Influences on Consumer Satisfaction with Products," *Journal of Consumer Research* (June 1980), pp. 49–54.

did years ago by positioning itself as the second-place car-rental company that has to try harder, and it's what Avis is doing again today by portraying itself as the rent-a-car outfit that tries harder because the employees own the company. Maytag has done the same, positioning its washing machines as so reliable that the Maytag repairman is bored to sleep, and so has Apple Computer by stressing how much easier it is to use a Macintosh than an IBM PC.

The tools used to position customer service operations are the same communications tools any marketer uses—advertising, promotion, public relations, and everything else that affects word of mouth. But sending messages about service is different from most forms of marketing communication. Since service is intangible, advertising has a special mission to dramatize service in ways that make the benefits clear and real. Moreover, all forms of communication should be focused tightly on the target segment because customers' expectations about service are affected strongly by the other kinds of customers they see—a business traveler checking into a budget motel revises his expectations radically if he sees a drunk asleep in the lobby. So does a housewife who notices that other shoppers in the supermarket are fashionably dressed. Thus communications that reach and attract the wrong segments can be a disaster.

Positioning customer service differs from normal positioning in other ways as well. Customers are hypersensitive to tangible clues like uniforms, repair trucks, brochures, and hotel lobbies. Often they can't tell that a service has been performed without some additional physical evidence like the elaborate receipts car mechanics make out or the strip of paper hotels wrap around toilet seats to let guests know the toilet has been cleaned. Customers' expectations of service rise and fall markedly because of seemingly minor clues or tipoffs like these.

The key to successful positioning of customer service is not to create expectations greater than the service your company can deliver. As customers gain experience and competition intensifies, expectations inevitably seem to rise. In the computer business, for example, surveys show that after-sale service has improved remarkably in recent years, yet customer expectations are so much higher that dissatisfaction also is on the rise.

Keeping expectations at just the right level—slightly below perceived performance—is a constant challenge. And lowering expectations without alienating customers is tricky, as one hotel chain discovered when it made the mistake of advertising that guests could expect virtually the same type of room across the country. Deluged with letters complaining of gross variations, the chain withdrew its claim but couldn't lower the expectations it had created. It still suffers from customers' perceptions that its service is below par. When Citibank set out to educate customers to expect ATM service instead of teller service, in effect lowering expectations, the effort cost millions and took about five years to succeed.[42] Given the difficulty of cutting back expectations, the cardinal rule must be to under-promise.

SUMMARY: THE THREE STEPS TO STRATEGY

Developing a strategy is fundamental to winning the customer service war. Companies that have clear, well-focused service strategies are better able to optimize the production and delivery of service. They have a leg-up in choosing the optimum mix of services for the customers they target and in driving to produce effective, efficient service.

There are three steps to developing a customer service strategy:

1 / *Segment.* Unlike classical marketing segmentation, segmentation for customer service focuses on customers' expectations more than their needs. Several customer service segments may exist within one market segment, and one customer service segment can cut across several market segments.

Segmentation suggests where to substitute low-touch for high-touch service, how to apply service capacity across segments, and how to get customers involved as co-producers of service. Once

[42]Alan Breznick, "Citibank the Impregnable," *Crain's New York Business,* vol. 3, no. 38, September 21, 1987, Section 1, p. 15.

customers are segmented, they can be tiered by their value and by the costs of serving them well.

Trying to serve more than one segment superbly is dangerous. If it must be done, make sure the segments and the services they expect aren't radically different. If there are big differences, consider abandoning the least valuable segments or creating different organizations to serve them.

2 / *Find out what customers expect.* Concentrate on the most important customers and highlight the differences between your company's notions of great service and theirs. When doing research, start with open-ended questions and focus groups, and move on from there to more formal methods, always seeking to preserve qualitative truth instead of generating thousands of highly accurate but largely misleading numbers.

As part of the research, look at competitors' strategies; understand where they are in the service life cycle and how to leapfrog them or to finesse their advantages. Avoid getting caught in a downward spiral of service, or cost/price squeeze; try instead to push competitors into the spiral.

3 / *Set customers' expectations.* Develop a communications plan that will influence customers to expect a little less service than they will get. If your company can consistently get a package door-to-door in eighteen hours, guarantee twenty-four-hour service; if your company's repair people respond to calls for help within two hours, promise three.

4

Words into Action: Leadership

Leadership helps make strategy a day-to-day reality. Unless top managers profess the religion of customer service, employees will view the most elegant strategy as just another easily ignored public relations campaign.

Leaders of companies that produce outstanding service incessantly pronounce their beliefs and back up their words with actions, often dramatic ones that become corporate legends. Their goal is to nurture a service culture that will shape employee behavior more effectively than rules and regulations can. They make service everybody's business and empower workers to make on-the-spot decisions in the customer's interest.

Effective service leadership can be hard on middle managers accustomed to giving orders instead of coaching employees to act independently. But cutting through red tape and blasting bureaucracy is key to delivering great service.

It's a phenomenal company. In a cutthroat, slow-growth industry, its sales have multiplied sevenfold over the last ten years, to more than $2 billion, and its profits have grown nearly as fast, to over $90 million, all without help from acquisitions. By most measures its operations are roughly twice as effective as the industry average. Its fanatically loyal customers sometimes travel hundreds of miles to patronize this firm; many say the experience is addictive. Shortly after moving into a new market it invariably seizes the biggest or second-biggest share. Rivals panic when they hear it's coming to town. Most react by trying to imitate its world-beating customer service. Thus the company is recasting an entire industry in its own image.

The marvel in question is, of course, Nordstrom, the chain of forty-eight fashion specialty retail stores that has branched triumphantly out of its home base in the Pacific Northwest to take over California's lushest markets and now is invading the East Coast. Thanks to a blizzard of case studies, magazine articles, and newspaper stories, Nordstrom is so famous for service that we almost decided to bypass it. Besides, Nordstrom's top managers have turned publicity-shy and refuse to grant interviews except to local newspapers in regions where a new store is opening.

But Nordstrom simply can't be ignored. The company and its managers epitomize the importance of leadership in producing outstanding service. And the stories customers tell about Nordstrom's extraordinary efforts to satisfy are too good not to repeat.

Consider returning merchandise. It's an activity everyone dreads because of the barriers most stores erect. They insist on seeing the original sales slip, ask the customer to justify his or her dissatisfaction, and refuse to accept used items, or old ones, or those that were marked down. Bringing merchandise back can be embarrassing, humiliating, and frustrating, as well as time-consuming. Just the thought of having to do it keeps people from buying things they might have to return.

Except at Nordstrom. The company's policy is to ask no questions and to make at least a full refund or exchange. Other stores say the same, but Nordstrom means it. When one customer brought back a $20 pair of earrings that broke after a month of wear and tear, she got new ones instantly. A businessman who returned a pair of squeaky shoes after wearing them for a year expected to get them fixed; he got a brand-new pair instead. When a part-time employee overheard a woman at her tennis club complaining about a blouse she had bought at Nordstrom two years earlier, the clerk broke in and insisted the woman return the blouse even though she had given it away to a friend.[1]

Heroic behavior is normal for Nordstrom employees. They're the Superwomen and Supermen of retailing, always on the lookout for chances to help. They have been known to iron a new shirt for a customer about to attend an important meeting; to serve lunch in a dressing room to a shopper busy trying on clothes; to buy merchandise at competing stores for customers who can't find exactly the right item at Nordstrom, and to resell it at a 30 percent discount; to bring large selections of clothing and shoes to shut-ins and others who can't shop at the store, including an executive who had time to try on a jacket only at the airport, between flights; to warm up cars when the weather's freezing so customers can do a little more shopping; and to make last-minute deliveries of party clothes to frantic hostesses. They even have paid tickets that shoppers incurred while parked outside the store.

Nordstrom spends freely to make up for failures that might offend customers. One executive, skeptical about the store's reputation, bought two suits just before a business trip. When Nordstrom failed to alter the suits in time for his departure, he was secretly gratified that the store was less than perfect. That is until he arrived at his hotel to find a Federal Express package waiting for him. Inside were the finished suits—plus three $25 ties by way of apology. Another businessman groused in a letter to co-chairman John N. Nordstrom that after several trips to get a suit altered, he had returned it because he was still dissatisfied. Nordstrom himself took a new suit and a tailor to the man's office; when the alterations were finished, the store delivered the suit, giving it to the customer for free. When an elderly lady asked a clerk for a shawl that wouldn't get caught in the spokes of her wheelchair, the clerk searched fruitlessly for the item throughout the Nord-

[1]Meg Grant, "The Customer Is Right," *California Business* (July 1986), p. 23; George Russell, "Where the Customer Is Still King," *Time,* February 2, 1987, p. 56; Interview with Cilla Raughley, former director of customer service at Nordstrom, November 8, 1987.

strom chain and spent a free day scouring other stores, all in vain. Finally the clerk knit the shawl herself.[2]

The non-heroic, day-in, day-out performance of Nordstrom employees is even more impressive. Each sales clerk keeps an elaborate "personal book," a profile of his or her repeat customers, from name and address to the clothing sizes, style and color preferences, birthdays, and anniversaries of the customer and his or her family. Armed with this information, the clerks call customers to announce the arrival of items that might please them, or to suggest an appropriate gift for an upcoming birthday. Referring to the book while the customer is buying, say, a dress, the sales clerk can make perceptive suggestions for accessories and other related merchandise and easily fetch items of the right size, style, and color from other departments. Days after making a sale, the clerk goes back to the book again in order to write the customer a thank-you note and to check that everything fits well and performs as promised. The result is a level of service that puts the most attentive doctors and lawyers to shame and leaves other department stores choking in Nordstrom's dust. The store's best customers are so hooked they call themselves "Nordies."

HOW NORDSTROM DOES IT. . .

To be sure, Nordstrom enjoys some strategic advantages. Consumers have turned increasingly to specialty retailers in preference to traditional, broad-line department stores, and Nordstrom has been a specialty retailer since 1963, concentrating above all on shoes and women's apparel. As a chain, Nordstrom got a late start and expanded strongly, so it has lots of new stores in malls

[2]Interview with Julie Connelly, marketing and consumer products editor, *Fortune* magazine, October 23, 1987; Nancy Yoshihara, "Chain Sets Itself Apart with an Old-Fashioned Service Policy," *Los Angeles Times,* September 30, 1984, part V, pp. 1 and 17; Laurie Itow, "Nordstrom: Shoppers' Delight," *San Francisco Examiner,* February 15, 1987, Section D, p. 4; Joan O'C. Hamilton, "Why Rivals Are Quaking as Nordstrom's Heads East," *Business Week,* June 15, 1987, p. 99; Pamela Abramson, "Where the Buyer Is King," *Newsweek,* January 5, 1987, p. 43; Tom Peters, *Thriving on Chaos* (Alfred A. Knopf, 1987), pp. 89–90; and interview with Cilla Raughley, former director of customer service at Nordstrom, November 8, 1987.

rather than a bunch of dowdy emporiums in decaying downtown locations. The company has had the wisdom—or luck—to operate in high-growth regions of the United States, not in weaker areas like the oil patch and the rust bowl.

Moreover, Nordstrom's service advantage flows from many factors besides the behavior of its employees. Compared with other stores, it keeps much wider and deeper inventories so customers have a better chance of getting what they want, and it assigns more clerks to the sales floor. Though its prices are competitive, and it will match any price a shopper finds elsewhere, Nordstrom deemphasizes price competition and the uncertainties it creates. The Nordstrom shopper can feel confident that she is not being ripped off; she won't discover that the $200 dress she bought last week is on sale this week for $120. Realizing that customers evaluate intangible service by judging the tangibles, Nordstrom pays close attention to atmosphere. The main floors of many stores feature formally dressed piano players who turn out a soothing stream of background music.

Yet the key to Nordstrom's success isn't strategy or tactics. As one department store analyst puts it, ". . . Nordstrom's service and quality of clothes are not a proprietary technology. Nordstrom just seems to be the only people who can pull it off."[3] The company's secret, neither obvious nor concrete, is the leadership its top managers exercise. They have shaped a culture and an organization that make superior service as natural as breathing.

The leaders form a committee of five: brothers John and Jim Nordstrom, grandsons of the store's founder; their cousin Bruce Nordstrom and cousin-in-law John McMillan; and an old friend of the family, Bob Bender. Mr. John, Mr. Jim, and Mr. Bruce, as they're known at Nordstrom, started at age ten as stock boys in what was then a chain of shoe stores. "We were raised kneeling in front of the customer," says Mr. Bruce.[4] Though Nordstrom went public in 1971, the extended Nordstrom family still owns

[3]Scott Conyers, securities analyst with the Charter Investment Group of Portland, Oregon, as quoted in Bill MacKenzie, "Nordstrom Leads Way as Specialty Retailer," *The Sunday Oregonian*, June 14, 1987, p. D8.

[4]Itow, "Nordstrom: Shoppers' Delight," p. 4.

nearly half the stock and tends to see the company as a family business.

Intensely competitive yet remarkably self-effacing, the Nordstroms view customer service as a religion and proselytize at every opportunity. Mr. John, like every employee, uses the stairs during peak hours rather than occupy elevator space a customer might need. Mr. Jim is famous within the company for insisting that Nordstrom accept any and all returns. Employees like to quote him as declaring, "I don't care if they roll a Goodyear tire into the store. If they say they paid $200, give them the $200."[5] The Nordstroms make it clear they will fire an employee for only two reasons—not taking care of the customer, and stealing—and they back up their words about service with their pocketbooks. Nordstrom doubtless could make more money if it didn't carry so much inventory, but that would be a disservice to the customer. The company accepts a "shrinkage" rate—the percent of merchandise lost to theft—at the high end of the industry norm because the Nordstroms think attaching electronic security tags to clothing, posting guards outside the fitting rooms, and limiting the number of outfits customers can try on would be insulting.

Nordstrom's leaders give constant proof of their belief that the sales clerk is the most important person within the company, since it's the clerk that directly serves the customer. They don't use the low-status term "sales clerk," preferring "sales representative," and they refuse interviews partly because publicizing executives diverts attention from the company's real heroes in the trenches. Every executive, except for the corporate lawyer, has gone through boot camp by selling at Nordstrom, including the few managers who have been hired in at senior levels from other companies.

The primacy of front-line employees shows up in the organization chart Nordstrom unfurls during training sessions. It's an upside-down pyramid. At the top, and greatest in number, come customers. The next layer is salespeople, then buyers and department managers, store managers, regional managers, and finally

[5]Yoshihara, "Chain Sets Itself Apart . . ." p. 17.

the committee of five, at the very bottom. The manager's job at Nordstrom is to support the front line and remove obstacles, not to issue edicts and push people around. Since the company is highly decentralized, front-line employees enjoy wide ranging authority and responsibility. In contrast to most department stores, where merchandise buyers are czars and salespeople are serfs, sales reps at Nordstrom strongly influence the decisions of buyers. Both buyers and department managers must spend half their time on the selling floor, interacting with customers.

If this sounds like an organization that's out of control, it is— and it isn't.[6] Training classes for new sales reps are rudimentary, lasting for one and a half days and consisting mostly of cash register training and lectures on company history and policy. The chain of command is primitive, and Nordstrom has precious few policies and procedures, since these tend to create red tape that slows employees' responses to customers. The top managers don't leverage their time by using ranks of assistants, nor do they force communications to rise to the top through proper channels. The top five answer their own phones, and they pride themselves on knowing the names of hundreds of customers and of many of the company's 20,000 or so full-time employees. With a straight face, Mr. Jim says that Nordstrom's top managers don't delegate responsibility because they generally have no control to begin with.[7]

In subtle ways, however, Nordstrom exercises iron-fisted control. Knowing that top managers are quite accessible to customers and prone to take dramatic action where service is concerned, employees do anything to keep customers from complaining to the top. Just one customer complaint about an employee's attitude can blight his career. Almost all the sales reps receive a large part of their pay through commissions, a scheme that cranks up the pressure to woo customers, especially for new hires. Fully 25 percent of them quit within a year, and another 25 percent are fired. The norms of Nordstrom's family-style culture create a well-defined

[6]An excellent though dated description of Nordstrom's management, and the source for some of the material we discuss, is a Harvard Business School case study: Manu Parpia, "Nordstrom" (Harvard College, 1979, rev. 1984; ICCH #9-579-218).

[7]*Ibid.*, p. 22.

mold. Taboos include chewing gum, pointing, pressuring customers to buy, and trying to steal customers from other sales reps. Employees who do well are markedly energetic, entrepreneurial, ambitious, attractive, friendly, and well dressed—in Nordstrom clothes, of course. Many adopt the image so completely that they're always over the limit on their Nordstrom charge accounts. When the computers break down, temporarily hiding their debts, the heavy spenders sometimes go on shopping sprees.[8]

In short, the Nordstroms run their company by means of a vibrant culture with customer service at its core. They summarize the culture's values in a few slogans, such as "The only difference between stores is the way they treat customers." The message is easy to grasp and uncompromising, and it hasn't changed in decades. Managers act it out in thousands of small ways, from keeping those high inventories to making dramatic service gestures to rewarding people who give outstanding service and punishing those who fail to satisfy customers. Everything about Nordstrom, from its organizational structure and process to its compensation plans, magnifies the authority, responsibility, and status of the people closest to customers and minimizes whatever might obstruct their efforts to serve.

. . . AND WHY MACY'S CAN'T

The culture of service gives Nordstrom a tremendous competitive advantage because corporate cultures are notoriously slow to build and hard to change.[9] Some stores trying to follow in Nordstrom's footsteps realize that. Over the years Marshall Field, the old-line Chicago-based chain, lost sight of its founder's famous slogan, "Give the lady what she wants." The company has been working to improve service since 1983 and admits it hasn't finished yet. Philip M. Hawley, chairman of Carter Hawley Hale

[8]Interview with former Nordstrom manager, November 1987.
[9]See Bro Uttal, "The Corporate Culture Vultures," *Fortune,* October 17, 1983, pp. 66 ff.

Stores, Inc., which has been bloodied by Nordstrom in California, figures that building up a service culture takes at least four or five years. "Service is an attitude, a kind of caring on the part of everybody in the store. It takes a lot of coaching and leadership," he says.[10]

Yet leadership and culture are "soft" subjects that most hard-nosed managers prefer to ignore, including the majority of those who compete with Nordstrom. The prime example is Macy's, once the undisputed king of California retailers. Seeing that Nordstrom always won when the two chains faced off in the same shopping malls, Macy's California decided to "Nordstromize" itself. It put sales clerks on commission, deepened inventories, adopted a more liberal returns policy, started talking up service, and hired people away from Nordstrom to train employees in the mysteries of coddling customers.

The Macy's effort was a flop. Some years after it began, Tom Peters sent researchers to compare the experiences of shopping at several Nordstrom and Macy's stores. This is what they found:

> . . . [At Nordstrom] clerks unfailingly approached shoppers within two minutes . . . one comparison shopper commented of Macy's, "I unwrapped, unpinned, and unfolded shirts and waved them like red flags in front of bulls. The salesgirl remained in her original position behind the counter." . . . Gift wrapping at Macy's generally required a trip to an out-of-the-way corner, a long wait and sometimes a charge of $3 or more. When one Macy's devotee took an unwrapped Macy's package to a Nordstrom store after a fruitless wait in line at Macy's, she was flabbergasted when a Nordstrom clerk offered to wrap it—conveniently, at the same counter—along with her Nordstrom purchases. . . .[11]

All of Macy's efforts to mimic Nordstrom couldn't overcome Macy's leadership, culture, and organization, according to our interviews with present and former employees. Senior managers, bred up to believe that success comes from smart buying, quality merchandise, and attractive presentation, never got the service

---

[10]Hamilton, "Why Rivals Are Quaking . . ." p. 99; Bill Saporito, "Makeover for a Plain Jane Retailer," *Fortune,* April 11, 1988, pp. 68–71.

[11]Tom Peters, "Store Is Where the Action Is," *U.S. News and World Report,* May 12, 1986, p. 58.

religion. They thought giving better service was up to the sales staff, not to them, and they did little in word or deed to support the service drive.

Even if they had, the organization would have sandbagged them. It's strongly centralized, strictly hierarchical, and plagued by what one Macy's manager calls "an incredible amount of policies and an incredible amount of procedures" that keep front-line workers from doing their jobs. At every level, people care most about what their bosses think, and they manage by dictating to their inferiors. Discussing Nordstromization, a former president of Macy's California once told a colleague it was simple—he'd just order salespeople to provide good service. "The problem goes straight up to the top," a company manager admits. "I'm trying to please my boss, every salesperson is trying to please their boss, so our focus is not on serving the people below us—or on the customer. Everyone does what his boss orders him to do, not what people on the selling floor need." Since the Macy's culture stresses tight control and assumes employees can't be trusted to do things right, store managers and salespeople lack the authority to make decisions quickly, and thus to keep customers happy. "Macy's is shackled by its culture, and over time the culture will always win," says a manager who spent many years vainly trying to Nordstromize the company.

WHY LEADERS MATTER

No company can produce outstanding service unless its top managers are visibly, constantly, and sometimes irrationally committed to the idea. Taking care of customers is so much work that it gets done only if the people at the top lead the charge. When they don't, the organization naturally turns inward and concentrates on internal processes that are less demanding to work on. Everyone succumbs to the pressure of just doing their jobs instead of catering to the customer. Reports, strategic plans, staff meetings, operations reviews—all the necessary bureaucracy of business diverts attention. At companies that aren't dedicated to customer service and organized around it, employees can imperil their careers by taking care of customers because they may not meet the deadlines for financial reports or make the slickest presentations to the strategic planning committee.

When a company lacks unremitting pressure from the top to realize a service vision, the daily, unglamorous job of caring for existing customers loses out in competition with sexy projects for winning new customers. It's the old story of grabbing for obvious, short-term profits at the expense of more subtle, long-term gains. As Jay Spechler, who oversees service quality for American Express, explains: "Service is a fragile commodity. You can have it today and lose it tomorrow. Without senior management behind it, it won't work. There are so many other things—new products and programs—driving the budget."[12]

It's no surprise that having a champion at the top is crucial to implementing a customer service strategy. The same could be said of any strategy: all of them need to be defended against competing pressures, all will be ignored unless leaders make them important. But leadership is peculiarly important to customer service for a couple of reasons. First of all, driving a company to produce outstanding service flies in the face of conventional wisdom. Instead of being told to keep their eyes glued to the bottom line of the income statement, employees are asked to forget purely financial considerations and pursue customer satisfaction at all costs. Few employees will respond unless they see that top managers are irrevocably committed to achieving a service vision.

More important, leaders shape culture, and culture is key to customer service. Much of service is a social process,[13] a web of interactions between employee and customer, like the behavioral exchanges that take place between a Nordstrom sales rep and her

[12]Interview with Jay Spechler, director, performance engineering, American Express Travel Related Services Company, February 2, 1988.

[13]The idea of service as social process has been stated most clearly by Richard Normann in *Service Management: Strategy and Leadership in Service Businesses* (John Wiley & Sons, 1984). Normann even characterizes new services, such as vacation clubs (Club Méditerranée) and contract cleaning companies (Service Master), as forms of social innovation.

client, or between the perplexed computer user and the problem solver who picks up the phone for a software company. Employees who have direct contact with customers perform what sociologist Arlie Hochschild calls "emotional labor,"[14] doing their jobs by performing believable roles, by using their emotions to act out unwritten scripts. It's a taxing kind of labor. Just imagine spending the work day being genuinely sympathetic and helpful to every customer who comes along, especially those who are upset about something the company has done.

Formal systems, rules, and methods do little to further effective social processes or to inspire emotional labor. When an employee's eyes glaze over and he refuses a customer's request because of "company policy," the social process—the moment of truth—screeches to a halt. When bank tellers and McDonald's clerks slavishly follow the rule of looking every customer in the eyes but don't perform any real emotional labor, the effect is gratingly false. Sometimes formal control mechanisms backfire in ludicrous ways. K-Mart once ordered clerks at check-out counters to tell every customer, "Thank you for shopping K-Mart" and posted signs saying "TYFSK" as reminders. Harried clerks just grunted a cryptic "TYFSK" after each sale, a contribution to the social process that no customer could understand.[15]

Formal controls are progressively less effective the more decentralized a customer service operation is, the more contact employees have with customers, and the more customers act as co-producers. All those traits increase employee uncertainty about how to produce service. Some fascinating research on nurses, trainers of airplane pilots, and retail clerks notes that task uncertainty increases anxiety, tension, stress, and dissatisfaction, and may even evoke "negative orientations toward clients/customers"—i.e., hatred of customers.[16] In those circumstances, the last thing

---

[14]Arlie Russell Hochschild, *The Managed Heart: Commercialization of Human Feeling* (University of California Press, 1983).

[15]Stephen Koepp, "Pul-eeze! Will Somebody Help Me?" *Time,* February 2, 1987, p. 55.

[16]Peter K. Mills, Thomas Turk, and Newton Margulies, "Value Structures, Formal Structures, and Technology for Lower Participants in Service Organizations," *Human Relations,* vol. 40, no. 4 (1987), pp. 177–198.

that helps is a set of formal controls that implies there is only one correct behavior for all the different situations employees encounter. The more uncertain the task, the more employees depend on values instead of formal controls to guide their behavior.

That's where culture comes in. Culture is nothing more than the values, beliefs, and norms a group of people share. A positive culture is what enables Nordstrom sales reps to take initiative and do so many pleasing and inventive things for customers. A negative culture, and an over-reliance on formal controls, is what leads Macy's clerks to behave toward customers like indifferent automatons. Leaders are crucial to customer service because their words and deeds are the touchstones of culture. If you doubt that, talk with any consultant who makes his living training companies how to give their customers better service. One of the first things you'll hear is that he won't take on an assignment unless the client's top managers participate along with the lowliest employees.

WHAT SERVICE LEADERS DO

When a company enjoys a reputation for treating customers royally, its leaders invariably speak of customer service as a philosophy or a religion. "There's a sign on my desk that reads, 'What have you done for your customers today?' " says Hervey Feldman, president of Embassy Suites, a new hotel chain that has won kudos for the way it treats guests. "I worship at my sign every day, and all my hotel managers worship at theirs." Heinz Adam, vice president for customer services at Federal Express, insists. "Customer service can't be justified on a p&l ledger . . . it's a philosophy." With startling consistency the same message comes from managers at all levels in companies that give outstanding service. They understand that unless a company's commitment to service transcends rational business analysis, the culture won't adopt service as a primary value.

Of course these leaders do more than preach and philosophize. They make service strategies real through "visible management."[17] As in a morality play, they exemplify for their employees what it means to produce great service. The Nordstroms handle dissatisfied customers personally. David Kearns, chairman of Xerox, answers calls from customers and fields complaints one day a month, a duty that rotates among Xerox's top managers.[18] Bill Marriott writes thank-you letters to his hotel's best guests, volunteering to fix anything they're unhappy with, and so do the general managers of Marriott hotels. Executives at Avis, from the president on down, spend several weeks a year on the front lines, manning a counter or servicing cars. When Citicorp was trying to improve customer service, it surveyed companies that seemed to have mastered the game, from McDonald's to IBM. Interviews with ninety managers at seventeen firms showed that "The CEOs . . . for the most part were deeply and personally involved in the customer service function of their business. They personally read complaint logs and letters, took phone calls, and were highly visible and available to the rank and file."[19]

Getting their hands dirty keeps top managers in touch with the problems of customers and the experience of the front line, and it shows everybody that serving customers is important. Never getting down into the trenches is dangerous. Critics of General Motors point out that its senior managers will remain aloof from the service problems customers must endure as long as they themselves get free, new cars every two years and have them serviced by dealers who know they're working on a VIP car.

What is most remarkable about service leaders is the way they treat employees. On the one hand, they set astronomically high standards for their employees and their companies. Federal Express guarantees absolutely, positively to deliver every package by 10:30 A.M. the next morning. Swissair's standard is that no more

[17]"Visible management" was first popularized by Edward Carlson of United Airlines in "Visible Management at United Airlines," *Harvard Business Review* (July–August 1975).

[18]John Hillkirk and Gary Jacobson, *Xerox: American Samurai* (Macmillan, 1986), p. 315.

[19]Robert L. Desatnick, *Managing to Keep the Customer* (Jossey-Bass, 1987), p. 103.

than 3 percent of the passengers it surveys should give negative ratings.[20] Frito-Lay insists that its route drivers be able to fill at least 99.5 percent of the orders they get for the company's more than 150 products. Guest Quarters Suite Hotels, which manages seventeen upscale hotels, surveys its 3,500 employees semi-annually. Whenever more than 10 percent of the workers say a Guest Quarters hotel is failing to achieve one of its goals, the company puts together an action plan with the manager that the manager is obliged to implement.

When it comes to standards, leaders of companies that shine in customer service are uncompromising. Ray Kroc, former chairman of McDonald's, once visited a branch and noticed a crumpled napkin in the parking lot, a clear violation of McDonald's standards for cleanliness. He stormed into the outlet, napkin in hand, and publicly fired the manager (whose immediate boss secretly reinstated him some weeks later). A Nordstrom sales rep who receives more than one warning about falling below standard for all sorts of behavior—sales performance, appearance, attitude, customer service, or goal setting—had better look for a new job. So had the IBM employee who fails to respond to a customer emergency.

On the other hand, these leaders go to extremes to get their people to act autonomously and take risks—to behave as though they own the business. Taking risks is the only way employees can provide effective and efficient customer service. Jan Carlzon of SAS relishes the story of Rudy Peterson, an American businessman who arrived at the Stockholm airport to discover he'd forgotten his ticket at his hotel. Instead of refusing him a boarding pass, the SAS ticket clerk took the responsibility of giving him a temporary one. While he waited in the departure lounge, she phoned the hotel, confirmed the ticket was exactly where Peterson said he had left it, and sent an SAS limousine to retrieve it. When Peterson boarded his plane, the flight attendant calmly delivered his

[20]Milind M. Lele with Jagdish N. Sheth, *The Customer Is Key* (John Wiley & Sons, 1987), pp. 58–59.

original ticket.[21] At the Amway Grand Plaza Hotel in Grand Rapids, Michigan, which is renowned for service, managers consistently reward risk taking. "It's paramount," says David Wheelhouse, director of human resources. "Each guest has different needs. To be successful, you have to stick your neck out, be personal, take risks to make the guest happy." It's the same with any customer service operation, whether it's after-sale repair or taking orders.

Getting people to take risks is a powerful way to improve efficiency. The bane of any customer service operation is the employee who says, "That's not my department," or, "I can't do anything about it," or, "I'll have to ask my supervisor." By passing the problem to somebody else, he not only alienates the customer but also multiplies the work a company must do to produce service. The way to avoid this disaster is to unshackle people. One of the quickest ways to shorten bank teller lines, for example, is to let the tellers themselves authorize more transactions, instead of forcing them to refer every questionable transaction to a bank officer. Most automobile makers insist their dealers get authorization for major repairs under warranty. The Acura Division of American Honda Corp. has surged to the top in service efficiency by declaring war on red tape and allowing its dealers to undertake most such repairs on their own authority. Ford has taken a cue from Acura: in 1988, it began authorizing dealers to spend up to $250 per car to fix unexpected problems. "We are giving back to the dealers total authority to handle customers on their own without any b.s.," says Joseph Kordick, head of Ford's parts and service organization. He admits "it's very risky and a big change from our old culture. We used to say, 'Audit the hell out of 'em because they'll lie and cheat and steal from you.' "[22] Presumably Ford's culture, like the cultures of most companies that offer great service, will be sufficiently powerful and positive that dealers will be

[21]Jan Carlzon, *Moments of Truth* (Ballinger, 1987), pp. 1–2.
[22]Thomas Moore, "Would You Buy a Car from This Man?" *Fortune,* April 11, 1988, p. 74.

able to make sound judgments on their own about when to fix something and when not to.

Service leaders use a full arsenal of motivational techniques to get employees to take risks (see the next chapter). They also set the stage for outstanding service with their own behavior. Basically, they treat employees as they wish employees to treat customers. They express the same values in their dealings with the front line that they want the front line to show in its dealings with customers. They realize that the world they create for employees is the world employees will create for customers. As Richard Normann has observed: "Climate is crucial, and climate must be pervasive. Anyone who has ever entered a French bank and studied the perfectly visible, deadly formal and almost deliberately destructive relationship between the front-line personnel, their superiors and the superiors of the superiors—all sitting one behind the other—will immediately give up any idea of obtaining good service there."[23]

Creating a positive climate for customer service means demonstrating concern for employees, enhancing their dignity, and solving their problems quickly and fairly. At the most specific level, it means calling sales clerks "sales representatives" and exalting their importance so they feel that "Nobody's going to look down on you because you work here," as a Nordstrom sales rep told us. More formally, it means installing a range of human resource policies—hiring, firing, promotion, compensation, benefits, grievance procedures—that employees view favorably. When employees feel those policies are positive, they produce service that customers view positively.[24] Above all, it means showing respect for employees daily. The most important criterion that Hervey Feldman of Embassy Suites uses in hiring general managers is whether they have the interpersonal skills to treat every employee

---

[23]Normann, *Service Management,* p. 47.

[24]David E. Bowen, assistant professor at the business school of the University of Southern California, demonstrated this correlation in a study of fifty-one branch banks: "Taking Care of Human Relations Equals Taking Care of the Business," *Human Resource Reporter* (November 1985).

as though he were competent. "Where you win or lose the ball game is with the way general managers treat employees," Feldman says. "If they treat 'em well, then the employees treat customers well, and the rest is merely scorekeeping."

TOOLS OF THE TRADE

Leaders of family businesses and those who have founded the companies they run generally have an easy time shaping corporate culture. They seem to understand intuitively the importance of service values and how to communicate them. When your name is on the building—or at least on your company's statement of incorporation—you tend to be hypersensitive about the image customers have of the company and to run the company like a family. Employees pay strict attention to your feelings. A surprising number of the firms that produce outstanding customer service were led by their founder, owner, or members of the founding family, including Shouldice, Nordstrom, and Network Equipment Technologies (see chapter 7).

Professional managers—i.e., non-owners—have a tougher time inculcating values. In place of intuition, and the profound authority of owners, they've got to use explicit techniques. Leaders who take culture seriously are bears for internal marketing, selling their points of view to the organization much as they would sell a product or service to the public, with slogans, advertisements, promotions, and public relations campaigns. The largest single chunk of their time is spent communicating values.

Again, slogans mean nothing without actions that exemplify them. Empty words are so common that some students of customer service find no correlation between the slogans leaders use and a culture's dedication to service.[25] Too many slogans and too little action quickly breed cynicism. Employees at one company became so inured to management's constant stream of unsubstan-

[25]See Karl Albrecht and Ron Zemke, *Service America!* (Dow Jones-Irwin, 1985), p. 48.

tiated slogans that whenever they heard a new one they would whisper among themselves the cryptic acronym "BOHICA"— "Bend over, here it comes again."

The companies that have the most effective internal communications don't just deliver the word from on high. They listen closely to employees, achieving two-way communication with a battery of procedures. Like Nordstrom, they insist that managers at all levels be constantly accessible. Guest Quarters has a program called "Straight to the Top," which encourages employees to ask the general manager of a hotel any question, even anonymously, and requires the manager to answer within forty-eight hours. (If the question is anonymous, the answer is posted for all to read.) A popular tool in companies that have many low-wage employees in constant contact with customers is the employee council. Employees from each department elect a representative, and the representatives meet weekly with the manager responsible for all departments. He updates them on everything he's doing; they ask questions, offer suggestions, voice opinions, and then go back to their departments to explain what's going on.

With or without employee councils, the weekly meeting of work groups or departments is a common practice of companies that produce superior service. The meetings serve several purposes. They keep managers in touch with the problems and experiences of the front line, and they break down barriers by making employees aware of what the rest of the company is doing. As one of the participants in the Citicorp study of service leaders put it, "If everyone knows what is happening throughout the organization, any chance encounter with a customer, even by a non-customer-service employee, turns out to be a benefit. The well-informed employee never says (and is never permitted to say) 'I don't know' or 'It's not my job.' "[26] The meetings also bake values into the corporate culture. They're inspirational, somewhat like old-fashioned revival meetings. At Nordstrom they may include short skits about working at the company. Many Nordstrom department managers use the meetings to wow sales reps with the latest

[26]Desatnick, *Managing to Keep the Customer,* p. 22.

merchandise, work out new goals with them, and develop contests for achieving those goals.

One of the most powerful techniques service leaders use to communicate values is the upside-down or concentric organization chart. Nordstrom and many other companies use the inverted pyramid, with customers and front-line employees at the top and top managers at the bottom. The Amway Grand Plaza Hotel uses a concentric chart, with guests in the bull's-eye—the most valuable position—employees in the next ring, and managers in the outermost circle. These aren't organization charts in the traditional sense. They don't clarify reporting relationships or functional divisions, and they don't accurately represent organizational structure. Their purpose is to show how organizational process is supposed to work. "Our round chart tells employees that their job is to make all the decisions needed for guests to be happy and that management's job is to support them, to make employees happy," says David Wheelhouse of the Amway Grand Plaza.

Leaders use all of these techniques—the internal marketing campaigns, the inspirational meetings, the charts—to encourage cooperation among employees in different departments and to blur the bureaucratic divisions and infighting that are death to customer service. Every company with outstanding service seems to be fanatic about the idea that it's everybody's business, not something that can be shifted to one department, especially not to the customer service department, the limbo to which employees assign those problems that they refuse to solve themselves. Ironically, companies that are most effective in customer service often don't have a customer service department. Chaparral Steel, which uses customer service to fend off fierce Japanese competitors, sends its production managers into the field to answer customer complaints.[27] Acura has just four people in its customer relations department, and its goal is to have none. "If we reach that goal," says Ed Taylor, Acura's general manager, "we'll know that prob-

[27]Judith Dobrzynski, "Fighting Back: It Can Work," *Business Week*, August 26, 1985, pp. 62 ff.

lems are being handled right where they occur—at our dealerships." American Express's card operation has never assigned customer service to any one department. Lou Gerstner, former president of American Express Travel Related Services, once proclaimed: "Other companies have customer service departments. American Express *is* a customer service department."

This doesn't mean that every company that has a customer service department should get rid of it. Giving customers one telephone number to call for service and assigning people full time to fielding those calls is a necessity when a company is large and its distribution methods entail little or no direct contact with the ultimate users of its products or services. Giants that sell through retail, like Procter & Gamble, or through other third parties, as many insurance companies and industrial suppliers do, can't rely entirely on their distribution channels. They need customer service departments to act as back-ups and to guide customers with problems through the corporate maze. Generally, the less after-sale service a product requires, the less customers will know where to turn for help, and the more sense it makes to maintain a customer service department.

Every leader, however, has to ask whether his company's customer service department actually improves the levels of service customers receive. Far too often such departments degrade service by acting as shields to protect companies from customers' problems. There are few quicker ways to improve service than to make everyone in your company responsible for it, no matter what department he or she is in.

Breaking down bureaucratic divisions helps energize front-line employees and, if it works, delights customers, but it can be highly threatening to traditional middle-level managers and first-line supervisors. When leaders do everything to shift power and authority to employees who serve customers directly, what's left for middle managers to do? They enjoy neither the satisfaction of shaping culture from the top nor the thrill of serving the customer. In many companies that use customer service as the ultimate weapon, the middle manager's job is unsatisfying, and few employees want to take it on. Predictably, when a company that has been producing poor service tries to reform and create more focus on customers, middle managers and first-line supervisors put up the most resistance.

The hard truth is that there's little place for the traditional middle manager in companies that go all out to serve customers. The skills that most such managers have mastered—protecting their fiefdoms, proving their importance by forcing all information and communications to flow through their offices, meticulously enforcing bureaucratic controls—become serious liabilities. Yet no matter how flat the organization, no company can function without middle managers.

The solution service leaders often take is to redefine the middle manager's job. Instead of acting like a boss, he is encouraged to behave like a helper. The watchword for companies that give great service is: "Whoever isn't serving the customer directly better be serving the people who do." At Amdahl Corp., which provides customer service rated even higher than IBM's, middle managers know that whoever has been assigned to handle after-sale service for a particular customer has carte blanche to rally the people, parts, and supplies needed to fix a broken computer. The seventeen service stars that Citicorp studied "paid a great deal of attention to the interdependence of service teams within their organizations. They measured the quality, timeliness, accuracy, courtesy, and responsiveness of the departments that service each other's needs for information, materials, supplies, and services."[28] They surveyed internal customers to see how well they were being served just as they surveyed outside customers, and they held middle managers accountable for the results in all cases.

The idea that a manager's main responsibility is to remove obstacles that keep people from doing their jobs will come as no surprise to anyone who knows the work of W. Edwards Deming and other gurus of quality control. Many of our findings about customer service—that it must be everybody's business, that a positive corporate culture is key to producing it, that work group meetings (the equivalent of quality circles) are proven tools for

[28]Desatnick, *Managing to Keep the Customer,* p. 91.

achieving two-way communication and finding better ways to serve the customer—are similar to findings in the literature of quality control. As companies that achieve total quality control often eliminate their quality control departments, so companies that shine in customer service often lack customer service departments. The point is that many managers already know how to lead the charge toward outstanding service because they know how to lead the drive for quality. The techniques, the obstacles, and the rewards are similar in many ways.

PRINCIPLES OF LEADERSHIP

No company can triumph in customer service unless its leaders drive the process and drive it hard. Giving great service often calls for employees to ignore short-term profits; it always calls for them to do hard emotional work in order to create positive social processes. Nobody will take his eyes off the income statement or put his heart on the line without constant demonstrations of support from the top.

Leaders of companies that shine in customer service adhere to three principles:

1 / *Foster a service oriented culture.* Leaders help create and nurture cultures by communicating values. They worship at the altar of customer service every day, and they do it visibly. They are personally involved in service activities. They back up slogans with dramatic, often costly actions. To inculcate values they stress two-way communications, opening their doors to all employees and using weekly meetings of work groups to inform, to inspire, and to solve service problems. They put values into action by treating employees exactly as they want employees to treat customers.

2 / *Make customer service everybody's business.* Unless every employee assumes responsibility for the customer's experience, service dies. Leaders encourage each employee to feel and act as if he or she owns the company. They set impossibly high standards. They push responsibility and authority for service as far

down into the organization as possible, often using upside-down or concentric organization charts to underline the idea that front-line employees are second in importance only to customers.

3 / *Declare war on bureaucracy.* Red tape and recalcitrant middle managers will sabotage service every time. To produce effective, efficient customer service, leaders keep policies, procedures, and other formal control mechanisms to a minimum, relying instead on cultural control. They re-educate middle managers and supervisors to focus on serving and supporting front-line employees, measuring their performance by surveying the service they render to internal customers.

5

Performance on the Line: People Policies

To customers, front-line workers embody service. Yet service workers often are the pariahs of corporate society, the lowest in the pecking order.

Not so at companies that lead in customer service. They pay extraordinary attention to their employees. Realizing that the production of service is hard emotional labor—an unremitting public performance—they take pains to hire people whose personalities predispose them to serve customers well. These companies minimize turnover, the bane of good service, with an impressive array of motivational and training programs. In the interest of increasing customer satisfaction, they give their employees lavish awards and genuine opportunities for advancement.

Hotels epitomize the service crisis, as any traveler knows. Blankly smiling receptionists seem to have a knack for losing reservations and shrugging their shoulders when distraught guests ask where else to find a room. Mute bellboys whisk baggage away and take the better part of an hour to release it. Maids who speak only in foreign tongues barge into rooms at awkward times then disappear, apparently forever, leaving the room uncleaned. Room service takes eons, especially when the traveler needs a cup of coffee in the morning, and what finally arrives often isn't what was ordered. Asking for any special service—a shoeshine, say, or sewing on a shirt button—may elicit a concerned response, but seldom the required action. Then there's the saga of checking out, which can seem to take longer than Moses' journey to the Promised Land. Unlike the patriarch, the hotel guest won't be set free until the "valet" who parked his car manages to retrieve it, a treasure hunt that can last for thirty minutes.

The facts are that hotels can't find enough workers, can't keep the ones they do find, and seldom succeed in training employees to be both courteous and competent. The number of hotel rooms in the United States is growing 3 percent annually, creating a demand for workers that will be at least 25 percent higher in the year 2000 than it is today. But the labor force of sixteen- to twenty-four-year-olds, the prime pool of entry-level hotel workers, is shrinking; it will be 26 percent lower by the end of the century than it is today. The population of older people who still have to work—the second most attractive source of hotel employees—also is contracting; it will be 10 percent smaller in 1995 than it is now.

Despite these scarcities, hotels do a terrible job of retaining their ever more valuable workers. Half of the typical hotel's salaried employees leave during the year, and so do 105 percent of all the hourly workers it hires during any twelve-month period.[1] Many hotel executives appear to have concluded that such astronomical turnover makes training uneconomic. They give their new hires, who often are illiterate in English, a day or two of perfunctory orientation before unleashing them on defenseless guests.

There are exceptions, particularly among hotels that aren't expanding at breakneck speed. Some individual operations stand out, like the Amway Grand Plaza in Grand Rapids, Michigan. Small chains of luxury hotels like Four Seasons, Inc., do a better

---

[1]Stephen J. Hiemstra and Lee M. Kruel, *Manpower Resources and Trends in the Lodging Industry: Past and Future* (a study prepared for the Hospitality Lodging & Travel Research Foundation of the American Hotel and Motel Association by the Department of Restaurant, Hotel & Institutional Management, Purdue University, 1986).

than average job, but at a much higher than average price for their rooms and services. A few big chains—Hyatt, Marriott, Stouffer, and Westin—usually transcend mediocrity, according to reliable surveys.[2] Generally, though, customer service in U.S. hotels is a nightmare. International travelers, familiar with the exquisite service at most Asian hotels and at many European ones, speculate that the culture and character of Americans are somehow inimical to giving good service.[3]

Of course the problem isn't with the character of American workers. It's with the practices of American managers, who usually have only the dimmest notions of how to help employees render outstanding service. For proof that a hotel chain can manage to produce outstanding service despite large size, swift expansion, and the putative shortcomings of American workers, consider Embassy Suites.

A Holiday Corp. subsidiary established in 1983, Embassy now manages and/or owns over 85 hotels with some 21,000 suites, and it plans to have more than 150 hotels open or under construction by the end of 1991. Embassy beats its competitors by almost any measure. Compared with the upscale operations of chains such as Hilton, Sheraton, and Holiday Inns, it boasts higher average room rates (because it has to offer fewer discounts), much higher occupancy rates, and fatter profit margins—13 percent higher than the group average. Embassy is growing more than ten times as fast as the entire hotel industry. The major reason for this stellar performance is simple: customers like Embassy Suites hotels better. When Consumers Union analyzed reports of 232,000 hotel stays by the 150,000 readers of *Consumer Reports* magazine, Embassy

[2]See, for example, "Where to Stay," *Consumer Reports* (July 1986), pp. 472–478.

[3]The contrast between service quality in the United States and elsewhere is just as strong among airlines, and it leads to similar speculations. According to IFAPA—the International Foundation of Airline Passengers' Associations—the airlines that render the best service are Swissair, Singapore Airlines, and Lufthansa, with British Airways, American Airlines, and Delta tied for fourth place. After flying to the Far East aboard Singapore Airlines, one of the co-authors returned to the United States on Pan American and was seated next to a Pan Am vice president. Asked why Pan Am's stewardesses produced service clearly inferior to Singapore's, the executive replied, "U.S. women just aren't brought up to serve people well." By pinning the blame on his workers, of course, he simply revealed his own incompetence.

came out first among twenty mid-priced chains ($40 to $79 a night) and first among eight high-priced chains ($80 and up).[4] NPD Research Co., which tracks the lodging habits of 10,000 travelers a month for Holiday Corp., finds that 62 percent of guests rate Embassy Suites "excellent," while the closest runner up, Marriott, garners "excellent" ratings from 53 percent.[5]

Embassy Suites' prime attraction is that it offers only suites, a concept that a predecessor company, Granada Royale, pioneered back in 1969. For the same price as a normal, upscale room with bath, guests get a room with bath, plus a separate living room, complete with desk, sofa bed, wet bar, and, in most cases, an icemaker and a microwave oven or small cooking range. The suite concept is so alluring that a score of other companies have jumped into the market, which is growing 15 to 20 percent annually.[6] Yet despite the competition, and despite not having hotels in every geographic market, Embassy Suites has held on to one fifth of the $2 billion suite hotel business.

What keeps Embassy Suites on top is the quality of service it produces for guests. While other companies have copied the suite hotel idea, few if any have figured out how to reproduce the competent, caring, responsive service that Embassy offers. In 1987, when a market research firm interviewed 5,900 of the hotel's guests, half of whom were staying with Embassy Suites for the first time, an impressive 58 percent rated the service higher than that of Hilton, Hyatt, Marriott, and Sheraton, and another 24 percent said Embassy's service was better than that of most of the competing group. During open-ended interviews, one fourth of the sample, 1,500 customers, volunteered that among the things they liked best about Embassy Suites was its helpful, friendly service. These findings are all the more impressive because Embassy Suites doesn't appear to be a high-priced, high-service operation with legions of parking valets, bellhops, and chambermaids dancing attendance on guests. Most of its hotels lack a concierge, a symbol

[4]"Where to Stay," *Consumer Reports* (July 1986), p. 475.
[5]NPD Research Co., *U.S. Lodger Panel Guest Satisfaction Survey, 1986–1987.*
[6]*Lodging Outlook* (Smith Travel Research), August 1988.

of outstanding service for some travelers. Neither is its staff deeply experienced in the hotel business. Many are part-timers, the second or third breadwinners in their lower-class families.

How does Embassy Suites do it? How does it beat the long odds against producing great service throughout a large chain of less than luxury hotels? To begin with, it has mastered the principles of strategy and leadership. The company's service strategy is clever and clear. It addresses two segments: business travelers in urban areas and pleasure travelers with families. The suite concept pleases business travelers, who usually expect some comfortable place in which to hold meetings, such as the suite's living room. It also pleases families, who expect some convenient way to accommodate their children, such as the living-room sofa bed. Since business travelers need rooms during the week, pleasure travelers prefer weekends, and suites delight both segments, Embassy succeeds in maximizing utilization of its capacity. Moreover, suites give the company flexible capacity. If an Embassy Suites hotel is close to being booked up, the manager can split a suite into two rooms and offer them to different customers at reduced rates.

Everything else about Embassy Suites is optimized to serve the two target segments. Valet parking is available, but most guests get quicker service by co-producing it: they park their own cars in a garage or lot linked directly to the hotel. Since business and family travelers insist on breakfast but have little other use for a hotel restaurant, Embassy provides free, full-service breakfasts in a pleasant dining area and doesn't waste money and effort trying to run a restaurant. Instead, it rents space to experienced restaurant chains such as Restaurant Associates. That way guests don't blame Embassy for shortcomings at lunch and dinner or in room service, and the hotel avoids full-blown restaurant operations, the least profitable of hotel activities. Tired business people who want a drink at the end of the day can take advantage of the free drinks Embassy serves at cocktail time.

Embassy Suites does perhaps the most extensive research in the industry about its guests' expectations and experiences, including interviewing five customers a day at each property. It has helped set expectations with an innovative advertising campaign. Hotel ads normally stress the beauty of the rooms and public facilities and the elegant, attentive service employees supposedly provide. Embassy Suites ads feature Garfield, a plump, scruffy cartoon cat known for his self-indulgence, to send the message that "the suite life" costs no more than staying in a traditional hotel. Images of grand luxury and Old World service are absent, so guests are less likely to expect those qualities and to be disappointed when they find out otherwise. Conversely, they're delighted by the service they actually experience because it tends to exceed the expectations Garfield has created.

Hervey Feldman, Embassy Suites' voluble, energetic president, has made the company a textbook example of service leadership. A thirty-year veteran of the industry and a former hotel management consultant, he calls customer service a religion and insists that employees practice the creed constantly. Like many outstanding service companies, Embassy Suites uses an upside-down organization chart to dramatize the idea that the customer is boss, that front-line employees are the most important ones in the organization, and that management's job is to serve employees. To reduce red tape and dramatize the primacy of customers, Feldman has created a new complaint policy. As he explains it:

> Most hotel complaint departments have battalions of people who investigate problems and promise to get back to the customer. They take your version of what happened, get a different version from the hotel manager or employee, and, if you're lucky, drop you a note offering an adjustment or saying that the insurance company won't permit one. We let customers adjust their own grievances. We ask for their opinion of what it will take to make things right, and if they can't think of anything, we often refund the room charge. This way we can save enormous amounts of employee and management time that would otherwise be wasted in an investigation. Employees and hotel managers learn about the adjustments we've made after the fact, and that may irritate them, but I really don't care about who's right. The customer is *always* right. Explanations, excuses, and alibis don't cut it.[7]

Feldman pushes authority and responsibility as far down into his organization as possible, emphasizing the duty of hotel gen-

[7]Interview with Hervey Feldman, October 16, 1987.

eral managers to support the front line. Because these middle managers have so much impact on employee behavior, they're more important to Embassy Suites than corporate executives who appear to be higher up in the pecking order. Embassy Suites takes remarkable pains in recruiting, training, and evaluating hotel general managers. Working with a team of psychologists that has studied the personalities of successful service executives, the company has developed a list of ten key "competencies" for hotel managers, from persistence to defining problems clearly. Recruiters use interviews, hypothetical situations, and psychological tests to find would-be executives who possess these abilities, and nearly every manager at Embassy Suites, regardless of title, undergoes training programs that stress the same ten abilities.

The most important skills are interpersonal ones, including the ability to consider the needs and feelings of others, to facilitate group activity instead of dominating it, and, above all, to treat everyone as though he or she is competent. That sounds like an odd criterion, but it's crucial to service. "Historically most managers in the hospitality industry, which has a large number of minimum-wage-type workers, believed that employees weren't too smart or too competent, even after being trained," Feldman notes. "That belief is false. Our workers do tend to be disadvantaged and inexperienced, but they have normal intelligence. With the right training and experience, they have the curiosity and competence to go beyond making beds."[8]

MOTIVATING THE FRONT LINE

The single biggest reason for the superior service Embassy Suites produces is the way it trains and motivates its lowliest workers. Like other chains, Embassy uses a one-day orientation session to familiarize new hires with the corporation and with their duties, and it relies on detailed manuals and instruction sessions to mold

[8]Feldman interview.

employee behavior. Unlike the others, Embassy provides all the opportunities for advancement workers can handle.

Feldman's secret weapon is SBP—the Skills Based Pay program, which encourages workers to learn the ten basic jobs of the hotel, from handling the front desk to cooking breakfast to inspecting newly made-up suites. After ninety days in a new job, the employee can apply for certification. If his or her supervisor approves, the employee takes a written test and performs a work sample, which the supervisor grades against the same standards that appear in training manuals, such as whether a housekeeper knocks before entering a suite and makes sure to greet guests in the corridors. Finally, the aspirant's co-workers discuss the results of the work sample and take a secret vote on whether or not to approve certification. If an employee fails, the supervisor must help him develop a written plan for succeeding and provide him with a study manual. Employees who win certification get an immediate, small pay increase—usually 25 cents an hour—and the opportunity to try out a different job or to train for it one day a week, with the chance to win another certification down the road and another pay increase. Embassy Suites has no problem getting workers to participate in SBP. "Minimum-wage people are going to get out of that pit as fast as they possibly can," says Feldman.[9]

The benefits of SBP for employees are obvious: increased feelings of accomplishment and self-worth, better pay, a visible career path that can lead to management (half of the people in Embassy Suites' Management Training Program rose from the ranks through SBP). The benefits for the corporation are perhaps even greater. Besides lower turnover, Embassy gets a work force competent in many aspects of hotel operations, which means they can solve a guest's problems on the spot instead of saying, "I don't know," or, "It's not my job." And because housekeepers can pitch in as bartenders or front-desk clerks when necessary, Embassy gains greater latitude than most hotels to vary its service capacity with variations in demand.

[9]Feldman interview.

Embassy Suites' other unusual motivational program is Success Sharing, which gives employees a stake in the company by linking part of their compensation to hotel performance. Embassy has taken a radical step by freely sharing vital business information with even its part-time workers. Every day they get to see the results of yesterday's guest interviews, along with their hotel's occupancy rate and cleanliness ratings. When a hotel meets or exceeds its quarterly targets for occupancy, customer satisfaction, and cleanliness—and 90 percent of Embassy Suites' operations do—employees get a bonus based on their hourly rate and the numbers of hours they've worked, not their position. The average front-line employee in a successful hotel gets a bonus of about $100 a month. Success Sharing is similar to other profit-sharing programs, but with significant differences. It applies to all employees, not just to supervisors and managers. Since workers get daily feedback on how their performance has shaped the hotel's overall business results, Success Sharing reinforces effective teamwork. But since bonuses are based on hours worked, Success Sharing also creates a direct link between individual effort and rewards.

Skills Based Pay, Success Sharing, and the other tools that Embassy Suites uses to train and motivate workers, such as selecting an employee of the month, are intimately linked with the company's culture. The tools express the culture and bolster its values, such as taking risks to solve guests' problems on your own. Other expressions of the culture, like Feldman's complaint policy and his declarations that customer service is a religion, help give the tools meaning.

Culture and tools cannot work in conflict with each other. If managers didn't really value and support front-line employees—if they didn't treat all workers as though they were competent—employees would quickly see Embassy Suites' innovative personnel policies as a sham. They would take the same skeptical view of Embassy Suites' statements about the culture of customer service if personnel policies were to close off chances for advancement and for sharing in the business's challenges and successes (as the policies of most hotels inadvertently do).

PEOPLE *ARE* SERVICE

The people problems hotels face, and the methods companies like Embassy Suites use to solve them, represent extremes. Hotel workers tend to come from the bottom of the labor barrel, yet they face extraordinary demands. The majority of hotel jobs entail frequent, high-touch contact with customers and lots of uncertainty, since customer needs and expectations are quite various. Hotel workers can't just follow standard instructions or methods for doing their jobs. They must make judgments, show initiative, and take risks in order to customize service for guests. The task of the hotel manager, bluntly put, is to transform frogs into princes.

Most businesses have it easier. They can draw on adequate pools of experienced workers, and the majority of their employees don't have direct contact with customers (though more of them probably should have such contact if top managers believe in service). Car manufacturers, for instance, don't have to turn assembly-line workers into paragons of courtesy, initiative, and resourcefulness, for the majority of them will seldom meet a customer. Even when workers must produce people-to-people service, standardizing, industrializing, or centralizing the job can reduce uncertainty and the need to make judgments.[10] Cashiers at McDonald's needn't worry about the right proportions for a milk shake or even about the cost of different items on the menu. There's just one way to make a shake, and the keys of the computerized cash registers show only the names of the items customers can order, not their prices, which the machine automatically retrieves and totals. Industrializing service reduces the levels of skill and emotional energy needed to do the job, though it also tends to create impersonal service that offends customers who have inappropriately high expectations.

At every company, however, somebody inevitably will contact customers directly and be asked to exercise judgment indepen-

---

[10]See Theodore H. Levitt, "The Industrialization of Service," *Harvard Business Review*, September/October, 1976.

dent of rules and regulations. When that service encounter occurs, the odds are good that it will be a failure—both from the customer's point of view and from the company's. Few organizations invest anywhere near enough time and money in hiring, training, and motivating customer-contact personnel, especially companies that try to finesse service problems by using a powerless customer service department as a buffer. There's a vast gap between the concern for customer service that many managers trumpet publicly and their willingness to invest in the people who are supposed to render service. According to Zenger-Miller, a California-based training and consulting firm that has studied the service expenditures of over two hundred corporations, spending on service training amounts, on average, to less than $1,000 per site, a pittance given the difficulties of educating people to produce good service.[11] Customer service departments often are staffed by part-timers, including retirees and housewives whose prime interests definitely don't include crushing the competition by producing superior service. The pay is low. Bonus or incentive programs are feeble, if they exist at all.

By now the folly of underinvesting in service employees should be obvious. Since service is intangible, customers judge its quality by the quality of their interactions with service providers. A grumpy airline ticketing agent in fact provides worse service than a pleasant, courteous one, even if she's just as accurate and effective in writing the ticket. Some fascinating research suggests that even when the system for delivering service breaks down, making effective service impossible, customers will be sympathetic and stifle their ire as long as they feel that the person who's trying to provide the service cares about them, understands their needs, and is doing his or her best to set things right.[12] Just think of how customers react when the airplane flight they've booked is canceled. If the ticketing agent gives a credible explanation for the

[11]Nancy Cushing, Carol Laughlin, and Roland Dumas, "Service Quality: The Future of Competitive Advantage," Zenger-Miller, Inc., January 27, 1987.

[12]A. Parasuraman, Valerie A. Zeithamel, and Leonard L. Berry, "A Conceptual Model of Service Quality and Its Implications for Future Research," *Journal of Marketing*, Fall 1985, pp. 41–50.

cancellation and makes every effort to get them onto the next available flight, they won't be terribly upset. But how do they feel when a stone-faced agent just announces the cancellation with the barest of apologies and hurries off to another gate?

Unfortunately, when managers approach the production of service just as they would the production of goods, workers have a natural tendency to give terrible service. Classical manufacturing absolutely requires a controlled environment. The steps of the production process must be laid out in minute detail, the workers must follow them to the letter, the whole process must be shielded from interference, whether that means refusing to mix different products on the same line or refusing to make minor alterations in the process to suit a customer's unique needs.

Excellent service is just the opposite: it absolutely depends on welcoming customer requests and responding flexibly. Many managers ignore this crucial difference in their quest for efficient production. Think of any well-run bureaucracy, where workers strive to push paperwork through a production line as fast as they can. In that environment, requests for special service become an intolerable form of outside interference. As one researcher puts it, "Most people who deal with paperwork feel the customer is a pain in the ass. They have resentment. It shows up in the voice. And if a customer hears that he's a bother, he'll be reluctant to ask for service again."[13] Dennis D. Pointer, professor of health administration at Virginia Commonwealth University, concurs that most service managers treat workers as though they were part of a 1950s style assembly line. But employees who provide service are not so much producers as they are performers, like stage actors. They have to behave, says Pointer, like Frank Sinatra at a concert, not just going through the motions or simply singing a song but putting their entire selves on stage in order to establish a direct connection, an intimate exchange with the audience.[14] In short,

[13]Interview with Wesley Henry, Educational Institute of the American Hotel and Motel Association, Michigan State University, January 7, 1988.

[14]Interviews with Dennis D. Pointer, Arthur Graham Glasgow Professor of Health Administration, Medical College of Virginia, Virginia Commonwealth University, January 1, 1988, and September 21, 1988.

they must perform a kind of emotional labor that's entirely foreign to production-line workers, and they need intense training and motivational help to do it. Walt Disney Co., known for excellent service at its theme parks, recognizes the special nature of service work by calling all of its employees "cast members."

Skeptics who doubt that service workers must be ready to put on a performance at all times should consider the experience of the Amway Grand Plaza Hotel. A huge and elaborate facility located in the secondary city of Grand Rapids, Michigan, Amway competes fiercely for lucrative convention business with hotels in Detroit, Chicago, St. Louis, and other Midwestern capitals. In 1987, the Michigan State Horticultural Society, a group of 3,500 commercial fruit growers, had just finished its annual convention at the Amway and was discussing the site for its next conclave, worth $200,000 to the hotel that won the contract. A room-service waiter who was delivering coffee to the society's chairman mentioned how much everyone at Amway looked forward to hosting his people next year. And even though the Westin Hotel in Detroit made a superb pitch for the business, the fruit growers returned to the Amway in 1988.[15]

The deadly enemy of great performance on the front line is high turnover. Nobody can be expected to shine when he's new on the job, doesn't know the technical aspects of his work or the organizational ropes, and lacks the confidence to take risks on the customer's behalf. What kind of service can hotels expect to produce when their hourly work force turns over more than 100 percent a year? How can restaurants ever hope to delight customers when the hourly work force of the food service industry turns over better than 200 percent a year?[16] Even much lower turnover can be a cancer on fast-growing organizations that try to provide expert service. If a department store, say, is expanding 20 percent a year and has a relatively low turnover rate of 30 percent, three out of five employees at any one time will have less than a year's

[15]Interview with David Wheelhouse, director of human resources, Amway Grand Plaza Hotel, January 20, 1988.

[16]Hiemstra and Kreul, *Manpower Resources and Trends in the Lodging Industry*, pp. x–xiii.

experience. They can hardly be expected to act as credible fashion consultants for picky shoppers. Besides, turnover is expensive. High Country Corp., which has turned around sixteen hotels, figures that the full cost of losing and replacing an average employee is $2,700.[17] Generally, the higher the skill and experience level of the employee who leaves and must be replaced, the greater the cost.

Curmudgeons may complain that high turnover is inevitable among low-skill, first-time workers, but the evidence suggests the fault is management's. Careful hiring, intensive and never-ending training, and a cornucopia of inexpensive incentive and motivational programs almost always slash turnover drastically. When High Country takes over a hotel and introduces its battery of morale and incentive programs, turnover normally falls by half and sometimes by 80 percent. Guest Quarters Suite Hotels, another specialist in turning around failing hotels, has achieved an average turnover rate of 42 percent, less than half the industry average, because of its outstanding employee-relations program. Effective personnel policies and lower turnover add up to better service. As one student of customer service has put it, "Managing an organization's human resources equates with managing its customer services. . . . Employee relations equals customer relations. The two are inseparable."[18]

HIRING SMART

Getting employees to produce great service sounds simple: Hire the right people, train them, and keep them motivated. But doing those things in practice is extraordinarily difficult, too difficult for most managers to master, apparently. How else to explain the Gorgonlike receptionist whose rotten personality repels custom-

[17]Other hotel chains cite much lower costs, yielding an industry average cost for turning over an employee of about $175. In many cases, these hotels have not counted the full costs of finding, hiring, training, and terminating an employee. In other cases, they are more efficient than High Country.

[18]Robert L. Desatnick, *Managing to Keep the Customer* (Jossey-Bass, 1987), p. 15.

ers, the dithering sales clerk who doesn't know how to poll the other stores in a chain for an item her store lacks, or the apathetic auto mechanic who can't be bothered to find the real problem with your car and is perfectly content to let you keep bringing it back? To understand how to avoid those syndromes, take a close look at the ways service leaders hire, train, and motivate their employees.

For Hewlett-Packard, McDonald's, Swissair, Guest Quarters, and most other companies that value customer service, hiring a new employee, at whatever level, is analogous to choosing a business partner. The focus is on finding those whose attitudes and personalities predispose them to serve customers well and make it likely the job applicant will fit the service culture. As in finding a mate for life, finding a promising employee means lots of screening and testing. After screening applications from would-be cabin attendants, Swissair invites groups of eight candidates to a full day of interviews, during which they are continually probed to see if their personalities "will fit into the company culture of putting the passenger first, being patient, not being authoritarian, not being bossy."[19] From dishwasher to auditor, people seeking jobs at Guest Quarters hotels must pass through four interviews, including one with the hotel's general manager. "We're not hiring," says Robert T. Foley, Guest Quarters's senior vice president for human resources. "We're entering into a fifty-fifty relationship with them. We will pay fairly and give them a good benefit plan, and their commitment to us is that they be customer oriented."[20]

Many outstanding service companies, like McDonald's and Embassy Suites, have defined sets of abilities and personality traits that help in producing good service. They probe management candidates for those characteristics with psychological tests and with "behavioral interviews," during which they ask applicants how they have acted or would act in various service situations.[21] Other

[19]Milind M. Lele with Jagdish N. Sheth, *The Customer Is Key* (John Wiley & Sons, 1987), p. 252.

[20]Interview with Robert T. Foley, January 18, 1988.

[21]See Desatnick, *Managing to Keep the Customer,* pp. 35–38. Desatnick claims that when he introduced behavioral interviewing at McDonald's, annual turnover among management trainees dropped from 50 to 30 percent.

companies use behavioral interviews to screen applicants for any job, managerial or not, that entails frequent customer contact. Still others, like Nordstrom's, go at it less formally. They have such strong cultures that they can rely on employees to sniff out the right personalities for the job. No matter the method, the goal is to find people who fit the culture.

Remarkably, relevant experience in previous jobs can be a negative. Foley of Guest Quarters explains: "Some 75 percent of the people we hire have never worked in the hotel business before. We want that. If they've worked at other hotels, they may come with predetermined ways of doing things that are very different from our ways."[22] Nordstrom also prefers people who haven't been tainted by working elsewhere. The store's department managers, who hire their own sales clerks, look more for personal chemistry and a sunny, upbeat attitude than for selling experience. Technical skill is less important than cultural fit.

To cut down on the amount of screening, companies that produce good service use ingenious methods to tap likely groups of potential employees. Hotels run by Guest Quarters, High Country, and Embassy Suites participate constantly in community affairs to broadcast and underline their dedication to service and to attract job applicants who feel the same way. The Amway Grand Plaza targets workers laid off from local manufacturers, as well as the handicapped; it finds both groups believe deeply in the dignity of labor and take well to intensive training.

Having studied the "personnel ideas" of numerous service companies, consultant Richard Normann concludes that finding an appropriate segment of the labor market means finding groups of people whose personal needs and life situations incline them to fit the behavioral profile a company defines for its customer service employees.[23] Service Master, the contract cleaning company, purposely hires people at the bottom of the social barrel and gives them a chance to improve their status by rising through the company's hierarchy of maintenance workers. Club Méditerranée tar-

---

[22]Interview with Robert T. Foley, January 18, 1988.

[23]Richard Normann, *Service Management: Strategy and Leadership in Service Businesses* (John Wiley & Sons, 1986), pp. 33–43.

gets young, restless, unmarried men who are still sorting out their lives to become the *gentils organisateurs* responsible for bringing a sense of fun and adventure to the Club's resorts. One British retailer has discovered that bright, frustrated, middle-class housewives whose children have left home make excellent sales clerks because they channel thwarted energy and affection into their jobs.[24]

Matching an employee's life situation with a service job sometimes means that turnover is an expected, natural consequence. When the life situation changes or evolves, the job becomes a mismatch. Young airline stewardesses who marry and have children may not make the best stewardesses, for they have found other outlets for their emotional energies, and they can't drop everything to fill in for an absent colleague. Workers at Embassy Suites who have mastered all the basic jobs, acquiring a broad overview of hotel operations and a newfound sense of competence, aren't content anymore just to make beds. In such cases the morale of all employees, and the company's attractiveness as an employer, depend on finding what Normann calls "beautiful exits." Stewardesses who have settled down can become trainers of stewardesses, the way they do at Singapore Airlines; hotel workers who have developed competence beyond the needs of their jobs can train to become managers, as they do at Embassy Suites. When there's no other place in the company for an employee who has grown and developed beyond the needs of the job, he or she gets help finding a job elsewhere.

DOUBLE-BARRELED TRAINING

Training—constant, intensive, lavish, and universal—is another hallmark of companies that produce great customer service. Most of the seventeen leading service companies that Citicorp studied spent 1 to 2 percent of their sales on training front-line employees,

[24]Normann, *Service Management: Strategy and Leadership in Service Businesses,* pp. 34, 36, 38.

managers, and executives.[25] Of course the kinds of training vary with the position. Customer-contact people get an education somewhat different from what people in the back office learn; front-line workers acquire some skills that differ from those taught to regional managers. In all cases, though, service leaders seem to have found a working balance between technical training, which covers the details of performing a job correctly, and social training, which focuses on the interpersonal values, attitudes, and techniques needed to render good service. And they understand that customer service training fails unless it includes lessons in how to treat internal customers, the people inside the company whose ability to serve outside customers depends on their getting service from colleagues.

Not all of the training is formal. Many companies that provide great service, like Nordstrom, rely on a kind of socialization process in which the new employee's peers and supervisors show him the ropes and inculcate the necessary values and attitudes. Informal or not, the training is consistent and tightly linked with the company's strategy, culture, and personnel policies, and it is supported by the design of the service delivery system.

Contrast that approach with what goes on in most organizations when managers decide workers could use some tips on coddling customers. The two hundred companies that Zenger-Miller studied generally used four types of social training programs in their efforts to improve service quality: teaching people to probe for customer needs so they can cross-sell other products and services; calling in motivational consultants to give two- to four-hour pep talks, emotional booster shots designed to increase positive thinking; running "smile-and-dial" sessions that show employees how to listen to, probe, and respond to complaints; and training workers to defuse irate customers, nearly always described as "problem customers," not "customers with problems." All four types of programs comprise several hours of classroom instruction, but little role modeling or on-the-job training, no follow-up, and few if any links with motivational tools like bonus programs.

[25]Desatnick, *Managing to Keep the Customer,* p. 51.

The training applies only to front-line employees, and sometimes just to the poor souls in the customer service department, not to supervisors and other managers who need it. It focuses exclusively on employee relations with external customers, ignoring their relations with internal customers and the importance of team building.[26] Is it any wonder such training has minimal long-term effects on the service that people actually produce? Or that customers who run up against graduates of these programs recoil from the insincere, ineffective treatment they receive?

Formal social training tends to work only when the customer service job is highly standardized. Teaching fast food clerks to make eye contact with customers, smile at three designated times during each transaction, and helpfully suggest a dessert can produce an impression of better service only if both the customer and the clerk clearly understand the outline and limits of the fast food transaction, the script, if you will. Teaching employees to behave that way in a fancy restaurant, where the transaction is richer and the script fuzzier, is sure to produce a negative impression. Who wants plastic responses from a waiter who's supposed to earn his big tip? Even in banks, where teller transactions might seem standardized, the script can be fuzzy enough that formal social training backfires. The mechanical smile and the automatic "Have a nice day" are irritating when they come from somebody who is supposed to recognize the customer's unique financial needs. In fact, the majority of outstanding service companies have discovered that the best social training is informal, the result of selecting people with positive attitudes toward customer service, teaming them up with old hands who know "our way of doing things," and barraging them with motivational programs. Even McDonald's finds that personal enrichment training—simply teaching managers and employees to be better at their jobs—is more effective social training for customer service than trying to teach people to have a good attitude.[27]

It's the opposite with technical training. No company that hopes

[26]Cushing, Laughlin, and Dumas, "Service Quality: The Future of Competitive Advantage."

[27]Desatnick, *Managing to Keep the Customer*, pp. 61 and 146–153.

to win through service can afford simply to dump an employee into a new position, hoping he will learn the technical aspects of his work by asking around. Producing great service means ensuring that everybody—not just customer-contact people, but anybody who can affect customer satisfaction—has a bone-deep knowledge of precisely how to perform his job. Savvy service companies frequently use massive instruction manuals that break down jobs into scores of discrete steps, and they reinforce the manuals with every type of written, oral, and non-verbal communication, from videotapes to role modeling. Hourly employees who attend Kentucky Fried Chicken's national training center must master ninety-nine technical lessons. Managers and supervisors at Guest Quarters Suite Hotels train new employees for forty to eighty hours. They prepare them with a detailed manual, then demonstrate how to do the job, watch while the employees practice, and check up again a week after the lessons. Guest Quarters, High Country, and lots of other companies make a point of asking new employees to rate the effectiveness of their training in confidential surveys, and some of them base a portion of managerial and supervisory pay on the survey results.

Training programs at companies that lead their industries in customer service tend to share two unusual characteristics. Most such programs emphasize cross-training, either vertical or horizontal. Delta Airlines and Singapore Airlines, for instance, use vertical cross-training: their aspiring cabin attendants must learn numbers of back-office jobs, from handling reservations to tracing lost baggage, before taking to the air. Hotels and fast food chains stress horizontal cross-training. They pay hourly workers extra to master most of the various hourly jobs. Creating switch-hitters gives these companies more flexible service capacity and increases the self-esteem of employees. More importantly, perhaps, it ensures that every employee has the knowledge necessary to solve the customer's problem, to span the boundary between the customer and the mysterious inner workings of the organization.[28]

Secondly, companies that produce great service insist that al-

[28]For an exposition of roles that span boundaries, see David E. Bowen and Benjamin Schneider, "Boundary-Spanning-Role Employees and the Service Encounter: Some

most everybody, from hourly workers to senior executives, share certain training experiences. Everyone at Nordstrom has done time on the selling floor, everyone at McDonald's has learned how to flip a hamburger, everyone at Embassy Suites understands how to inspect a room for cleanliness, and every officer at Xerox has fielded customer complaints. Sharing archetypal experiences like these keeps managers in touch with the challenges of producing customer service, inspires the front line, and creates a strong cultural bond.

TURNING PEOPLE ON

Serving customers skillfully is hard emotional labor, and it demands frequent bursts of extra effort. Companies that provide superior service use a wealth of motivational programs to keep employees' energy flowing. The higher the degree of customer contact a group of employees has, the greater the number and power of motivational programs it can use. At companies that are fanatic about service, and where employees have frequent, intense contact with customers, managers seem to invent new programs constantly. For example, the five U.S. regional operating centers of American Express Travel Related Services Company, which handle charge card business, have developed a suite of more than one hundred customized motivational tools to charge up employees.

At AMEX and elsewhere, the most popular programs offer public praise and material rewards for workers who have gone out of their way for customers. Many companies, of course, select employees of the week, month, and year. Companies that have mastered customer service go further. The Amway Grand Plaza Hotel gives out a Golden Plate award for excellent service in its restaurants and an emerald-studded lapel pin in the form of a sunburst,

Guidelines for Management and Research," in John A. Czepiel, Michael R. Solomon, and Carol F. Surprenant, eds., *The Service Encounter* (Lexington Books, 1985), pp. 127–147.

the hotel's logo, for workers who exemplify service quality. Every month the employees themselves select a five-star team of workers who have put Amway's values into action by exceeding the confines of their job descriptions in order to please customers. Pictures of the five-star teams are posted in the employee cafeteria and the hotel lobby, and the teams get a free tour of a neighboring city, where they check out service at competing hotels. At Nordstrom, when one employee notices another making heroic efforts to please a customer, she writes up the incident, which is printed in a weekly circular. Employees elect one salesperson a week to the VIP Club for having performed outstanding service. Once a month an employee is named a Service All Star, and his or her picture is hung near the store's customer service desk.

The most elaborate awards program anywhere may be the Great Performers program at American Express. Periodically, AMEX regional managers select employees who have rendered extraordinary customer service to be semi-finalists in the Great Performers competition. The managers send descriptions of the award-winning feats to headquarters, and AMEX verifies the facts and selects the most praiseworthy employees to be Great Performers of the year. The winners get a week's vacation in New York, a "Great Performers" certificate and platinum pin, an awards banquet, and $4,000 apiece in travelers checks. The twenty-six winners at the 1988 banquet included a Beirut AMEX representative who helped passengers after an airline hijacking by approving the captain's charge of $50,000 for food and lodging costs; a worker in the Arizona collections office who spotted an unusual pattern of purchases on a card member's bill and helped nab some thieves; and a Manila manager who broke up a fight in a store, keeping a newlywed who was using her husband's American Express card from spending the night in jail. Lou Gerstner, then president of the Travel Related Services Company, handed out the awards, declaring, "Every year the stories get more dramatic." More than 425 AMEX employees have been dubbed Great Performers.

Awards programs often are linked with contests in order to keep the competitive juices flowing. The Pride campaign at High

Country hotels, for instance, starts every quarter with a pep rally during which the general manager selects six Pride commissioners, three of them employees, three department heads. They wear badges of their rank, and whenever they spot an employee serving customers with distinction, they pass out one or two "Pride dollars." At the end of the month, employees turn in their dollars and are ranked by the wealth they've accumulated. Those in the top two quartiles get prizes—a day off with pay, a free weekend in the hotel, a TV set—and they're featured during the next pep rally. The employee at each hotel who has the most Pride dollars at the end of the year gets an all-expenses-paid vacation in Acapulco. The Best Treatment program at Guest Quarters hotels asks guests to vote for the employee who has treated them best. The one with the most ballots for the week gets $50, and the monthly victor gets $100.

Awards programs are formal expressions of the encouragement and praise that effective front-line supervisors mete out continually. By creating service heroes and service legends, the programs charge up all employees, not just the winners. But far too many awards programs fall flat because they lack credibility, frequency, or psychic significance. Unless the process for selecting winners is careful, obviously meritocratic, and tightly linked to customer perceptions of service quality, employees will view the awards simply as management's way of playing favorites. Unless awards come soon after an outstanding service performance has occurred, the connection between employee behavior and awards will be obscure (that's why Guest Quarters hotels pass out "Pride dollars" immediately). And unless the award has material and emotional significance—tangible value like a day off, and active recognition and applause, not just a name on a plaque—nobody will care.

Are awards programs expensive? Just the opposite, say managers who have used them successfully. Listen to Richard Knight, vice president for operations at High Country: "It costs more if you don't do it. Prizes for our incentive program cost $25,000 to $35,000 a year for an average property of 250 rooms. That comes back in hundreds of thousands of dollars in customer satisfaction, repeat business, word of mouth advertising, and image. We constantly hear our guests say not just 'I'm coming back because the service is good,' but 'I'm coming back because John knows how I like my breakfast eggs or Jane knows just what I need for a meeting.' "[29]

Nonetheless, some managers view award programs suspiciously. They fear that by inciting workers to break the rules on behalf of customers, awards will produce chaos and cost the company enormous sums. Of course no company could survive with a bunch of loose-cannon workers, each seeking to please customers in his or her own way, at company expense, and with no regard for standard operating procedures. But the problem never seems to arise among companies that understand the production of customer service. Thanks to powerful social and technical training, their employees tend to develop an unfailing sense of when going the extra mile is going too far.

In the long run, employees need more than praise and awards to keep them going. They also need reasonable pay and a visible future. That's not what they usually get. People who have primary responsibility for serving customers, whether it's in a customer service department or a field service organization or a teller's cage, often inhabit a corporate ghetto. The pay is poor and there's no escape.

Great service companies have razed the ghettos. They tend to pay more than their shortsighted competitors—Frank Mancari, owner of an outstanding Chrysler dealership in Chicago, pays his telephone receptionist $400 a week, well above the going rate, because he knows that how she handles customers has an enormous impact on his business.[30] And service leaders usually provide a credible career path for their customer-contact employees. It can be a policy of promoting people from customer service to general management, the way Amway, Marriott, and Guest Quarters do—half or more of the managers at those companies have risen from the ranks. Other companies have created career lad-

[29]Interview with Richard Knight, January 20, 1988.

[30]Richard C. Whiteley, Forum Corporation, "Creating Customer Focus" (undated speech).

ders within customer service operations so people can rise through a hierarchy as their skills develop, eventually achieving management positions comparable to those in other departments. However it's done, employees can see a future, and they can get as much training as they want in order to achieve it.

PRINCIPLES

Customers judge service by the quality of their interactions with the people who provide it. The more contact employees have with customers, the more critical employee behavior is to perceptions of service quality. The prime shaper of behavior is culture; personnel policies are particular tools that express the culture. If they don't express it accurately—if they're inconsistent with the values and norms of the culture—the policies won't work, and the culture itself can be weakened.

A major goal of these people tools is to reduce turnover, which is hugely expensive in terms of dollars and service quality. The more the work force churns, the heavier the burdens of teaching people to produce good service. High turnover is especially crushing for fast-growing companies that need to keep hiring new employees. Fortunately, effective personnel policies can reduce turnover dramatically.

Most companies invest far too little money and effort in hiring, training, and motivating their employees. Companies known for great customer service outspend their competitors to ensure that customer-contact workers do a superior job. They generally adhere to three principles:

1 / *Work ceaselessly to hire the right people.* Service leaders take as much care in hiring customer service employees as they would in selecting business partners. Since attitude is more telling than experience, they look for people whose personalities predispose them to produce good service and to fit in well with the service culture. The most sophisticated companies search out target groups whose life situations fit well with the job requirements (frustrated housewives can make great retail clerks).

2 / *Train, train, and retrain.* Companies that produce superior service strike a balance between social training, which is usually informal, and technical training, which must be formal and highly specific. Their training activities emphasize service to internal customers, as well as to external ones (i.e., corporate teamwork). Unless their transactions with customers are highly standardized and industrialized, these companies avoid "smile-and-dial" programs, which tend to produce behavior that customers feel is phony. They cross-train employees to increase their abilities to solve customer problems on their own. At some point in their careers, managers and supervisors will have participated in at least some of the training programs that front-line workers undergo.

3 / *Motivate lavishly.* Customer service calls for heroic emotional labor, and the more contact employees have with customers, the more motivation they need. To create service heroes and legends, the service leaders use a panoply of awards programs, and they make the awards frequent and meaningful, both emotionally and materially. They pay customer service workers well enough to show their importance to the company's success, and they give employees genuine career paths instead of making service a dead-end job.

6

Service by Design

When a core service or product is designed without customer service in mind, the task of producing outstanding service becomes virtually impossible. Constant breakdowns drive up costs. The difficulty of repair frustrates service employees and customers alike.

Design for service means giving front-line service workers a voice in design from the beginning. Smart designers strive to give customers a role in producing service, to provide flexible service capacity, and to seize every opportunity for substituting technology for costly labor.

Designing core services to optimize customer service is harder than designing serviceable products, but the tasks are similar. In both cases the key is to pinpoint likely points of failure and provide for quick response and repair.

Design has no obvious connection to customer service. When consumers and corporate customers think about service, they tend to consider only the summary question of satisfaction: Were they served competently, caringly, and at reasonable cost—or not? The answer to the question often comes down to the behavior of the people who serve. If the field engineer can't get the computer up and running within two hours, he's viewed as a bumbler.

The same goes for the waitress who brings your food forty-five minutes after you ordered it, the auto mechanic who can't fix your car right the first time, the sales clerk who doesn't know where the department store keeps button-down shirts. All of them, obviously, render terrible service. They may say it's not their fault, that the system's to blame, but any customer knows the service providers are the problem. They're incompetent and inefficient, and they don't give a damn.

Except in most cases the "bumbling" service provider is right. He's just as much a victim as the customer is. They've both been zapped by poor design—products whose design makes them difficult or impossible to maintain and repair, services based on systems that force the most able and willing human being to produce lousy service. As W. Edwards Deming, the patriarch of quality control, pointed out long ago, "Workers are never to blame for flaws in a process. Process design is management's responsibility." And it's the same with product design. When the mechanic can't fix your car, it's seldom his fault and almost always the fault of the car designer and the managers who set up the service department.

That's not something design engineers want to hear. Making products serviceable or designing service procedures to be fail-safe are challenges that don't interest most engineers. Their motives, typically, are aesthetic. They strive for the most elegant design, the one that solves a problem or meets a set of performance specifications with the fewest components, processes, or systems. It's a very demanding goal, one that can never be achieved (the ultimate elegance, after all, is zero components).

Unfortunately, aesthetic motives seldom lead to products that are serviceable or service systems that don't break down. It's the rare company that can get a design engineer to listen to a field service technician or to a frustrated do-it-yourselfer or to a customer service representative. In those few cases when the engineer is willing to listen, it's usually too late. The basic, elegant design is already complete; modifying it to improve service will be an afterthought. The decoupling of design and customer service is a fact of corporate life.

The price for ignoring the impact of design on service can be staggering. At best, customers become so frustrated and irate with the poor serviceability designed into a product, or the unresponsiveness designed into a service, that they'll refuse to buy again. Listen to the expletives that an auto mechanic spews when he discovers that replacing a particular spark plug on a van means removing the engine from its mounts. Ask any business traveler if he wants to return to a hotel that doesn't provide wake-up calls on time. At worst, the failure to make serviceability a cornerstone of design can result in catastrophe.

That's what happened to McDonnell Douglas and its DC-10 widebody plane. The DC-10, which has the worst reputation of any modern commercial aircraft, was designed in a hurry to compete with Boeing's 747, the first—and the most successful—widebody. The rush showed up in details like the unsafe location of hydraulic and electrical lines needed to control wing flaps, ailerons, and rudder. A series of "problems" with cargo doors that popped open because of poor design gave the DC-10 a black eye early in its career. One such "problem" caused the 1974 crash of a DC-10 near Paris, an accident that took 346 lives, a world record at the time.

On May 25, 1979, a DC-10 operated by American Airlines made another sort of history. Heading for Los Angeles with a capacity load of passengers, Flight 191 rolled onto Chicago's O'Hare Field at 2:59 P.M. The plane started taxiing down the runway four minutes later. When it reached 159 knots, it began to lift off. Then, just one second before its wheels left the ground, an engine ripped off the left wing.

The DC-10, designed to be flyable with only one of its three engines working, kept climbing, clawing for air. But when the 16,000-pound engine broke free, it had been carried up, into, and over the wing, taking a huge chunk out of the wing's leading edge and severing control lines. The trailing-edge flaps necessary to keep the plane climbing were fully extended on the right wing, but they had retracted on the crippled left wing. As the plane climbed to 370 feet, it started yawing. The right wing kept lifting strongly while the left wing dipped and dipped until it was perpendicular to the ground. Exactly thirty-one seconds after takeoff, Flight 191 crashed to earth, its left wing plowing into an abandoned airfield. The crew, all the passengers, and two bystanders were killed. The death toll came to 273.

Investigators quickly discovered why the engine had flown off. The under-wing engines on DC-10s are attached to the wing by means of a pylon, a 2,000-pound ovoid structure. The top side of the engine bolts to the underside of the pylon; the top side of the pylon, in turn, attaches to the underside of the wing. What holds the pylon to the wing are L-shaped flanges, or brackets. One leg of the L is bolted to the top of the pylon. The other leg extends upward and slips into a fixture that looks like an upside-down U. A bolt secures the assembly, passing from one side of the U-shaped fixture, through the leg of the L, and out the other side of the U.

In the case of Flight 191, the aftermost of the L-shaped brackets had developed a severe crack, 10½ inches long. Subject to the thrust of takeoff, the bracket had broken, leaving the aft end of the pylon—and thus of the engine—hanging free. Without any support from the aft flange, the forward flange broke. And then the engine assembly, pylon and all, flew up and into the wing.

Why had the aft flange cracked? Investigators couldn't say immediately, but a swift examination of the U.S. fleet of DC-10s turned up eight other planes that had experienced similar fractures. On June 6, Langhorne Bond, head of the Federal Aviation Administration (FAA), suspended the "type certificate" of the DC-10, the plane's license to fly. The effect was to ground every DC-10 in the world until further notice. The cost to airlines in terms of lost revenue was estimated at $5 to $7 million a day.

Three weeks later, FAA investigators had solved most of the mystery. The connection between the L-shaped bracket and the U-shaped fixture on a DC-10 needs to be inspected and, if necessary, lubricated or replaced after about 20,000 hours of flight. McDonnell Douglas's maintenance manual instructed airlines first to remove the engine from the pylon and then to remove the pylon from the wing in order to perform the inspection. That procedure takes roughly 400 man-hours and represents a big chunk of time and money for an airline that wants to keep planes flying.

American Airlines had invented a way to cut the time in half.[1] Instead of detaching the engine from the pylon, it would cradle the engine in a forklift, detach the pylon from the wing, and lower the whole assembly, engine plus pylon. To reattach the engine, American's maintenance crew would raise the forklift, guiding the vertical leg of the L-shaped bracket between the arms of the U-shaped fixture. It was a delicate procedure: there was less than an inch of clearance between the L and the U. But American had developed the operation with the knowledge of McDonnell Douglas and had performed it over forty times without apparent mishap.

The FAA investigators found that American's procedure was too imprecise for the DC-10's tight clearances. Injuries to the L-shaped bracket had caused the fatal crack, as well as cracks in other American DC-10s and in some DC-10s owned by Continental, the only other U.S. airline that used American's maintenance method. The American way was a killer. Of the FAA investigators' six main recommendations, three prescribed changes in the maintenance procedure.

But American wasn't the only culprit. The FAA also found that the design of the pylon assembly made sound maintenance and inspection very difficult. Their final recommendation, couched in pure bureaucratese, was that "McDonnell Douglas Corporation should reevaluate the design of the entire pylon assembly to minimize design factors which are resulting in sensitive and/or critical maintenance and inspection procedures."[2]

Six months later, the National Transportation Safety Board amplified the FAA's stricture, noting: "McDonnell Douglas should have foreseen that the pylons would be removed, and . . . should have . . . designed [the pylon assembly] to eliminate, or at least minimize, vulnerability to damage . . . the maintenance operation, regardless of the procedure used, would be difficult to perform and

[1]National Transportation Safety Board, *Aircraft Accident Report #NTSB-AAR-79-17,* December 21, 1979, p. 26.

[2]Hearings Before the Subcommittee on Commerce, Science, and Transportation, U.S. Senate, July 11 and 12, 1979 (serial no. 96-51), p. 308.

would be particularly vulnerable to damage-producing errors. Thus the Safety Board concludes that the basic design of the aft attachment of the pylon to the wing was unnecessarily vulnerable to maintenance damage."[3]

THE NOSE DIVE

Was McDonnell Douglas chastened? Did it rush to redesign the pylon so the airlines, its customers, could service the assembly easily, without incurring heavy costs or causing accidental damage? No. The company seemed not to recognize that its design engineers had forgotten serviceability. In testimony before the U.S. Senate, John Brizendine, then president and chief executive officer of Douglas Aircraft, the commercial aircraft division of McDonnell Douglas, asserted that recent tests had proven the design of the pylon was "a good design and a good structure that performs as we originally intended. . . ."[4] Responding to a suggestion that Douglas redesign the pylon to be foolproof, he huffed, ". . . it is contrary to the concept of designing and producing efficient machinery. . . . I don't believe that the design of the aircraft should be unduly compromised to take care—if a guy is going to abuse it, if that is going to occur. If you take that philosophy throughout the airplane, you are never going to get it off the ground."[5] He had conveniently forgotten the irksome, grubby realities of aircraft maintenance. As one airline vice president commented, "These planes are serviced in steaming jungles and remote spots all over the world—sometimes by people who aren't terribly competent in sophisticated techniques—and you just shouldn't have a structure that can't take some knocks."[6]

[3]National Transportation Safety Board, *Aircraft Accident Report,* December 21, 1979, p. 56.

[4]Hearings before the Subcommittee on Commerce, Science, and Transportation, U.S. Senate, July 11 and 12, 1979, pp. 74, 76.

[5]*Ibid.,* pp. 77, 81.

[6]William M. Carley and David P. Garino, "DC-10 Grounding Gives McDonnell Douglas, Carriers New Problems," *Wall Street Journal,* June 3, 1979, p. 27.

For McDonnell Douglas, the consequences of poor design for service went far beyond a few embarrassing moments in the congressional spotlight. The company had to bear partial responsibility for 273 deaths—and to watch its insurance company pay out over $100 million to satisfy the claims of crash victims' families. McDonnell cost its customers, the airlines, at least $200 million in lost revenues during the thirty-seven days that the DC-10 remained grounded. Worst of all from a business standpoint, passengers started avoiding the DC-10. Sales of the aircraft went into a nose dive.

During the first half of 1979, before the crash, McDonnell had received twenty-four new orders for the $40 million DC-10 and was close to producing a total of four hundred planes, the minimum needed to break even on development costs. Soon after the May 25 disaster, Alitalia, American Airlines, and several big carriers in the Pacific region either canceled their options to buy DC-10s or announced plans to sell off their DC-10s and replace them with Boeing 747s or widebodies made by Airbus Industrie, the European aircraft consortium.[7] All told, new orders in the second half of 1979 fell to ten planes.

The next year McDonnell Douglas managed to pick up merely twelve new orders. By May 1981, the second anniversary of the crash and the sixth year of production for the DC-10, the company had delivered or had firm orders for a total of only 366 aircraft, some $1.4 billion short of breakeven.[8] Meanwhile Boeing's orders for 747s held firm at about eighty a year, increasing Boeing's share of the cyclically depressed aircraft market. Lockheed and Airbus also picked up sales from the DC-10.

McDonnell's loss of the widebody market had long-term consequences. Without DC-10 profits, the company couldn't develop totally new aircraft to compete with the smaller, medium-range widebodies that its competitors were launching. Ultimately,

[7] Winston Williams, "The Pall Over a Plane: McDonnell Douglas and the DC-10," *New York Times,* May 11, 1980, Section 3, pp. 1 ff.

[8] Lydia Chavez, "Crash Still Clouds McDonnell Future," *New York Times,* May 23, 1981, Business Section, pp. 1 ff.

McDonnell Douglas's failure to design for service helped knock it out of the number two position in commercial aviation.

SECOND-GUESSING YOUR FAILURES

The DC-10, of course, is an extreme case. The design failures of most companies don't cost them hundreds of lives, hundreds of millions of dollars, or entire markets. By the same token, most industries don't go to the lengths the aircraft industry does to ensure effective maintenance service for its products. Before a plane can be certified, its manufacturer and its buyers recommend maintenance guidelines. The FAA's Maintenance Review Board scrutinizes and modifies the guidelines. Both the FAA and the manufacturer send staffers to work full time with the airlines on refining maintenance and repair procedures in light of experience. And as long as an aircraft is in service, its maker alerts operators to service problems and methods with a blizzard of bulletins.

With all this review and double checking, how could a service catastrophe overtake the DC-10? The short answer is that the designers of the pylon-wing attachment, of the recommended service procedure, and of McDonnell's entire customer service function didn't account for their customers' view of what would constitute a satisfactory maintenance program. Even if they understood the time and monetary pressures on the airlines, they failed to reflect those realities in the design of the pylon attachment and of the maintenance method. Nor did they realize how McDonnell's approved service procedure might overtax the skills of aircraft maintenance crews. The designers of McDonnell's service function assigned their customers the primary role in producing maintenance and couldn't see that doing so created pitfalls or potential failure points that the company would have to guard against.

This kind of blindness—tunnel vision design—isn't at all an extreme case. It plagues many companies in every industry. It's the reason many customers, experiencing service failures ranging from out-of-stock spare parts to unfixable cars to interminable lines at ticket counters, scratch their heads and wonder, What in the world were they thinking of when they set up this system? By creating products and services that serve their company's needs instead of their customers', designers afflicted with tunnel vision short-circuit great service. If Nordstrom, like most department stores, had designed its service system with a thirty-day limit on returning merchandise, the best returns clerk in the world would be unable to produce superior customer service. If General Electric had achieved big savings in manufacturing cost by designing a dishwasher with the rotary sprayer welded to the motor shaft, the most talented repairman would leave customers gnashing their teeth after he announced that replacing the sprayer meant replacing the motor as well.

Designing products with service in mind isn't easy. It adds a whole new layer of activity to the traditional design process. First you have to figure out what costs product failure imposes on your particular set of customers, both the immediate costs of a breakdown and the ongoing costs (see chapter 3, pp. 63–64). Both types of costs will vary depending on how and when a product is used. The immediate cost to a customer when a wristwatch, say, stops ticking will differ depending on whether the customer is watching TV or watching his air supply while skin diving, which is why divers' watches are designed with higher reliability than ordinary watches. The ongoing cost to the customer when a harvester fails is very high during the first five days of downtime. Farmers often decide to harvest just before a weather change will ruin their crops, and when a harvesting machine fails, they keep farm workers standing by in hopes the machine will be fixed quickly. After five days, however, the weather crisis usually has passed and the farmer has given up on getting the harvester fixed quickly, so he lets the workers go. His ongoing costs then become much lower.[9]

The costs of product failure, combined with the cost of buying the product, determine what kind of design to pursue. If the product is inexpensive and if failure burdens the customer with fairly low costs, it makes sense to design a throwaway product that

[9]Milind M. Lele and Uday S. Karmakar, "Good Product Support Is Smart Marketing," *Harvard Business Review,* November–December 1983, pp. 124–132.

can't be repaired but only replaced (remember the Timex watches in chapter 3?).

If the product is expensive, and so is the cost of initial failure, then designing for maximum reliability is the ticket. That's what Tandem Computer does, since its machines are used by banks, insurers, and other businesses whose daily operations crash to a halt when the computer goes down. Aircraft makers do the same by incorporating multiple back-up systems in planes.

Conversely, when the product costs a lot to begin with and the ongoing costs of failure outweigh the initial costs, the design target is quick and easy repair. That's what savvy designers of copiers, cars, and washing machines strive for.

Of course, when both the initial and the ongoing costs of failure are high, the product that embodies the best customer service is one that's inexpensive enough in relation to the costs of failure that the customer can afford to buy back-ups, or the manufacturer can afford to offer loaners.[10]

Most companies that know their customers well and understand the service implications of design choices find that picking an appropriate design target is straightforward. The really subtle part of designing for superior service is understanding what's likely to happen in the field. Will repair people have enough skill to fix a product properly? If not, then the design had better be simplified. Can the company or the customer afford to stock the variety and volume of spare parts needed to service the product? Maybe several components of the product can be combined into one, thus reducing spare parts inventories. Will repair people need to buy special tools, or to take new training courses? If the customer demands service at his location, how does that requirement affect a supplier's ability to make repairs? Can the customer be induced instead to bring the product to a central repair depot? The questions go on and on.

The only way to answer them is to involve service and repair people in the design process from day one, and sometimes customers as well. The idea seems so sensible and simple that you

---

[10]Lele and Karmakar, "Good Product Support is Smart Marketing," pp. 124–132.

might imagine it's standard operating procedure. Not at all. Xerox develops service procedures only after starting production of a new machine, and it doesn't get the reactions of service technicians until shortly before the product is launched.[11] By contrast, Fuji Xerox, the company's Japanese affiliate, brings service technicians into the design process at the beginning. Until three years ago, Cadillac used a disastrous serial-design method. The designer of the car's body would leave a hole for the engine, then the power-train designer would try to fit the engine into the cavity, then the manufacturing engineer would try to figure out how to build the design, and finally the service engineer would struggle to invent ways of repairing the car. The results were predictable. On one model, the exhaust manifold blocked access to the air-conditioning compressor, so seasonal maintenance of the air conditioner meant removing the exhaust system. On another model, the connection between the spark plugs and the spark plug wires was so tight that mechanics tended to break the wires when they pulled them off to check the spark plugs. Although Cadillac recently switched to "simultaneous engineering," bringing all parties into the design process at the beginning, it's the only division of General Motors that has done so.[12]

Designing a core service to avoid breakdowns and to recover from them quickly is even harder than designing a product for easy repair. With a product, the technical specifications give a designer good hunches about where and how the product will fail. Bringing customers into the design process early on can show how actual use of the product may cause failures and indicate what kind of service will be most satisfactory. Bringing in service technicians casts light on how product design can be optimized for repair. Sending prototypes into the field can be a useful test of the product's serviceability.

Just try doing any of those things when designing a service. The technical specifications of a service mean very little. A bank may

[11]Gary Jacobson and John Hillkirk, *Xerox: American Samurai* (Macmillan, 1986), pp. 263–264, 307.

[12]Interview with Rosetta Reilly, director of customer satisfaction, and John Guttenberger, president, Cadillac Motor Division, General Motors, Inc., October 26, 1987.

specify that tellers handle most deposits within thirty seconds and achieve 98 percent accuracy. But tellers aren't machines; their performance varies widely. And the service they produce is co-produced with customers. The customer who hands over an illegible deposit slip instantly changes the teller's production function. Prototypes of services can't be banged together in the lab and subjected to various stresses in order to reveal failures; they have to be developed in the field and tried out with actual customers. Moreover, customer perceptions of service quality are more complex and more personalized than perceptions of product quality. A car that looks good, performs well, seldom breaks down, and can be repaired cheaply and quickly is obviously a great car. But does a teller who handles your transaction within thirty seconds, achieves invariable accuracy, and fixes any problems fast produce great service? Not if the teller is surly, or the bank lobby is dilapidated, or the teller line stretches around the block—or if the customer is in a lousy mood to begin with.[13]

A great help in designing a core service, or the system for servicing a product, is to chart the steps of providing the service and how those steps interact. In a highly influential paper, G. Lynn Shostack, a senior vice president at Bankers Trust Company, showed how to blueprint services in order to design and control them more effectively.[14] Using elaborate flow charts to diagram services, Shostack placed special emphasis on specifying the stages of the process where failures might occur, often because of the customer's role in service, and on laying out steps to recover from failures. Her point applies even in cases where it's not worth building a complex flow chart of a service: Look closely at every step in the service process, find the potential failure points, and design back-up steps. If McDonnell Douglas had done that for the DC-10 maintenance procedure, the company might have noted that customers could reattach engines inaccurately, and it might

[13]For more on how customer moods affect customer satisfaction, see Robert A. Westbrook, "Intrapersonal Affective Influences on Consumer Satisfaction with Products," *Journal of Consumer Research,* 7 (June 1980), pp. 49–54.

[14]G. Lynn Shostack, "Designing Services That Deliver," *Harvard Business Review* (January–February 1984), pp. 133–139.

have been able to modify the pylon's design, the maintenance procedure, or both.

WHERE DOES THE CUSTOMER FIT?

Obviously customers play roles in producing every service, from a shoeshine to the maintenance of a nuclear reactor. Not so obviously, it's the designer's responsibility to figure out what kinds of roles and how many of them the customer will play. Will a shoeshine service be more effective and efficient for a given set of customers if the customer simply walks up to a shoeshine machine and drops in a quarter, if he visits a shoeshine parlor and specifies what color of polish he wants, or if he calls an itinerant shoeshiner to visit his office? Does encouraging airlines to run their own maintenance shops produce superior service? Or will service be better if the airline manufacturer takes on that role? If the manufacturer runs the maintenance shop, how will the airline participate in setting schedules, designing procedures, and controlling safety?

The customer's role in producing service has sparked a great debate. To traditional, manufacturing-oriented managers, customers are an intrusion and a disturbance, a bunch of uncontrollable inputs that undermine production efficiency. In their view, the people and systems that produce service should be sealed off from customers as much as possible. The less contact the customer has with the production system—the lower touch a service is—the more efficient production will be. At the least, a clear division should exist between service producers and the service deliverers who interact with customers in high-touch ways.[15]

To more market-oriented managers, involving the customer is the key to increasing service productivity. While admitting that the more high touch a service is, the less efficient and controllable it tends to be, members of this school point out that self-service

---

[15]The production-oriented position appears most strongly in Richard B. Chase, "Where Does the Customer Fit in a Service Operation?" *Harvard Business Review* (November–December 1978), pp. 137–141.

is often better service. Designing self-service operations that encourage and support customer participation, they contend, is the only way to achieve big leaps in service productivity without sacrificing quality and effectiveness. Striving to isolate customers from the production system is woefully misguided. As Christopher Lovelock and Robert Young write,

> In their search for operating efficiency, there is a risk that managers of service organizations may come to see consumers as a nuisance, a constraint, and even as a barrier to productivity. The reductio ad absurdum of a mindset that stresses operating efficiency at the expense of the consumer is pungently illustrated in this newspaper report from the Midlands of England:
>
> "Complaints from passengers wishing to use the Bagnalls to Greenfields bus service that 'the drivers were speeding past queues of people with a smile and a wave of the hand' have been met by a statement pointing out that 'it is impossible for drivers to keep their timetable if they have to stop for passengers.' "[16]

Everything else being equal, a system produces service more effectively and more efficiently when the customer participates as much as he can. That's less true, of course, when the service is ambiguous. If the customer has trouble telling whether the service is any good, he won't have a criterion for his own performance or a clear idea of how to help in producing the best service. Customers can't participate much in their own gall bladder operations or in fixing automatic transmissions or in executing trades on the floor of a stock exchange. Neither does customer participation help much when a service organization and its customers have conflicting goals. In the case of the Internal Revenue Service, for instance, asking customers to take responsibility for performing their own audits would produce no audits at all.[17] But in the vast

[16]Christopher H. Lovelock and Robert F. Young, "Look to Consumers to Increase Productivity," *Harvard Business Review* (May–June 1979). The bus story comes from Patrick Ryan, "Get Rid of the People and the System Runs Fine," *Smithsonian* (September 1977), p. 140.

[17]For an explanation of performance ambiguity and goal incongruence, see David E. Bowen and Gareth R. Jones, "Transaction Cost Analysis of Service Organization-Customer Exchange," *Academy of Management Review,* vol. 11, no. 2 (1986), pp. 428–441.

majority of cases, encouraging the customer to co-produce is a key to successful service design.

Making the customer an effective co-producer means designing a service production system that treats customers in some ways like employees. The designer must give customers clues about what they should do, such as signs in bank lobbies, instruction manuals for computers, and training courses for airplane mechanics. The system should accept only the "right" customers, ones that have the ability to co-produce. If an industrial customer, for instance, can't communicate his needs for components frequently and accurately, he's the wrong customer for a supplier that wants to provide just-in-time shipments of components. Similarly, the shopper who hasn't done her homework about the features of an appliance is the wrong customer for a deep discount store. And just like employees, customers need incentives to perform, such as savings of time and money, or the possibility of producing higher-quality service for themselves than anybody else could.[18]

JUGGLING CAPACITY

Managing capacity is the bugbear of customer service operations. When demand overburdens capacity, service quality plummets. But putting enough capacity in place to handle the highest level of demand will bankrupt most service operations. Good design for service emphasizes making the service system as flexible as possible, giving it the ability to reconfigure capacity as demand fluctuates. Citibank, for example, has laid wires under the carpets of its lobbies in New York City. The wires monitor the amount of time customers must spend waiting for a teller, and when the wait gets too long, Citibank lays on more tellers. Nordstrom has designed its retail service system to use a large number of temporary employees during the busiest seasons of the year, and it doesn't guarantee its sales clerks any particular schedule. As a result,

[18]See David E. Bowen, "Managing Customers as Human Resources in Service Organizations," *Human Resources Management,* vol. 25, no. 3 (Fall 1986), pp. 371–383.

Nordstrom can vary capacity. But Macy's, by guaranteeing schedules and hiring relatively few temps, has locked itself into providing service that matches demand only during certain times of the year.

Designing swing capacity into a service system is often the answer to a capacity conundrum. A field service organization large enough to handle almost every emergency call within two hours will have lots of spare capacity during the troughs of demand. That's the time to get the service engineers working on preventative maintenance. Embassy Suites, like most hotels, has loads of idle capacity in the form of desk clerks who aren't very busy and housekeepers who have finished all their work by mid-afternoon. Unlike many other hotels, Embassy has designed a service system that uses cross-training so that housekeepers, desk clerks, and other functional specialists can pinch hit for each other when demand for one of their functions soars.

Swing capacity isn't always the answer. Produce managers in a grocery store can't do much to help out the harried butcher department. Most airline baggage handlers aren't qualified to fill in as flight attendants, and it would be a waste of money to have pilots take meal orders and check that everyone's seat belt is fastened. As W. Earl Sasser has pointed out, you're essentially stuck with level capacity whenever a job requires high levels of skill, training, judgment, and compensation.[19] In those cases you have to try smoothing demand by fiddling with prices, requiring reservations, and promoting service during off-peak times. Parisian department stores, an Alabama-based chain, reduces the Christmas shopping rush by offering November shoppers free shipping of their gifts. One of the largest U.S. packaged food companies offers retail stores fast delivery for an extra charge, normal delivery at no charge, and slow delivery at a discount. The stores also get discounts for ordering by telephone instead of waiting for a salesman to call, and for allowing the manufacturer to place a certain number of out-of-stock items on back order, instead of

[19]W. Earl Sasser, "Match Supply and Demand in Service Industries," *Harvard Business Review* (November–December 1976).

canceling them.[20] All those demand-shaping strategies ease the burden on the food company's service capacity.

What if a company is stuck with level capacity and has few options for smoothing demand? How much of peak demand should its service system be designed to satisfy? Certainly not all of it, unless the company has bottomless pockets. The best the designer can do in this case probably is to tier customers by their sensitivity to bad service and by the costs of losing their business, then set the capacity level just high enough to serve the most important customers during the peaks of demand.

TAKING THE LABOR OUT

Many students of customer service are closet Luddites, believers that automation can't do much to improve service productivity and is certain to degrade service quality. They view the unstoppable invasion of high tech as dehumanizing. Automated teller machines, banking by personal computer, information dispensed by push-button terminals in department stores, answering machines—all such service developments are seen as cold and impersonal. They must be offset by designing services to include lots of "high-touch" human interaction.

The Luddites are only half right. Most customers appreciate high-touch service, provided it's well performed by the emotional laborers who produce it. But neither customers nor service suppliers would be willing to give up the service improvements made possible by technology. Indeed, every designer should be grateful for the opportunity to substitute electronic work and intelligence for the human variety.

Part of the job of designing service into a product is to seize opportunities for making the product smarter, more able to care for itself. Electronics companies were the first to realize the compelling economics of smart products. The fully loaded cost of a

[20]Randy Myer, "Repairing Manufacturer-Retailer Links," *Wall Street Journal*, June 2, 1986.

field engineer or technician is well over $50,000 a year; throw in training, and the figure is close to $100,000.[21] Hiring, training, and compensating a field force is a heavy constraint on the growth of most electronics companies. Anything that cuts the need for putting bodies into the field is a boon. That's why nearly every maker of computers, instruments, and other sophisticated electronic gear has designed self-diagnostic hardware into its products.

At the lowest level, that hardware is just a communications link that enables technicians at a central service center to test a machine without leaving the office. More sophisticated systems record the machine's performance so technicians waste less time pinning down intermittent errors. The most exotic systems incorporate circuits on each chip that allow a machine to diagnose problems and recover from most failures without human intervention, in effect fixing itself. The large computers sold by Amdahl Corp. have special diagnostic processors that automatically dial up Amdahl headquarters to report failures, potential failures, and failures that were averted because the computer took automatic action. When a problem is beyond the powers of the computer to fix by itself, technicians at Amdahl's service center link up with the ailing computer over the telephone lines. In 70 percent of such cases, technicians can get the machine up and running within a half hour, without visiting the customer's site.[22]

As electronics infiltrate cars, washing machines, gas meters, and many other products, the opportunities for endowing those machines with intelligence multiply. GM's top-of-the-line cars now include circuits that keep track of mileage and engine performance in order to tell customers when service is needed and to give mechanics a record of how the car has been used. The electronics revolution also has increased the opportunity for customers to co-produce many services. With a personal computer that talks with other computers over the telephone, for example, customers can search for products and order them, make travel

---

[21]Howard Bierman, "Field Service Booms Despite Shortage of Technicians," *Electronics Week,* May 13, 1985, p. 54.

[22]Interview with Jack Lewis, president, and Richard Ferone, vice president, service, Amdahl Corp., October 28, 1987.

plans and buy tickets, and acquire software programs, news reports, and other information without leaving home or dealing with
a human being. Industrial customers with computer links to their
suppliers can reorder automatically, without the intervention of a
salesperson. These computerized services certainly are impersonal, but they can also be remarkably convenient for customers
and remarkably inexpensive for service providers.

KEEPING YOUR EYE ON THE CUSTOMER

The list of factors that designers of customer service systems
should consider is virtually endless. One student of service suggests designers have to take into account no fewer than eight
issues:

✓ the role of intermediaries, such as travel agents;
✓ whether the service is high contact or low contact;
✓ whether the customer is an individual or an institution;
✓ how long it takes to deliver the service, and how much information
  customers need about work in progress;
✓ how much capacity may constrain delivery of the service;
✓ how often customers repurchase the core service or product;
✓ how complex the service is; and
✓ how much a service failure will affect customers.[23]

The great simplifier for designers is a clear service strategy. If the
set of target customers is well defined and if their service expectations are well understood, the design often falls into place easily.
On the other hand, without a clear strategy and a solid concept
of the service customers expect, the most exhaustive check list
won't produce an effective design.

Consider American Express. The company is well known for
the innovativeness and effectiveness of its service. A main reason
American Express hits the bull's-eye so often is that it knows

[23]Christopher H. Lovelock, "Developing and Managing the Customer-Service Function in the Service Sector," in John A. Czepiel, Michael R. Solomon, and Carol F.
Surprenant, eds, *The Service Encounter* (Lexington Books, 1985), pp. 265–280.

exactly who its customers are and bases all of its innovations on extensive market research. AMEX's drive to streamline authorization of charges was rooted in surveys that showed its customers placed a high priority on effortless, invisible authorization. (Few experiences are more embarrassing, after all, than having to listen to a hotel clerk spend ten minutes trying to get approval for your charges.) Market research also led American Express to develop speedy card replacement, as well as a program to authorize hotel and similar charges for customers who have just lost their cards.[24]

Or consider Shouldice Hospital. Because of its exclusive focus on hernia patients, Shouldice naturally knows what kind of service will be most satisfactory. Or look at Jan Carlzon's Scandinavian Airlines. Having decided to pursue the intra-European business traveler, Carlzon had little trouble figuring out what kinds of service to develop. His clarity extended even to the basic design of passenger aircraft. Noting that business travelers often complained about the cramped seating and headroom on conventional jets, Carlzon pushed Boeing to design a "people-pleasing plane," which would sacrifice cargo space for more passenger space.

As in Carlzon's case, rigorous pursuit of a customer service strategy may have major consequences for a company's methods of producing a core product or service. If your target customers place a high value on quick delivery, designing an effective service system may mean relocating your plant closer to customers' factories. If quick turnaround is more important to your customers than low prices, you may have to replace all your expensive production equipment with models that have shorter set-up times. Just as important are the things a clear strategy will prevent you from designing into a service system. If UAL (United Airlines) had spent more time refining its target market and understanding that market's expectations, it never would have branched out from airline service into hotels and travel agencies, operations that it eventually had to sell off.

[24]Interview with MaryAnne Rasmussen, vice president, quality assurance, American Express Travel Related Services Company, February 27, 1988.

PRINCIPLES OF DESIGN

Designing products and service systems to maximize customer satisfaction goes against the grain of most designers. Effective design for service calls for accommodating customer behavior, but customers behave in quirky, unpredictable ways. They always seem to be polluting the designer's unsullied vision. Fortunately, designers respond well to clear rules. Here are three that will ensure they keep customer service and satisfaction in mind:

1 / *Chase the failure points.* First get a clear understanding of how the core product or service can break down. Pay special attention to the ways in which customers may cause unexpected failures. Then design the company's responses to failure so they will exceed customer expectations.

2 / *Sign up the service staff.* Only the people who have to fix products or compensate for failed services know the real problems. Get them to join the design team from the start, and let them participate as equals with team members from R&D, manufacturing, and marketing. Don't let pressures for attractive, low-cost products—or elegant, high-priced ones—overwhelm the importance of designing products for serviceability.

3 / *Share the work.* Producing outstanding service at reasonable cost is almost impossible without the help of customers and of labor-saving devices like electronic intelligence. Savvy designers get customers to co-produce, to do more of the work themselves. They also grab every chance to incorporate diagnostic equipment into the core product or service.

7

The Backbone of Service: Infrastructure

———

The largest cost of producing great service is that of creating infrastructures—networks of people, physical facilities, and information that support the production of customer service. Because the investment is so great, building infrastructures makes little sense until most other elements of service are in place.

Yet the competitive rewards of establishing service infrastructures, or factories, are enormous. Like classical factories, service infrastructures show significant economies of scale—the bigger the factory, the lower the costs of production—and of scope—the more services an infrastructure produces, the easier it is to add new services. Thus infrastructures can become potent barriers to competition. Companies that lead in the infrastructure race have achieved a head start that followers seldom can overcome.

Bruce Smith knew that the 1.5-inch-thick operating plan he had placed on the boardroom table wouldn't delight his backers. The assembled venture capitalists had already sunk over $10 million into Smith's attempt to develop a complex switching system that large companies could use to create their own communications networks. The technical and business risks were sobering: investors in Network Equipment Technologies had no guarantee that NET could make the switch work as promised, launch it before a window in the market closed, or compete effectively against other suppliers.

Now Smith was asking them to take on an entirely new kind of risk, one certain to make the bravest investor flinch. Instead of playing it safe by contracting with third parties to sell and service NET's products, the way other start-up companies in the switching business had done, Smith proposed creating his own sales and service organization. The cost would exceed $11 million, nearly half the total investment needed to get NET off the ground. Of that amount, service operations alone would consume around $6 million of capital, and projections showed service wouldn't turn a profit for years. Even so, Smith was suggesting that NET do whatever it took—including cutting back spending for attractive R&D projects—to beef up service. And he wanted the company to start building service operations well before launching its first product and thus before bringing in any revenues that might offset the cash drain of setting up service.

As the investors leafed through NET's plan, they knitted their brows and started to grumble. One gasped, "My God!" The discussion became heated, then a huge argument broke out. How could Smith justify such a gamble, one investor demanded. As leader of a high-tech start-up, how could he possibly recommend scrimping on R&D for the sake of service? Another investor laid out the advantages of not building up an elaborate service operation; NET, he insisted, should call on an established company to sell and support its switches because that course promised faster time to market, less investment at risk, and a proven entree to rich accounts. A third backer pointed out that NET's grandiose service plan would cost so much that the company would have to jack up its prices for switching gear. Why not take a less expensive approach to service, price the hardware lower, and reach a broader market?

But Smith would have none of it. NET's potential customers expected service every bit as good as they were getting from IBM, he asserted, and only an in-house service operation could achieve such quality. NET's business wasn't selling telecommunications gear but solving customers' communications problems. To do so with the necessary reliability, Smith said, would mean providing the world's best customer service. As for offering lower-quality service and lower prices, that was a contemptible alternative for a company like NET, which had a chance to produce superior service and reap hefty premiums.

At last Smith saw that he wasn't getting anywhere. The investors were digging in their heels. It was time for an ultimatum. He tossed his employee badge on the table and declared that if the investors couldn't endorse the operating plan and help raise the money needed to set up service operations, then they could just go and find themselves a new chief executive. He wouldn't stick around to watch them ruin the chance of a lifetime.

THE PAYOFF

In the end, Smith won the battle. And NET's investors have every reason to be thankful for his stubbornness. By 1988, some three years after the fight, NET had become a phenomenon. With revenues close to $100 million, it had seized one fourth of the market for large switches used to run private communications networks. Profits had ballooned to $15 million and were doubling every quarter. NET's stock, first offered to the public in 1987 at $16 a share, was trading for more than $22, a price that gave the company's original backers at least a thirteenfold return on their investments.

The biggest reason for NET's success is its outstanding service factory, or infrastructure. Thanks to Smith's lavish spending, NET can keep its switches working more than 99 percent of the time. The hint of a breakdown that the customer can't fix himself will bring a NET service engineer running; within two hours, the equipment will be humming away again. Such responsiveness has built invaluable word of mouth. To make a sale, the company asks prospective buyers to call any organization that has bought NET equipment—and then to ask NET's competitors for the same privilege. When prospects take up the challenge, they hear nearly incredible encomiums about NET. As one potential buyer told the company, "I've never heard such praise. You must be paying your customers a lot to say things like that." Perhaps the ultimate accolade came in mid-1987, when IBM formally agreed to act as a huge, extra marketing and service arm for NET's equipment.

Moreover, NET's service factory has become a formidable barrier to competitors. Having spent millions on infrastructure, NET is able to command a premium for its products of 20 percent or more above prevailing market prices. The premium helps NET continue to beef up its service factory. Competitors who have failed to risk so much on their service infrastructures get no premium, which means they can't afford to start building their own infrastructures, which means they'll probably never be able to deliver service good enough to command a premium, which means . . . By using its infrastructure to set the standard for service in its industry, NET has pushed its competitors into a vicious cycle from which they're unlikely to escape.

PUTTING THE ELEMENTS IN PLACE

To be fair, Smith's backers had solid reasons for questioning the wisdom of heavy investments in infrastructure. Simply having a service factory doesn't automatically mean you can produce great service. Even if you do, customers won't necessarily reward you for it. Betting on infrastructure can be a fatal error, especially for a fledgling company with no track record in the marketplace. If customers don't respond, the service factory becomes a millstone, dragging the company down to its death in an ocean of overhead expense.

NET pulled off the gamble because it put in place most of the other elements needed to produce outstanding service even as it was building an infrastructure. To begin with, Smith had a clear vision of what customer service is and why it matters so much. After years of experience running a division of G. D. Searle that sold and serviced medical imaging equipment, he had concluded that customer service means more than fixing broken products or fielding complaints. In his view, "Customer service is whatever helps the customer get the benefits he expects from a product."[1] Smith also had an uncanny understanding of how the battle-ground in many markets has shifted from features, cost, and quality to service. As he describes the fourth battleground,

> [Customers] expect more from their vendors. They expect a consulta-tive market approach, more effective application of technology, better training, and exemplary support. In short, they seek a partnership with their chosen vendors. . . . Those of us at NET welcome this market maturation. We see the market responding to real value provided and recognizing that vendors can provide and charge for value they add beyond the "iron" they physically bolt to the floor. If a vendor is not prepared to sell more than iron or is unwilling to think about being in partnership with his customer, that vendor has not done the tough stuff. Indeed, that vendor has missed the real problem.[2]

Nearly every element of service we have discussed so far is present at NET. From the day of its foundation in 1983, the company had a finely honed service strategy. Its customers would be the world's largest private users of telecommunications, compa-nies whose businesses critically depend on accurate, reliable transport of information, primarily in the financial services, trans-portation, and electronics industries. These customers expect— and will pay for—networks that work better than 99 percent of the time. Most important, they comprise a crisply defined service seg-ment: most are sufficiently large and sophisticated to manage their own, private "telephone companies" and to learn how to service their networks independently. As long as any network failure can be repaired instantly, they don't care whether service is high tech or high touch.

Part of NET's strategy was to set customers' expectations at levels that differentiated the company from competitors yet al-

---

[1]Interview with Bruce D. Smith, February 2, 1988. We were astonished—and en-couraged—to find Smith's definition of customer service was very close to our own. See chapter 1, p. 22.

[2]Bruce D. Smith, "The Religion of Customer Service," from remarks delivered at the 1985 Dataquest Telecommunications Industry Conference (Network Equipment Tech-nologies, 1985), p. 9.

lowed NET to exceed expectations. While most vendors of switching equipment promised repair within four hours, NET promised two-hour response. Though salesmen for other companies in the switching business had disappointed customers by promising delivery of nonexistent equipment, NET kept its salesmen from setting expectations too high by forbidding them to mention any gear that wasn't already in production. It also dissuaded them from selling switches in locations where NET couldn't provide superior service, and it made sure they kept the customer's interests first by delaying half of their sales commissions until after customers verified that the equipment was working as promised.[3]

Smith has provided remarkable leadership. Believing that "service is a religious issue [which] starts at the top," he has built a powerful service culture. Like others at NET, he calls customers "clients" in order to underline the trusting, ongoing relationships the company seeks to build. He never tires of saying that "everything you do, from raising money to the way you design, make, and market the product, has to reflect the philosophy of customer service."[4] He insists that all reports of service problems cross his desk within four hours of receipt—a policy that drives NET employees to solve most problems before he can see them.

Smith, who tells customers to call him any time at home, has contributed his share of heroic stories to the growing book of service legends at NET. One Sunday morning at 4:00 A.M., he recalls, a frantic customer woke him up with a tale about a NET switch that had failed because of a flood. By Monday morning, NET had installed a standby switch, and the customer's operations hummed along as though no disaster had occurred. Smith and NET's other founders have labored to make service everybody's business. Every officer takes responsibility for satisfying a group of customers and visits them three times annually to see how well NET is doing. Their visits are reinforced by customer

---

[3]Smith also has found that a simple accounting method gets every NET employee to focus tightly on customer satisfaction: NET doesn't record a sale until the customer officially accepts a switch, showing that he is satisfied with the equipment.

[4]Interview with Bruce D. Smith, February 2, 1988.

satisfaction managers who also visit customers to inspect NET's service performance. Finger pointing—blaming the other guy for a network failure—is forbidden. When a customer's system goes down, NET will fix it, even when the failure was caused by the customer's own blunders or by equipment or services provided by another vendor. If NET's field engineers find fault with the quality of a NET switch, they don't blame the factory. Instead, they work with the factory to clear up the problem. (Since the service and the quality assurance groups report to the same executive, infighting is minimal.)

Like other great service companies, NET takes extraordinary pains to hire the "right" people and to train and motivate them constantly. Jerry Davis, vice president of quality and service, looks for field service engineers with five to seven years of experience and the classic personality of a Mr. Fixit—pride in getting things to work, a penchant for tinkering, and an affection for gadgets (Davis gets his kicks from flying stunt airplanes). A candidate undergoes interviews with five or six NET employees; if just one of them expresses doubt, even if it's just a negative gut feel, the candidate flunks.

The hard economic reason for being so picky is that NET spends $30,000 or so to train first-year service engineers and $15,000 a year thereafter to keep them up to date. Wasting that investment on employees who leave the company would be a shame. To make sure they stick around, NET has established an attractive career path that runs up through the service organization and out to other parts of NET; in the past few years, the company has promoted one third of its service engineers. As a result of careful picking, extensive training, and savvy motivation, turnover in the service organization runs less than 5 percent a year (compared with an industry average of 15 percent).

Consistent with Smith's philosophy that customer service must pervade all operations, NET has done a bang-up job of designing its products with service in mind. Members of the field service force sat in on design meetings from the beginning to make sure the switches could be fixed easily. Of the $12 million NET spent to develop its first product line, nearly $2 million went for service features. As a result, the complicated switches are notably easy to maintain and repair. The design is highly modular. Replacing a failed component usually takes no tools, not even a screwdriver. It's simply a matter of pulling out one printed circuit board and inserting another by hand.

Finding out which board needs replacing is almost as easy. Thanks to diagnostic hardware included with each switch, NET's central computers constantly monitor the performance of thousands of modules in the field and flag problems automatically. When a customer calls NET's Technical Assistance Center, technicians sitting in front of computer workstations bring up the complete performance history of the problematic switching system, including an analysis that shows which past repairs could be creating present problems.

THE SERVICE FACTORY

With a fair amount of luck, money, and talent, nearly any of NET's competitors might equal the company's achievements in strategy, leadership, people management, and design. But they would have far greater difficulty successfully imitating the element that ties all those other elements together, produces service, and delivers it to the customer—NET's service factory.

For a $100 million company, the infrastructure is awesome. It has four main parts. First come the people—seventy-five field service engineers, plus an elite of 40 engineers at the company's Technical Assistance Center (TAC), and twenty-eight instructors for training customers and NET's engineers as well. Keeping one engineer in the field costs about $100,000 in salary and overhead.

Then there are physical facilities: NET has thirty-five field offices to support the 1,500 or so switches it has installed, plus the TAC and several classrooms. Thanks to remote diagnostics and the TAC, NET can solve most customer problems over the phone. For every one hundred calls the TAC receives, it sends out field engineers only twenty-four times. Thus NET has substantially improved the productivity of its service factory by investing in technology, and by making customers effective co-producers of service.

Equipment is next. Each field engineer carries some $15,000 of test equipment and about $50,000 of spare parts. Most field offices keep "disaster nodes"—or loaner switches—on hand, at a value of $40,000 to $200,000 each, depending on size. Each classroom uses roughly $1 million worth of NET switching gear to give students hands-on experience.

Last and perhaps most important is the Service Information Management System (SIMS), an extensive database NET has built up to keep track of its customers and their service records. SIMS records all interactions with the customer, not only the service history of his equipment, but also every keystroke the engineer in the Technical Assistance Center has used to diagnose the customer's problem. If a call for help has to be switched to another NET employee with a special set of skills, SIMS provides an on-screen summary of previous efforts to solve the problem. The customer doesn't have to endure the tedium and frustration of re-educating every new party who tries to help him. Instead, he is soothed by an environment of apparent understanding and competence. The bill for SIMS: $200,000 for custom software and at least as much for hardware to run the program.

In total, NET has invested $15–20 million in plant and equipment for its service factory. In addition, it spent about $14 million in 1988 on salaries and other expenses needed to keep the factory running. Although the company offsets some of those expenses by charging for training and service, the investment costs have been so great that NET is just beginning to break even on service operations. These are heavy numbers for any company. It's doubtful that NET's competitors have the will—or the wherewithal—to ante up.

It's also doubtful they have the discipline. To build its service factory while keeping customers satisfied, NET did something few companies have the guts to do: it throttled back on sales growth. The company has a firm policy of making sure the infrastructure—people, offices, equipment, information—is in place before shipping switches to a new geographical location. Thus it built the service factory ahead of sales growth, not behind it, the way most companies do. That tactic doubtless cost NET lost revenues in the short run, but it also bolstered the company's reputation for unmatched service.

Even supposing competitors had the will, wealth, and discipline to go up against NET's infrastructure, most of them would find they had entered the game too late. As we suggested above, NET has established a self-perpetuating advantage and pushed its competitors into a position of self-perpetuating disadvantage. Thanks to its service factory, NET can charge customers a premium, which it reinvests to keep building the factory and to make it more efficient. Competitors, meanwhile, have no justification for premium prices and probably will never be able to build factories as efficient as NET's (unless they receive windfalls through merger or acquisition). In contests like this, infrastructure can be the deciding advantage.

NET has triumphed by building a well-oiled service factory. But isn't it a special case? Does NET's approach to building a service infrastructure have anything to teach an airline, an appliance manufacturer, or an insurance company? Surprisingly enough, it does.

HEAVY INVESTMENTS

When most people think about the economics of service, they think of people-intensive businesses with relatively low levels of capital investment. But while it's true that service operations employ lots of people, the infrastructures needed to provide service also make those operations surprisingly capital-intensive. One exhaustive survey of pure service businesses, from restaurants to electrical utilities, has concluded that "services equaled or exceeded manufacturing in capital intensity."[5] Granted, the survey

---

[5]James Brian Quinn, Jordan J. Baruch, and Penny Cushman Paquette, "Technology in Services," *Scientific American,* vol. 257, no. 6 (December 1987), p. 52.

results were skewed by the inclusion of utilities, airlines, and similar businesses that provide service mainly by enabling customers to share the use of hugely expensive equipment. Yet even more classically people-intensive service businesses—restaurants, retail stores, insurance companies—showed formidable levels of capital investment, much of it devoted to substituting technology for labor.

The lesson for customer service in both manufacturing and service industries is that infrastructures are a major cost. When setting up customer service operations, simply hiring and training platoons of people and sitting them down before a bank of telephones won't work. It's also necessary to sink serious money into the infrastructures they need to do their jobs economically and well—powerful computer systems for keeping track of customers, a network of field offices, inventories of spare parts and repair equipment.

The driving force for making those investments is the cost and difficulty of using people alone to produce customer service. Varian, a company that supplies equipment for manufacturing semiconductors, estimates that it spends $100,000 to train a single field service engineer. While training costs in other, less technical industries run much less, they're still significant—and they're unavoidable. Trying to make employees productive without training them thoroughly is a sure route to disaster. The untrained auto mechanic can't fix cars right the first time, the untrained department store clerk can't tell customers where to find merchandise, the untrained cashier drives customers crazy by taking forever to complete a credit card transaction.

Training is hardly a quick fix. New employees frequently need months and even years to become maximally productive. Until they do, they'll take longer to repair equipment or to move a customer through a check-out line. They won't understand products and services deeply enough to explain them to customers. Every "moment of truth" with a service neophyte is probably a moment when precious reputation—and future sales dollars—are lost. Thus to the extent that infrastructures can make service employees more productive—and reduce the need to hire new employees—they cut both the expenses of hiring and training and the costs of lost sales.

Infrastructure costs themselves can be reduced by paying attention to the other elements of service. A service strategy that segments customers according to their need for service and their competence to perform self-service can enable a company to drastically reduce the extent of its infrastructure. For example, Amdahl Corp., which enjoys high ratings for the service it supplies to users of its mainframe computers, has controlled the size of its infrastructure by offering at least three levels of service, depending on customer needs and abilities. Those who need instant service but don't wish to provide it themselves buy on-site service, where an Amdahl field engineer works full time at the customer's site. Other customers whose needs are less urgent rely on Amdahl's repair centers, which dispatch service engineers on request. Large customers who can justify the up-front expense send employees to Amdahl's service school and use them instead of Amdahl's field force to perform periodic maintenance and repairs. The more the customer is willing to tolerate delays and to produce his own service, the less Amdahl charges. It has matched its costly service capacity with demand by segmenting customers, and so it has avoided sinking more and more money into its infrastructure in a doomed effort to provide every customer with instant service.

In addition to segmenting, many companies drive to reduce the underlying costs of their infrastructures. Here's where people policies and product design can play crucial roles. A major infrastructure cost, for example, is inventories of spare parts. After all, not having enough spare parts in the field is a quick and easy way to destroy the quality of customer service. Among the reasons for BMW's plunge from sixth place in customer satisfaction in 1986 to eleventh place in 1987 was that owners of the 325e model were more likely to experience "service delays due to lack of spare parts."[6] Yet keeping every repair shop stocked to overflowing is an expense no company can afford.

[6]Power Report, August 1987 (J. D. Power, Westlake, California).

More training and smarter design can have dramatic effects on spare parts inventories. In the case of electronic equipment, for example, inexperienced service engineers often drive up the size of inventories by playing replacement roulette with spare parts. Not knowing what's wrong with a failed system, they blindly swap out components until they get the system to work. Frequently over one third of the supposedly defective components that they return to the factory work just fine. Though the customer may be happy with the repair, removing perfectly good components drives up the size of inventories required in the field and forces the supplier to retest the good parts before reshipping them. Personnel policies that produce better-trained, more seasoned field engineers are one way to combat this hidden problem of mistaking good components for bad.

Another way is clever design. The diagnostic hardware that NET and other makers of high-tech equipment tuck into their products can pinpoint the exact locus of a failure before the field engineer leaves his office. The engineer needs to carry only a few components from office to customer site, which reduces spare parts inventories. And he doesn't waste time playing replacement roulette. Diagnostic hardware increases the number of service calls he can make, and thus the effective capacity of the infrastructure. Effective design also eschews excessive complexity. While products designed to be highly serviceable may seem complex, like NET's switches, they are never so complex that a company's service organization can't repair them.

ECONOMIES OF SCALE AND SCOPE

Like factories that churn out physical goods, service factories often exhibit significant economies of scale—they can produce incremental service at marginal cost—and of scope—they can handle new types of service at something close to marginal cost. Those economies can become powerful advantages for companies willing to spend heavily on customer service infrastructures before their competitors do.

Consider Sabre, the American Airlines computerized reservation system that many travel agents use. American was early to market with its system, designed originally to improve service to the airline's own customers. To defray the huge costs of setting up and maintaining Sabre—the system represents more than $1 billion of investment—and to persuade travel agents to accept Sabre computer terminals, American recruited other airlines to use its system. American soon discovered that the incremental costs of handling reservations for travelers' other needs, such as rental cars and hotel rooms, were negligible, so it added those services as well.

Now Sabre handles so many transactions that American can price the service very low and still turn a handsome profit. Although competitors have created at least four similar systems, only one of them—United Airlines' Apollo—is anywhere near as successful as Sabre. All the rest, forced to compete with Sabre's awesome economies of scale and of scope, have faltered. Even Texas Air, the hyper-aggressive holding company that has become the largest domestic carrier by gobbling up other airlines, has failed to crack Sabre's stranglehold. Texas Air simply got to the market too late to counter Sabre's self-reinforcing growth. It's the same for many other businesses, like distribution companies that create computer networks to handle ordering from their suppliers and delivering to their customers, or providers of computerized databases, who can add new services at almost no cost. There's room in the market for one and maybe two companies, but usually that's all. By the time latecomers join the fray, the early leaders are so far out ahead, and their costs have dropped so low, that there's no contest.[7]

Unfortunately, setting up effective infrastructures usually means putting up with losses for years. NET expects its service factory to break into the black for the first time in 1988, nearly five years after the factory started up. Amdahl Corp.'s infrastructure took nearly a decade to start generating profits instead of losses.

[7]See Peter Petre, "How to Keep Customers Happy Captives," *Fortune*, September 2, 1985, p. 42 ff.

When First Interstate Bank, the nation's largest super-regional bank, began to use automated teller machines, each ATM transaction cost twice as much to handle as a transaction with a human teller, and ATM costs didn't drop below the teller level for years.[8] Citibank, of course, suffered a similar drain when setting up the ATM network that has helped make it the most powerful consumer bank in the United States.

The economies of scope in a customer service infrastructure aren't so broad that companies can hope to take on a large number of different customer segments. Service infrastructures are tightly coupled to the market segments they serve and seldom work well for substantially different segments. The service infrastructure of a company that sells computers to business users, for instance, seldom can offer top-notch service to engineering users because their needs are so different. The Men's Wearhouse, a California-based men's clothing store, guarantees that it sells many of the same clothes upscale retailers do at significantly lower prices. Men's Wearhouse locations and inventory are attuned to the budget shopper. Efforts to provide good service to more upscale customers are doomed to fail unless the company revamps its infrastructure from the ground up (or, even better, creates a separate infrastructure for the upscale customer, as Honda did by creating the Acura division). In fact, infrastructures are so customer-specific that students of service assert the only way companies can realize economies of scope is to develop "new core services to be sold to the existing market segments," not to new ones.[9]

A MIGHTY FORTRESS

Business theorists often say that the size of a barrier to market entry is measured by how much a new entrant must pay to

[8]Mard Naman, "Competitive Banking," *San Francisco Business Magazine,* April 1, 1986, p. 16.

[9]Donald Cowell, *The Marketing of Services* (William Heinemann, London, 1984), p. 130.

achieve parity with the existing market leader. But in the real world, few businessmen seem to know what that number is. As a result, companies frequently jump into new markets ill-equipped to overcome the barriers their competitors have erected. That's especially true when the primary barrier is a service infrastructure, rather than a manufacturing investment or a market position. It's the rare strategist who sees how important customer service is to market success and how large the bill can be to create a service infrastructure.

Look again at NET. The company was able to bootstrap itself into the market for private switching gear partly because its products had certain technical advantages. But an equally important reason was that no direct competitor had yet constructed a service infrastructure. If one had, NET would have had to match the competitor's investment in order to succeed. And if the competitor had been in the market for a while and had invested, say, $20 million in infrastructure, NET's original investment of about $6 million, or 25 percent of its equity, would have been woefully inadequate to achieve substantial market share. The company would have been out-serviced at every turn by a competitor with radically lower costs of service.

Intel was able to weather the customer service mistakes it made in microprocessor development systems because of its forbidding infrastructure. The company had invested heavily in applications engineers to help customers design systems around Intel microprocessors. It had spent millions to set up customer training centers around the world, each one equipped with hundreds of thousands of dollars of computer gear. Competitors who entered the market late never had much of a chance. Either because they didn't understand how much a comparable infrastructure would cost, or because they just couldn't afford it, none of them except Motorola was able to penetrate Intel's defenses.[10]

Or look at Frito-Lay. The main reason that company dominates

[10]See William H. Davidow, *Marketing High Technology* (Free Press, 1987).

the market for salted snacks—potato chips, tortilla chips, and so forth—isn't its broad product line or the millions it has spent on building a brand image. It's Frito-Lay's distribution system, which enables the company to trounce competitors by providing unmatched service to smaller stores. "It would be awfully hard to start a Frito-Lay system today," says W. Leo Kiely III, the company's senior vice president for sales and marketing. "You must have an efficient organization for delivery and a network of plants close to the outlets. That kind of distribution system is hard to duplicate."[11] Unilever, a global giant in detergents and products for personal care, enjoys a similar bulwark against competitors. As Sharon L. Morgenstern, Unilever's consumer service manager, explains, "We have moved into an era where consumers expect service. It makes a difference if there is service behind a product, especially in the case of new products. Smaller companies moving into new markets are at a disadvantage because they don't have the infrastructure to back it up."[12]

It isn't just consumer product companies that barricade themselves behind heavy investments in infrastructure. One reason why no company has made lasting inroads against Boeing, the world's largest aircraft manufacturer, is that company's massive service factory. Boeing fields 2,000 phone calls and telexes a month from 400 airlines around the world. It pumps out thousands of pages of documentation and notices to the airlines on how to do their job better. In all, the company employs 2,000 people and uses a gaggle of computers to keep its products running well. At headquarters, "[service] engineers work at long, orderly rows of militarily stark metal desks. . . . Another room is a library filled floor to ceiling with maintenance manuals. In yet another, typists work at computer keyboards, methodically logging the telexes and sending replies. If the problem is a faulty toilet, it goes to [an] assistant who handles payloads; if it involves landing gear, it goes

[11]Interview with W. Leo Kiely, senior vice president, sales and marketing, Frito-Lay, Inc., October 23, 1987.

[12]Interview with Sharon L. Morgenstern, consumer service manager, Unilever, October 23, 1987.

to the engineer in charge of 'flight control.' Information worth keeping goes into Boeing's data bank."[13] Obviously, competing against Boeing's infrastructure takes megabucks.

SALVATION BY TECHNOLOGY

Spending big on infrastructure isn't enough; service leaders also spend smart. They seize every reasonable opportunity to invest in labor-saving technology.

Much of that technology slashes infrastructure costs by improving the quality and availability of the information employees need to produce service. Digital Equipment Corp., the world's largest maker of minicomputers, equips its disk storage units with self-diagnostic hardware that detects declining performance and automatically alerts DEC's service organization. DEC sends a service engineer to fix the disk drive before it fails. The customer doesn't suffer a catastrophic failure that could bring his computer system to a total halt. And DEC improves the productivity of its service organization since it can send out service engineers to maintain disk drives during slack times, when they have no urgent calls.

American Express also relies on technology to boost the productivity of its infrastructure. The dozens of computer systems at its regional operations centers include sophisticated database systems that automatically spit out customer information when the customer calls and thus increase the chances that an employee can answer an enquiry on the first call. MaryAnne Rasmussen, an AMEX vice president, says, "We strive for productivity but don't do it by saying 'hurry up and get the next call.' Instead, we put in place systems that allow you to service the customer in a split second."[14]

Technology frequently enables customers to co-produce service. The diagnostic hardware in NET's switches helps the cus-

[13]Laura Parker, "Boeing Monitors Health of Its Aging Jumbo Jets," *The Washington Post,* December 25, 1986, p. A3.

[14]Interview with MaryAnne Rasmussen, October 16, 1987.

tomer fix the equipment by himself, with telephone advice from NET experts. Xerox and its competitors equip their copiers with self-diagnostic circuits and display screens that detect malfunctions and show users how to repair them. That investment in technology saves millions of service calls annually.

THE TIES THAT BIND

Infrastructures are most effective when they're designed to serve particular segments, when they fit tightly with the expectations, needs, and abilities of the kinds of customers a company attracts. Such specialized infrastructures are bulwarks against competitors who try to enter your market with their existing infrastructures. But they also can be powerful constraints. Highly specialized service factories act to unite company and customer in an economic bear hug. Once a customer has invested time in learning to deal with a service infrastructure, especially one that requires him to play an active role in producing service, he's reluctant to switch to a different infrastructure. By the same token, companies that create infrastructures optimized to particular segments find themselves in a pickle when their markets change or when they drive to serve new markets. They're stuck unless they spend heavily to change their infrastructures, which can mean starting from the ground up.

AT&T is a prime example. Its infrastructure was optimized to serve residential customers in every corner of the country. Thanks to regulation, customers were forced to use a homogeneous set of communications services, and AT&T developed a specialized infrastructure to support just those services—monumental databases showing which equipment was installed where, huge warehouses that stored spare parts and remanufactured faulty equipment, fleets of repair trucks. Then technological change and deregulation transformed the market. Customers began buying non-standard equipment from companies other than AT&T and installing it themselves. Geographical responsibility for service was split among the BOCs, the Bell operating companies. Instead of an asset, AT&T's old infrastructure became a liability. The BOCs had to shed thousands of repair people and cut back on their warehouse operations. With all the "foreign" gear customers were buying, the operating companies no longer knew which equipment was installed where. They had to devise new service commitments to their customers, with different responsibilities and prices. Customer service often suffered as the BOCs struggled to revamp their infrastructures. Even today AT&T's transformation is incomplete.

Or consider Shouldice, the specialized hernia hospital we discussed in chapter 3. Shouldice's infrastructure fits the needs and abilities of its customers as closely as a surgical glove. The buildings are designed to encourage exercise and social gatherings, both of which promote healing. Patients take care of themselves to a large extent, cutting Shouldice's costs and building their own sense of autonomy. The doctors, having performed thousands of hernia operations, seldom make mistakes, and the operating rooms constitute a hernia repair production line. This infrastructure enables Shouldice to offer what is undoubtedly the world's best service for hernia patients. But would the hospital's service factory be as effective for other kinds of patients? Almost certainly not. Although Shouldice has considered performing related kinds of operations, it has always turned down diversification for fear that it couldn't render the same quality of service it gives to hernia victims.

Building an infrastructure is something like building a battleship—it costs a bundle, you can't switch to another design halfway through construction, and the final product locks you into a particular strategy. So, when planning infrastructures, it's important to make them as appropriate and as flexible as possible. Looking closely at customer expectations and needs, as well as company capabilities, are obvious ways to ensure a good fit. More subtle is the matter of how willing and competent the customer is to participate in producing service. Co-production usually saves money, but it can't be imposed willy-nilly. Customers are more or less willing to help themselves depending on the image, price, and complexity of a product or service. Differences in customer competence also shape appropriate service factories. A fancy restaurant catering to naive diners needs to provide much more help—explanatory menus, patient waiters, simplified place settings—than a restaurant for the cognoscenti. NET's infrastructure works well for that company's skilled, competent customers, but it would be disastrously inappropriate for, say, small businesses.

Infrastructures need to be as flexible as possible because of the classic difficulty of matching service capacity and service demand. Using outside contractors to provide swing capacity can be a relatively easy way to achieve flexibility. NET, for example, signs up third parties to service its switching equipment in remote areas where the company itself has too few customers to justify investing in its own field office. (To ensure quality, NET screens the outsiders carefully and requires that they take three weeks of training.) Another solution is to use customers as swing capacity. Hotels gain flexible capacity by placing minibars in their rooms. Come evening, a customer can get a drink without taxing the capacity of room service, which tends to be strained right then because other guests have ordered hot meals.

Since it's difficult to build infrastructures that are flexible enough to accommodate fluctuating demand, most companies with extensive customer service operations strive to shape demand to fit their infrastructures. Peak and off-peak pricing are the usual tools. Airlines, hotels, and car-rental agencies offer special rates on weekends, when demand from businessmen is low and they're stuck with idle capacity. Computer companies offer different levels of response times and different hours during which service is available, pricing these services according to the burden they place on the service infrastructure (slower service during off-hours is the cheapest kind).

INVISIBLE INFRASTRUCTURES

Certain infrastructures that are essential to customer service have nothing to do with field offices, inventories of spare parts, or fleets of repair trucks. Instead, they consist of the information that a company gathers about its own activities and about its customers. Investments in information can be just as much a competitive edge as investments in a physical service factory. The possessor of a solid information infrastructure is able to personalize dealings with customers, speed the delivery of service, and adjust service offerings to changes in customer preferences well before competitors catch on. And the right kind of information, intelligently organized, can lock in customers more effectively than any other kind of infrastructure.

Again, consider NET. The company took several years to bring up its SIMS database, which records everything about the locations, configurations, and service histories of the company's switches. Now that SIMS is running, the effectiveness of NET's remote diagnostic service is much greater, for details about system characteristics and prior repairs give valuable clues as to what has gone wrong. NET's customers are pleased both with more accurate diagnoses and with more personalized attention. Since engineers at NET headquarters see a complete history of the customer's problems as soon as he calls in, they give the impression of providing more caring, attentive service.

Information infrastructures are the linchpin of customer service in industries characterized by large numbers of relatively small transactions, such as financial services and retailing. K-Mart, for instance, intends to use superior customer service based on information systems to pass Sears, Roebuck in sales and market share by 1991. The company is spending $1 billion on its plan. Some of the investment will go for updating K-Mart's point-of-sale terminals so they can read the bar codes on merchandise and instantly supply the sales data needed to adjust inventories. The intended result: fewer stock-outs of hot items, which will doubtless increase customer satisfaction. K-Mart is spending another chunk of its $1 billion on a satellite network to link its stores to headquarters, enabling the stores to speed up credit authorization and shorten waiting lines.[15]

[15]"K-Mart's New Strategy: Concentrate on Core Biz," *Crain's Detroit Business,* vol. 3, no. 41, October 12, 1987, Section 1, p. 14.

Some information infrastructures that aren't marvels of high technology are nonetheless quite effective. Companies like Marriott, Nordstrom, and Alcott & Andrews, a chain of specialty clothing stores for the professional woman, all make clever use of information to personalize their service and build customer satisfaction. Salespeople at Nordstrom and Alcott & Andrews keep detailed notes on their customers' tastes, backgrounds, wedding anniversaries, and family birthdays. These "personal books" enable the sales clerks to give their customers more intelligent recommendations, and even to remind them when members of their families are expecting gifts. Marriott is using notes on its customers to construct profiles of their needs and expectations that will allow the hotel chain to create new services.

The most powerful information infrastructures are those that become an integral part of the customer's business, the way American Airlines' reservation system has become a lifesaver for travel agents. Distributors like Bergen-Brunswig, American Hospital Supply, and NAPA—the National Automotive Parts Association—have tied themselves to customers by giving them computer terminals hooked into the distributors' mainframe computers. In some cases, customers use the terminals simply to speed up ordering and to keep abreast of delivery schedules. The most sophisticated systems, however, keep track of all the customer's sales and inventories and automatically reorder items that are running low. Once customers come to rely on these systems and to appreciate the superior service technology makes possible, they almost never take their business elsewhere. To do so would entail great inconvenience and high costs for learning to deal with a new distributor's system.

DISTANT INFRASTRUCTURES

Frequently an infrastructure for customer service doesn't belong entirely to the company that produces the core product or service. Airlines use travel agents. Makers of washing machines rely on appliance stores. John Deere, Caterpillar, and all automobile companies use dealers. For a great many products and services, intermediaries provide the bulk of customer service. If they do a good job, customers tend to praise the core product or service. By the same token, when the intermediary fails, customers normally blame the company whose name is on the product or service, not the organization that sold it. Thus word of mouth about a company often depends on third parties that the company controls only in part.

Manufacturers that want to provide great service through quasi-independent channels of distribution go to great lengths to support—and co-opt—their channels. Deere and Caterpillar have built deep and lasting relationships with their dealerships, many of which have been in the same family for generations. In exchange for steadfast financial and marketing support, the dealers offer loyalty. When Deere, for instance, launched a problem-plagued line of four-wheel-drive tractors, its dealers came to the rescue. Rather than blaming the company for saddling them with a shoddy product, they placated customers with an endless willingness to fix the dud machine. Deere lost hardly any market share because of its blunder.[16]

Inspiring the loyalty of independent channels and helping them produce outstanding service can be tricky. Manufacturers and their dealers have a basic conflict of interest: they're both scrapping to squeeze a profit from the same sales dollar, and that conflict often looms larger than their common interest in satisfying customers. Manufacturers that are truly dedicated to service go to great lengths to ensure their intermediaries will take care of customers. They pick and choose them as carefully as they select their own employees, making sure that would-be dealers have the capital and the skills needed to produce outstanding service. They refrain from over-distributing their products, which could cut into dealers' profits. They provide elaborate support for dealers—computerized communications with headquarters, extensive service

[16]Milind M. Lele with Jagdish N. Sheth, *The Customer Is Key* (John Wiley & Sons, 1987), pp. 164–165.

equipment, unceasing training programs. In effect, they make their intermediaries part of the corporate infrastructure.

Companies that deliver outstanding service through third parties often go over the heads of their intermediaries to establish direct contact with customers. The tool they use is information. General Electric, for instance, binds consumers more closely to itself by giving them critical information they need to use GE appliances more effectively. GE's Answer Center in Lexington, Kentucky, comprises a database of some 750,000 answers to common customer questions, a bank of toll-free telephone lines, and 250 permanent employees, all of them dedicated to solving customers' problems the first time. The Answer Center is a way for GE to get closer to the hundreds of thousands of small customers that buy products through GE dealers. Procter & Gamble, General Motors, and scores of other companies that use indirect channels of distribution have made similar investments in centralized information centers.

NEVER ENOUGH

Building an infrastructure is a task that never ceases. Sales growth creates inexorable pressure to expand the service infrastructure. Technological change constantly threatens to render existing infrastructures obsolete and inefficient. Competitors are always on the prowl to out-service your company by investing more heavily and more intelligently in their own infrastructures. Given all those forces, it might seem that building an infrastructure is like throwing money into a pit that yawns ever wider the more cash it swallows.

Companies that produce outstanding service strike a precarious balance between over- and underinvesting in infrastructure. They time their investments so that sales growth and the growth of the service infrastructure leapfrog each other slightly. Intel, for example, used a four-part classification—A, B, C, and D—to guide its investment in field offices. D offices were one- to two-man service operations that did too little business to make money; C offices broke even; A offices were very profitable; and the Bs fell somewhere in between. Intel geared the growth of its service operations to demand for service, which was a function of sales, by opening no new offices when it had too many C and D operations. Companies like NET use third parties to provide service until demand at a particular location is high enough to justify setting up a company-owned field office. Whatever way a company chooses to pace the expansion of its infrastructure, sales growth and service capability will be slightly out of phase. The key word is slightly: service capability that seriously leads or lags sales is the sign of a poorly considered investment strategy.

Until recently, technological change in service infrastructures tended to be gradual. United Parcel Service, for instance, succeeded for many years with a low-tech infrastructure whose primary features were clever methods for consolidating pick-ups and a fleet of trucks specially designed to minimize the time a UPS driver spends locating and unloading packages.[17] But as service factories have come to depend more on information technology, the pace of change has quickened. UPS, under pressure from Federal Express's investments in information systems, has been forced to make major new investments in computers and communications networks. In New York City, Citibank got a jump on competitors by becoming the first consumer-oriented bank to offer an extensive network of automated teller machines. Now that other New York banks have responded with their own ATM networks, Citi has spent some $30 million to replace its old terminals with new, more versatile models, and to build up a network of ATMs located in supermarkets.[18] In short, the more an infrastructure depends on information systems, the faster it must change, and the more investment it will absorb.

Given the huge costs of infrastructures, and their dramatic economies of scale and scope, it's important to know when *not* to invest. There's little sense in trying to outspend a competitor with a much larger and more efficient service factory unless it's abso-

---

[17]Kenneth Labich, "Big Changes at Big Brown," *Fortune,* January 18, 1988, p. 56 ff.

[18]Alan Breznick, "Citibank the Impregnable," *Crain's New York Business,* vol. 3, no. 38, September 21, 1987, Section 1, p. 15.

lutely necessary to the survival of your business. Consider Borden, which holds a healthy 14 percent of the salted snack market. With a network of ten regional potato chip companies that run a combined fleet of 3,000 delivery trucks, the company might seem to be strong enough to go toe-to-toe with Frito-Lay. But Borden has no such intentions. Frito-Lay's infrastructure is simply too strong, and its service levels too daunting. As direct owner of some 10,000 delivery trucks, Frito-Lay has an intensity and breadth of coverage that would take Borden many years and many millions of dollars to match. So Borden has decided to focus on distribution channels such as supermarkets, where it suffers less of an infrastructure disadvantage.

PRINCIPLES FOR BUILDING INFRASTRUCTURES

Infrastructure is the backbone of customer service. Clearly, no company can deliver service without building a service factory. And thanks to economies of scale and scope, the few competitors that possess the most efficient service factories also possess a self-reinforcing advantage.

Investments in infrastructure are always heavy, and they're usually much heavier than naive managers expect. Some of the burden can be shifted by hiring third parties that already have infrastructures in place and that rent them out to different manufacturers. But that's just a stopgap solution for any company that intends to control its own destiny, bind itself closely to customers, and achieve a competitive edge through service. In the end, scrimping is no solution, and service cheapskates almost always lose out. The keys to erecting an efficient, affordable service factory are to make sure all the elements of service are in place, and to plan the growth of the infrastructure meticulously.

When creating infrastructures, keep in mind three principles:

1 / *Plan for the long haul.* Very few investments in infrastructure begin to show a positive return in less than three years. Even five years of negative cash flow isn't unusual. So building an infrastructure calls for deep pockets.

Of course, there are many ways to manage and moderate this investment. Third-party service organizations often can be used to handle locations where volume is too low to justify a full-blown field office. Information systems and electronic hardware almost always reduce levels of investment in physical facilities and levels of spending for service employees. The size of the infrastructure needed to meet a given level of demand can be reduced by offering customers different tiers of service and charging less for tiers that burden the infrastructure less.

The lesson is simple: Don't underestimate the amount of investment your infrastructure requires. Underinvesting may permit a smart competitor to push your company into an eternal game of catch-up.

2 / *Match the infrastructure to the customer.* The more a service factory reflects the needs, expectations, and abilities of the customers it's supposed to serve, the more effective and efficient that factory will be. More effective because the factory will do a better job of meeting and exceeding customers' expectations; more efficient because the customized factory is streamlined, and because it helps customers co-produce service.

One measure of how tightly an infrastructure is tailored to the customer is whether that infrastructure would suit quite different customers. If it would, then it's probably not well matched to the customers you're trying to serve. NET's service factory does a great job for large companies that use a lot of communications, but it wouldn't do much for residential telephone customers; Shouldice's infrastructure works well only for hernia victims, not for people with gallstones; Frito-Lay's service factory meets the needs of smaller grocery stores but gives the company little advantage among giant supermarkets.

Tightly tailored infrastructures have a hidden advantage. If they meet customer needs and expectations uniquely well, customers are happy to pay whatever premium is needed to fund the first-rate service factory.

3 / *Leapfrog the growth of sales and service.* It's impossible to match exactly the demand for service that sales create with the supply of service that infrastructures make possible. One always

leads or lags the other. The gap gets dangerous when it grows too large. When sales explode, the service factory breaks down as frantic employees scramble to deal with far more customers than the infrastructure was designed to handle. When the infrastructure mushrooms far faster than sales, it will gobble up all a company's cash, and then some.

The secret is timing. When sales threaten to overwhelm service, get the sales force to lay off until the growth of the infrastructure catches up. Otherwise, their very success will tarnish your company's hard-won reputation. When the infrastructure has mushroomed so much that the company is awash in idle capacity, turn off the money faucet until sales create enough demand to take up the slack. It's impossible to achieve perfectly balanced growth; frequent little leapfrogs will do just fine.

8

Keeping Track: Measurement

Measurement is both the last and the first step in producing superior service. There's little sense in creating extensive measurement systems until all the other elements of service are in place, until there's something to measure. But drafting an effective strategy—the first step toward better service—is difficult without some measure of current service performance.

Measuring service performance or quality is quite different from measuring product quality because service is an experience. The best measurement systems focus on three different aspects of service: process, product, and customer satisfaction.

The challenge sounds impossible to meet. Every year more than 14,000 employees of American Express's Travel Related Services (TRS) Company—the AMEX division responsible for charge cards, travelers checks, tours, and other services—come into contact with some 29 million customers around the world. The workers field over 21 million telephone calls, 5 million letters, 311 million requests to authorize charges, and 650 million transactions.[1] That's nearly 1 *billion* moments of truth annually. The vast majority of them require quick, accurate reviews of complicated accounts, both of card members and of businesses that accept the American Express card, some of them on the other side of the world. Many of these service encounters are problematic, fraught with potential for disaster. Customers who call or write TRS seldom do so unless they're puzzled or irate to begin with. Each decision to reject a charge can outrage a card member, each decision to authorize a charge can sock TRS with a loss. Collecting from delinquent debtors is especially hard to accomplish with grace. What bill collector can make a deadbeat feel better, not worse, about the company that's doing the dunning?

Yet despite the volume and potential difficulty of its customer contacts, the Travel Related Services Company has achieved a matchless record. Its service is leagues ahead of what the competition produces, according to students of the charge and credit card industries.[2] Customers clearly agree. TRS's core service isn't a particularly good deal for customers: compared with Visa and MasterCard, the bank-sponsored cards that are its main competitors, American Express charges higher annual fees and requires immediate payment. It has signed up far fewer retail establishments than the bank cards. Yet American Express's card operation has been growing at better than 15 percent a year and retains over one fifth of the $200 billion U.S. market for charge and credit card transactions.[3] A big reason, independent surveys say, is that the company has soundly beaten Visa and MasterCard in ease of use and prestige.[4] It's not just card members who prefer American Express. Businesses that accept plastic—"service establishments," or "SEs," in AMEX lingo—rate TRS above the competi-

[1]MaryAnne Rasmussen, "Service Quality: Our Most Strategic Weapon," *When America Does It Right: Case Studies in Service Quality* (Institute of Industrial Engineers, 1988), pp. 105–113.

[2]See, e.g., *The Nilson Report* and Michael Weinstein, "American Express Is Voted First Among Equals," *American Banker Consumer Survey*, 1987, pp. 54–56.

[3]Patricia Winters, "Credit Card War Looms," *Advertising Age*, March 16, 1987, p. 84.

[4]Michael Weinstein, "Consumers Give High Ranking to American Express Card," *American Banker*, September 21, 1987, pp. 1 and 60.

tion because it authorizes charges faster and rejects fewer requests for authorization.[5] To get such superior service, businesses are willing to pay a commission of up to 5 percent on their sales, far more than Visa and MasterCard charge.

How does TRS stay ahead of the pack? As you might expect, the company has a service strategy sharply focused on caring for its customers' travel and entertainment needs. American Express is so closely identified with the idea of security while traveling that U.S. citizens who find themselves in trouble abroad are more likely to turn to the local AMEX office than to the U.S. Embassy.[6] TRS has intimate knowledge of the markets it serves. It researches customer needs exhaustively in order to create a wealth of new services, such as the Global Assist program, which refers card members traveling in foreign countries to local doctors and lawyers, or Enhanced Country Club billing, which reports details of the month's charges on a few sheets of paper rather than forcing card members to plow through stacks of jumbled receipts.

American Express is so sensitive to the need for focused strategy that it has divided its customers into several different segments and devised unique service programs for each of them, based on whether they hold a regular, Gold, Platinum, or Optima card. By creating separate organizations to serve those segments, the company has been able to optimize its operations much as Shouldice Hospital does. American Express doesn't offer day-and-night travel agent service to the holders of regular cards, who fly four times a year, on average. But customers with Platinum cards, who typically fly twelve times a year, can book reservations through American Express anywhere, any time. Employees in the TRS groups that deal with holders of the different cards follow different procedures and get different training; people in the Platinum card division, for example, sometimes visit the poshest restaurants and hotels to gain first-hand knowledge of how their customers live and how they are likely to use the Platinum card.

[5]Paul S. Nadler, "Banks Must Charge Off Authorization Woes," *American Banker,* August 10, 1987, pp. 4–5.

[6]Rasmussen, "Service Quality: Our Most Strategic Weapon," p. 106.

American Express obviously understands the principles of leadership, training and motivation, design, and infrastructure and their roles in producing outstanding customer service. Chairman James D. Robinson III is fond of saying that his company's success depends on four factors: quality, quality, quality, and quality. Robinson and other top managers review the quality of American Express's service every month, and TRS publishes a glossy annual report entitled "Quality Assurance and Customer Service." The report is more than window dressing. Besides reviewing everything TRS has done in the previous year to improve service, from creating quality circles to investing in new technology, it contains a dozen charts showing how well the company's six geographic divisions have performed against standards for accuracy and timeliness in processing applications, bills, payments, changes of address, and requests for replacement cards. Although TRS pushes responsibility for customer service far down into its organization, a quality assurance team from headquarters works with the company's thirty operations centers around the world to review and improve their methods.

Employee training is constant—TRS's training bill in 1987 came to $40 million—and normally includes cross-training for other jobs and "up-training" for better ones. The variety of motivational programs TRS uses to keep its workers turned on is mind-boggling, extending well beyond the Great Performers program we described in chapter 5. The U.S. Consumer Card Group alone uses sixteen different employee recognition programs, from passing out gift certificates to workers whom managers spot going beyond expected performance levels, to selecting an employee of the month who gets $100 in travelers checks, a reserved parking space for the month, and a photo portrait that's displayed near the cafeteria.

TRS makes massive investments in the infrastructures needed to support outstanding service. In 1987, for instance, the company poured some $300 million into technology. A computer program that scores card members' account activities and behavior patterns allows TRS to minimize unnecessary contact with low-risk customers and custom-tailor its communications to reflect a card member's creditworthiness. The Authorizer's Assistant, another computer program, automatically responds to charge authorization requests by reviewing a card member's recent charges and suggesting an appropriate decision to the human authorizer. (TRS estimates that Authorizer's Assistant helped slash bad judgments about authorization by 75 percent.)

RIDING HERD ON
MILLIONS OF MOMENTS

The key to TRS's mastery of millions of moments of truth is the way the company measures service performance. Although American Express has a long tradition of producing extraordinary service, it started slipping in the 1970s. The company was growing very fast, doubling its business every three years or so, and it had underinvested in systems to support that growth, especially for its burgeoning international operations. Shaky quality meant unhappy customers, which meant lost revenues and higher expenses. So in 1978 American Express decided to develop better methods for ensuring service quality.

The result was a learning process that hasn't stopped. When the team charged with improving quality began studying TRS's Phoenix, Arizona, operations center, a test bed for AMEX's quality improvement efforts, everything seemed up to par. All the center's departments were meeting their performance objectives, pushing paper right on schedule. Yet customers weren't happy. Then it dawned on the team that customers don't care whether internal operations are performing well; they care only about getting the service they want. Ray Larkin, a member of the quality improvement team, recalls: "What we realized was that we had been looking at service all along through the wrong end of the telescope. We had been measuring the work of individual departments; and individual departments were, in fact, performing well ... people were doing a good job at their individual tasks. But the customer does not care about individual tasks. The customer cares about end results. . . . That realization in and of itself was the first big step in our quality transformation process. We called it our enlightenment phase."[7]

"Enlightenment" led to a sweeping reform of TRS's approach to quality. With the help of McKinsey & Co., the management consulting firm, American Express redefined its card services to focus on discrete transactions that customers could see and that TRS could measure. Instead of looking at each separate activity needed to replace a lost card, for example, AMEX started looking at the process of replacing cards as it cut across departments—in short, as the customer saw it. After defining these basic service outputs from the customer's point of view, the quality team did some market research to establish what characteristics of those outputs really mattered to customers. Like British Airways, AMEX confirmed its suspicions—customers cared deeply about timeliness and accuracy—but also discovered, to its surprise, that customers cared just as much about the responsiveness of employees, about their ability to act knowledgeably, caringly, and politely.

The next steps were straightforward. Using its market research, AMEX developed an elaborate set of service standards, such as replacing lost cards within two days and getting bills to card members within three days of closing the books. Larkin's team helped the Phoenix operations center redesign its activities and restructure its organization to match up more closely with the customer's view of service; instead of one accounting department, they created separate operations for billing card members and for paying service establishments. They set-up quality circles and launched a blitzkrieg of internal communications that included "everything from posters, buttons, and cartoons to highly visible progress charts showing a department's statistical improvements."[8] A videotape entitled "Quality—I Take It Personally" proclaimed the new creed, and so did "Tickets to Quality," slips of pasteboard given to employees that bore the signature of Chair-

[7]Raymond J. Larkin, "The History of Quality at American Express," speech delivered to the American Productivity Center Quality Forum, New York, N.Y., July 14, 1987.
[8]*Ibid.*

man Robinson and the message, "Quality . . . You're Part of It, I'm Part of It . . . I Take It Personally."

Seeking some general metric for product quality that would be equivalent to the scrap rate or reject rate in a factory, Larkin's team zeroed in on "avoidable input," the time-consuming, frustrating inquiries that the operations center received whenever some aspect of its output confused customers or failed to please them. Tracking "avoidable input" led to many reforms. When TRS noted that lots of card members got in touch because of their confusion about charges they had incurred overseas, the company started sending frequent travelers a booklet explaining the cultural and legal peculiarities of making purchases abroad. "Avoidable input" about foreign purchases dropped quickly.

Transforming the Phoenix operations center took a full year. AMEX needed another two years to roll out the new quality program to each of its worldwide operations centers. By that time the company had made stunning progress. Over the three-year rollout period TRS as a whole improved the quality of its service delivery by 78 percent, according to the new service standards, and reduced costs per transaction by 21 percent. Over the last ten years, the quality program that started in Phoenix has added hundreds of millions of dollars to AMEX's bottom line.[9] In light of those results, AMEX has had no difficulty extending the quality assurance program that started in card operations throughout its highly diversified business, from travelers checks to insurance and securities brokerage.

Today's Service Tracking Report (STR), American Express's monthly summary of performance, probably is the most thorough and sophisticated quality analysis produced by any customer service organization. The measures are specific, demanding, and tailored to the special circumstances of each operations center. (In Japan, where customers tend to have higher expectations than elsewhere, the local standard for processing new card member applications is half again as fast as the standard that prevails in most parts of the world.) The Service Tracking Report gives man-

[9]Larkin speech.

Total Customer Service

agers at all levels, from Chairman Robinson on down, a customer's-eye view of operational problems wherever they occur. And since a big part of every employee's compensation is tied to achieving the standards, the system has teeth.

Even the exhaustive STR was not enough for quality-obsessed managers at American Express. No matter how elaborate and finely tuned to customer concerns, the report depends on American Express's measuring its own performance. Self-measurement is vulnerable to all sorts of errors. Market research, for instance, may indicate that replacing most lost cards within two days is an appropriate service standard, but certain groups of customers can and do feel differently. Besides, the STR is bound to fall short as customers' needs change and as competitors' innovations modify customer expectations.

To capture the impact of its service on customers' attitudes and behaviors, and to ensure that the STR stays on track, AMEX began in 1986 to perform follow-ups on some 12,000 transactions a year, interviewing customers shortly after they have dealt with the company to discover their satisfaction with the encounter and the impact it's likely to have on their future use of the card. As one TRS officer explains it, "[C]ustomer satisfaction surveys accomplish what the rest of our methodology does not. They bring us closer to the Cardmember . . . and—most importantly—do not wind up on the shelf. They wind up providing the specific actions necessary to improve present levels of service delivery and new ideas for added or enhanced service programs. They are a leading edge quality-assurance tool."[10]

IT'S HARDER THAN YOU THINK

Reading about American Express's Service Tracking Report, anyone who has run a factory or a manufacturing business may

[10]MaryAnne Rasmussen, "Ensuring Quality on a Worldwide Basis," speech given to the American Productivity Quality Forum, New York, July 14, 1987.

react by shrugging his shoulders and muttering "So what?" Setting up standards for the different phases of a production process, measuring achievement of those standards, and making regular reports is a time-honored way of controlling quality in plants that turn out physical goods. Even the follow-ups that American Express performs with its customers may seem banal to seasoned plant managers. After all, isn't that just like the practice of tracking a product's defects or breakdowns once it leaves the factory and reaches the customer's hands?

Not at all. Analogies between quality control in factories and in customer service operations may be easy to make, but they're highly misleading. For one thing, the objectives of a service quality program have to be different because service quality as a concept is different from product quality.

The basic aspects of quality in a physical good are the object's conformance to specifications and its fitness for use. It's fairly easy to tell if a car door doesn't close solidly or if a barbecue grill is so poorly designed or manufactured that it's liable to break after a few cook-outs. When shopping for cars or barbecue grills, a customer can reach some conclusions about the product's quality simply by looking at it or by pantomiming the actions he would go through when using it—say, raising and lowering the cover of the grill. Academics call these easily gauged traits "search properties," since customers can size them up to a large extent while searching for a product and before buying it.

Customer service possesses few search properties. You can't size up the quality of customer service that comes with a washing machine until you have bought the machine and gone through the experiences of installation, use, and breakdown—or lack of breakdown. You may reach some tentative conclusions about the quality of service on an airplane flight by checking out the length of lines at the ticket counter and the freshness of paint on the aircraft, but you can't really make a judgment without participating in the entire cycle of airline service, from checking in and taking off to landing and collecting your baggage. When buying subassemblies, a corporate customer can readily measure the quality of sample parts before signing a contract, and even try to gauge the supplier's service by asking other customers. But promises of good service remain just that until after the contract is signed and deliveries have begun.

The majority of traits that determine service quality in the customer's mind require experience with the service. In one of the few pieces of research on the subject, professors from the marketing department at Texas A&M University conducted twelve focus-group interviews with customers around the United States, asking them to discuss their perceptions of the quality of service rendered by retail banks, credit card issuers, securities brokerages, and product repair and maintenance operations. The focus groups generally agreed on ten attributes of service quality, ranging from tangibles, such as the physical facilities and the other customers visible at the service site, to responsiveness and competence. As the researchers observed:

> Only two of the ten determinants—tangibles and credibility—can be known in advance of purchase, thereby making the number of search properties few. Most of the dimensions of service mentioned by the focus group participants were experience properties: access, courtesy, reliability, responsiveness, understanding/knowing the customer, and communication. Each of these determinants can only be known as the customer is purchasing or consuming the service. . . . Two of the determinants that surfaced in the focus group interviews probably fall into the category of credence properties, those which consumers cannot evaluate even after purchase and consumption. These include competence (the possession of the required skills and knowledge to perform the service) and security (freedom from danger, risk, or doubt). Consumers probably are never certain of these attributes, even after consumption of the service.[11]

Since most attributes of service quality are so closely linked to customers' experiences, you can't do a final inspection for service quality in the absence of customers. Thus setting up service standards and monitoring variations in service production, just as companies monitor variations from a set of technical standards

[11]A. Parasuraman, Valerie A. Zeithamel, and Leonard L. Berry, "A Conceptual Model of Service Quality and Its Implications for Future Research," *Journal of Marketing,* 49 (Fall 1985), pp. 41–50.

when manufacturing a product, is a myopic way to control service quality.

To complicate matters further, customers weight the attributes of service quality differently according to their expectations. Partly because of all the advertising American Express has done, card members expect more responsiveness than they do from, say, Visa. If a customer loses both cards and American Express replaces its card in two days while Visa takes three days, the customer may well downrate American Express for inferior service and praise Visa's "superior" responsiveness. From a technical point of view, AMEX's service was superior; according to the experience and expectations of the customer, it was second-rate.[12] The same dilemma of differing expectations confronts any customer service operation. The attributes that matter most to Mercedes customers differ from the attributes that matter most to Hyundai buyers.

Since service quality consists of a bundle of experience qualities weighted by customer expectations, classical, product-oriented quality control programs are impotent. If that seems like an extreme statement, think again about the distinguishing characteristics of services:

- ✓ In contrast to goods, they're intangible—they can't be stored and they can't be inspected at some time after they're produced.
- ✓ They're delivered to the customer at the same time they're produced, so it's hard for workers to inspect their work before it's shipped. If the clerk at the ticket counter doesn't smile when producing a service, there's no way to add the smile later on.
- ✓ The customer usually plays a role in the production process, which means that controlling service quality entails controlling customer behavior, a thorny job at best. Incompetent customers can doom service to be incompetent, as banking customers do if they make no effort to understand banking procedures.
- ✓ The production of customer service usually relies more heavily on the worker's behavior than on any system of machinery. Since a person's behavior can vary radically depending on how he or she feels, you can't control service production just by imposing stan-

[12]See Richard T. Garfein, "A Company Study: Evaluating the Impact of Customer Delivery Systems," *Journal of Services Marketing,* vol. 1, no. 2 (Fall 1987), p. 23.

dards. You have to get employees to internalize a set of norms that allow them to respond flexibly and effectively to customers, which is why outstanding service companies have such strong cultures (see chapter 4).

PROCESS, PRODUCT, AND SATISFACTION

Despite the serious difficulties of measuring and controlling the quality of customer service, service leaders have figured out ways of doing it. Generally, they use three different metrics: *process* measures, *product* measures, and *satisfaction* measures.

The most primitive measures focus on controlling the process of creating service. American Express monitors how long its operators take to answer the phone, how quickly they respond to customer inquiries, and whether the operator can resolve a problem without passing the customer on to somebody else. NET and other suppliers of electronic equipment monitor how long their repairmen take to respond to a customer call and how many repair trips they can manage per day. Every bank pays close attention to the speed and accuracy of its tellers, and airlines that are known for their service, like Swissair and American, have developed extensive standards for how long baggage handlers should take to unload a plane, how quickly reservations clerks should answer their phones, and how fast maintenance crews should finish cleaning an aircraft so it will be ready for the next flight.

Product measures focus on outcomes of the service process that a company can assess without involving its customers. Ideally, product measures summarize the effects of the process from the customer's point of view and are closely linked to customer satisfaction. Most computer companies measure the mean time between failures for their equipment and the mean time to repair broken gear. American Express's Service Tracking Report essentially is a compendium of product measures, and so are the forms that Embassy Suites' housekeeping inspectors fill out when they visit a freshly made up hotel room. When Federal Express uses the standard of delivering all its packages by 10:30 A.M. on the day after they were sent, and when Kraft measures how close its deliverymen come to filling 100 percent of a grocer's order, they do so on the assumption that achieving those goals will create higher customer satisfaction.

That's an assumption, however, that needs to be tested constantly, which is why outstanding service companies incessantly survey their customers' reactions to the experience of dealing with the company. They realize that service quality ultimately is whatever the customer says it is and not just whatever the service supplier can measure. Satisfaction surveys give companies the most meaningful picture of how good their perceived service quality is, and they are a crucial check on the relevance of product measures. When a discrepancy regularly crops up between quality achievement as measured by customers and quality achievement as measured by internal product measures, it's time to change the product measures. Quality assurance analysts at American Express, for example, monitor telephone transactions to check for politeness, tone of voice, accuracy, respectful treatment, and so forth. But AMEX frequently checks the relevance of these measures and calibrates the accuracy of analysts by comparing analysts' judgments of transactions with the judgments of customers, as revealed in post-transaction interviews.

AVOIDING THE PITFALLS

The good news is that process, product, and satisfaction measures can be used to control the quality of customer service; the bad news is that setting up those measurement systems is full of pitfalls. The deepest trap is suboptimization—or, in plain language, the tendency of people to perform to whatever measures you pick at the expense of the larger reasons for measuring things. Remember the K-Mart clerks who were asked to say, "Thank you for shopping K-Mart" to every customer and responded by blurting out "TYFSK"? Or the legions of cashiers, tellers, and sales clerks who lavish customers with the smiles and eye contact that managers are measuring, all the while producing service that most customers perceive as mechanical and impersonal? Process standards are especially vulnerable to suboptimization because they are so narrow, so specific, and so visible. Managers find it easy to push hard on process standards, and employees find it easy to concentrate on nothing else.

The more elaborate the process standards, and the more managers push them, the greater the likelihood of gross suboptimization—and grossly poor service. Before the break-up of the Bell telephone system, companies like New York Telephone had developed elaborate, three-inch-thick policy manuals that specified literally hundreds of process measures supervisors would use to measure work group performance. The complex, functionalized organization of telephone operating companies seemed to make the manuals necessary, and suboptimization was tolerable in the days of monopoly. Once exposed to competition and forced to respond to customers, however, the Bell process measurement system became an enormous liability. Operating company managers gradually realized that getting employees to go by the book made them terrible at serving customers. Public perception of the customer service rendered by telephone companies was epitomized by Ernestine, the character that comedienne Lily Tomlin invented to personify operators. Confronted with an outraged customer, Ernestine invariably replied, "We don't have to care. We're the telephone company."

It wasn't that the Bell system companies didn't care. They cared about the wrong things. As the vice president for quality measurement at U.S. West Communications put it, "the company had very rigid standards of quality—but they were based on management's (and regulators') perceptions of quality. The target of the prescribed levels was internal efficiency . . . customers were told the 'rules' rather than granted the exception. The rules were seen as necessary to maintain control of the vast Bell network of wires— and workers. . . . Instead of focusing on customer satisfaction, management monitored the level of customer complaints. . . . So the 'Bell culture' provided a long list of standards against which employees, managers, and regulators measured almost every step of every task. There was a lot of emphasis on quality—as defined by everyone but the customer."[13] For U.S. West, overcoming its non-quality culture meant reorganizing to manage markets instead of products, services, and territories. Rather than defining quality as "excellent adherence to engineering (or regulatory) standards," the company switched to viewing quality as the satisfaction of its customers, and it started tying management compensation to service quality as customers perceived it.

Of course, process measures are necessary. Every company needs them just to keep track of what's going on. To minimize suboptimization, companies that produce great service counterbalance process measures with a wealth of product and satisfaction measures that keep employees' eyes fixed on the customer. They strive to ensure that the measures they use for process and product aren't self-defeating, poorly structured, or unrelated to customer needs and expectations.

That's a strong contrast to the way most companies operate when trying to measure service quality. In a series of papers, John Goodman of Technical Assistance Research Programs has outlined the wealth of measurement errors committed by customer service organizations for which he has consulted. Among Goodman's most egregious examples:

- ✓ The financial services company that adopted a standard of responding to its customers within 14 to 21 days, although 60 percent of its customers expected 7 day response;
- ✓ The utility that set a standard of meeting 92% of repair appointments, even though meeting the standard meant that repairmen would anger over 3,000 customers a month by not showing up on time or at all;
- ✓ The health insurance company that evaluated managers on how fast they could turn around claims, ignoring the fact that customers don't care about speed if the payment is less than they expect and there's no explanation;

[13]Ed Tharp, "Redefining Quality in an Industry in Transition," *When America Does It Right: Case Studies in Service Quality* (Institute of Industrial Engineers, 1988), pp. 566–567. See also in the same volume, Robert F. Cummins and Joseph F. Riesenman, "Telephone Company Quality Measurement in the Post-Divestiture Era," pp. 543–549.

✓ Another health insurer that labored to provide physicians with extra-fast turnaround, even though doctors only review their accounts receivable every 30 days.[14]

These standards failed because they were unrelated to customer expectations. But the most frequent error made when selecting measures is to focus on averages. Setting up average performance targets appears to make sense because it recognizes the variability that afflicts service production. Companies that strive, say, to ship orders an average of three days after receiving them or to answer the telephone within an average of three rings doubtless believe they have set themselves stringent product and process goals that surely will result in high quality service. The problem is that averages *do* accommodate enormous and possibly quite damaging extremes. Even if the standard is relevant—if customers actually expect three-day shipment—an average of three-day shipment can include many orders that were shipped in one day, incurring expense with no commensurate increase in customer satisfaction, as well as many other orders that were shipped so late that customers became annoyed and started talking down the quality of service.

The problem of averages crops up regardless of whether the standard in question measures time, accuracy, or numbers of customers. In all cases the average can conceal vital extremes that managers need to know about. The solution is to set standards in absolute terms, to require that all orders leave the factory within three days of receipt and to leap with fury on any deviation from standard. Again, American Express is a model. Its Service Tracking Report measures how often the operations centers achieve absolute targets, such as two-day card replacement, and sets 100 percent achievement as the standard.

[14]John A. Goodman, "Working Paper: The Bottom-Line Implications of Upset Customer Expectations and How to Meet Them" (Technical Assistance Research Programs, June 1983); John A. Goodman, "Working Paper: Issues in the Development of Valid, Actionable Satisfaction Measurement and Incentive Systems" (Technical Assistance Research Programs, October 1985); and John A. Goodman and Arlene R. Malech, "Working Paper: Requirements for the Establishment of Customer Service Standards Which Maximize Customer Satisfaction and Minimize Corporate Expense" (Technical Assistance Research Programs, February 1987).

Structuring the standards carefully isn't enough. After looking at hundreds of process and product measures, we've concluded that even the best ones eventually lead to suboptimization unless they are combined with frequent measures of customer satisfaction. It's not just that employees tend to do exactly what the measures tell them to do, ignoring the purpose of the measures, or that the measures are designed primarily to serve the needs of internal operations. Rather, all measures are imperfect representations of customer expectations because they don't get inside the customer's head. Even reasonably close representations eventually drift out of alignment with expectations because those expectations keep changing in response to advertising, competition, and experience. A system for measuring the quality of customer service that doesn't include large doses of feedback from customers isn't an effective system.

Once again there's a pitfall. As Goodman and others have noted, most companies tend to address customer satisfaction by analyzing complaints and by conducting sporadic random samplings. Complaints fail to give an accurate picture of customer satisfaction because most customers who are upset with your service don't complain (and almost nobody who's satisfied pipes up). Random samplings are misleading for another reason. They may accurately represent the population of a company's customer base, but they don't represent a fair cross section of customers who have dealt with your company recently. For that reason, random samplings are essentially popularity polls that measure the general perception of a company's service, more or less independently of the service it actually is producing.

The solution is to eschew random sampling in favor of follow-ups on recent transactions, as American Express, Hewlett-Packard, and scores of other service leaders have discovered. Limiting customer surveys to those customers with recent service experience ensures that what's being measured is service performance, not general perception, and it pinpoints service quality problems quickly. The results of valid satisfaction surveys aren't just academic. Toyota dealers, for example, measure satisfaction with their service by calling customers shortly after their cars have left the dealer's shop and asking about the repair experience. The dealers keep track of how they're doing and dispatch service managers to fix any problems. By contrast, Oldsmobile's approach to measuring service quality relies on postcards that new car owners voluntarily send in. Is it any wonder that Toyota has achieved much higher perceived levels of service quality than Oldsmobile has?

MEASURES THAT MATTER

Managers who are obsessed with the quality of customer service normally keep discovering new measures and adding them onto the existing ones. Over time, the number and variety of quality measures tend to mushroom close to the point of unmanageability. That's natural. Customer service quality is so elusive that you can only measure it by successive approximations, much as particle physicists can only show the existence of subatomic phenomena by batteries of subtle calculations. Complex, wide-ranging measurement programs like American Express's Service Tracking Report are common among service leaders. Hewlett-Packard, for example, traditionally measures the quality of its products with two systems. The FURPS system concentrates on the product attributes of functionality, usability, reliability, performance, and supportability. The AART system focuses on the quality of H-P's relationships with customers and measures the company's ability to anticipate customer needs before they become problems, to make available whatever's required to meet those needs, to respond quickly and effectively, and to ease transitions from one generation of products to another. Now H-P is applying versions of FURPS and AART to its field service operations.[15]

All serious systems for measuring service quality run the risk of not being taken seriously. Front-line employees and supervisors have a lot on their minds besides filling out endless reports;

[15]Phil Carter, "Service Quality at the Hewlett-Packard Company," *When America Does It Right: Case Studies in Service Quality* (Institute of Industrial Engineers, 1988), pp. 326–327.

hard-boiled operations managers are innately skeptical of market-oriented satisfaction studies.[16] Simply cooking up a long, rich list of quality measures and baldly announcing them is a sure recipe for failure. Most people won't pay attention to the list and even those who do will gradually stop furnishing the necessary data as they become overwhelmed by daily crises.

Companies that make the measures matter usually pay attention to four tools for implementation. First, they ensure that the measurement programs have strong support from top management. The officer responsible for quality control often reports directly to the chief executive, and senior managers review service quality reports frequently. Second, when developing measures of quality, service leaders seek the help of the employees who will be measured. The Amway Grand Plaza Hotel, for example, asks employees to set their own standards for service (and finds that they pick more demanding ones than managers would ever dare suggest). Thirdly, service leaders strive to develop measurement systems that depend on the information that employees and managers need to do their jobs. Customer engineers at Hewlett-Packard use portable computer terminals to enter data about each repair call they make. Their managers need the data to plan service capacity and to restock inventories of spare parts; H-P's quality supervisors use the same data to measure the quality of service H-P is producing. Companies like U.S. West Communications have even reorganized their operations in order to reflect the customer's viewpoint and to create a closer alignment between the information needed to measure service quality and the information needed to operate the business.

Finally, quality measures take on vibrant meaning when managers close the loop, when they demonstrate the impact of the measures on the company and its employees. Nearly every company that shines in customer service links part of its workers' and managers' compensation to their achievement of quality standards, not just process and product measures but customer satisfaction scores as well. Achievement of quality standards also is

[16]See Carter, *ibid.*, p. 328, and Garfein, "A Company Study," p. 24.

the basis for employee-of-the-month awards and the other motivational programs we examined in chapter 5. In a more negative way, service leaders often close the loop with SWAT teams. When an operations center, dealership, hotel, or branch office falls behind in service quality, the SWAT team descends from headquarters to help local managers work out their problems and improve their scores. Yet another way of closing the loop is to use the results of satisfaction surveys in developing new products, services, and methods of operation.

THE PRINCIPLES OF MEASUREMENT

Effective measurement isn't the essence of high-quality customer service. It can't take the place of having a solid core product or service to begin with, nor is it a substitute for strategy, leadership, motivation, infrastructure, and design. Measurement is only part of the process of achieving quality, as any student of total quality control will know. Without strong support from the top, dedication to zero defects, and some form of quality circles, the best measures will have minuscule impact. In sum, measurement is an insufficient condition for the creation of quality service.

But it is absolutely necessary. Lacking good measures, no company can assess its progress or adjust to changes in customer expectations. No manager can reward employees appropriately, tune his strategy and infrastructure to customer needs, or design products and service delivery systems that support outstanding service. Without valid measurement systems, it's impossible to know what actions are required to improve customer service.

When designing measurement systems, keep three principles in mind:

1 / *Let your customers say what counts.* Most measures are designed by and for the company that uses them. They serve the needs of operations managers and administrators, not the needs of customers, and they ensure that front-line workers will wear blinders. To avoid this syndrome, make customer satisfaction measures an integral part of the measurement system and check

constantly to see that process and product measures are aligned with what matters to the customer. Don't target ten-day delivery when most customers expect next-day service.

2 / *Beware the wrong carrot.* It's a funny thing: people tend to do what they are told to do and what they're rewarded for doing. Unfortunately, they tend to do those things to the exclusion of everything else. Unless you pick individual measures very carefully and design a system that balances process, product, and satisfaction measures, suboptimization is a certainty. Instead of dangling a single carrot, hold out a garden salad of complementary measures.

3 / *Close the loop.* Measurement systems come and measurement systems go, but bureaucracies endureth forever. And they usually view any new measures with a jaundiced eye. The only way to get people's attention and positively affect their behavior toward customers is to make the measurement systems matter. Tie them to compensation, both psychic and monetary. Back them up by promoting managers who exceed the standards and investigating—or "helping"—those who don't. Use feedback from the measurement systems, especially from customer surveys, to develop and promote new processes, products, and services. Eventually you'll persuade the most cynical paper pusher to take notice.

9

Forging
the Ultimate Weapon

———

Sometimes it seems as though organizations that have triumphed by providing superior customer service—Shouldice, Nordstrom, Singapore Airlines, Frito-Lay, IBM, Caterpillar—achieved their preeminence mysteriously. Thanks to luck or divine providence, they just happened to have leaders who believed in service, made the heavy investments needed to realize their beliefs, and created strong service cultures. These companies, given decades to refine their methods and hone their competitive edge, seem naturally to have developed employees who are dedicated to service, core products designed to make service easy, and elaborate infrastructures that give them a decisive advantage in service battles. Managers at less fortunate companies, you may think, can only doff their hats to the service leaders and resign themselves to an eternity of finishing second.

But impotent admiration is both unnecessary and dangerous. As we have tried to show throughout this book, companies that provide outstanding service don't do it by dumb luck. They *manage* to do it. They put into action the six elements of customer service: strategy, leadership, personnel policies, design, infrastructure, and measurement. They trounce their competitors by spending more effort and money on service, and by spending them in smarter ways. They "spoil" customers not from altruism but purely out of self-interest. By leading customers to expect ever better service, and by exceeding those expectations, they build strong customer loyalty. In the same way, they make less able competitors look worse and worse and lose more and more business.

That's why it's dangerous simply to admire the service leaders without taking action. Companies that are content to remain service followers teeter on the edge of a precipice. A few nudges from the service leaders in their industries, a few years of rising customer expectations, and the followers tend to topple. At the bottom of the cliff lies an ocean of vicious circles. There's the vicious circle of employee behavior, where dissatisfied customers vent their rage on employees, who react by producing shoddier service, which only makes customers more dissatisfied. There's the vicious circle of bad word of mouth, where unhappy customers pass around tales of service disasters that feed upon themselves, leading thousands of potential customers to shun the offending company and deny it an opportunity to prove the rumors wrong. There's the vicious circle of infrastructure investment, where service followers find they can't charge enough to pay for service factories that would improve their competitiveness and enable them to charge enough to fund their service factories.

Thus the question isn't whether or when to start striving for service excellence. It's how to do it. And here we have a confession to make. Though we've tried to simplify the elements of producing outstanding service, and their subsidiary principles, putting them into practice is never simple. On the one hand, all the elements hang together. The best infrastructure in the world is little more than a drag on profits if employees snarl at customers. The most elegant service strategy is so much hot air if it's not based on accurate measurement of customer expectations and corporate service performance. The most inspiring leadership can't compensate for a product so poorly designed that it breaks down often and takes forever to fix.

On the other hand, no company striving to improve customer service can implement all the principles of service at once and with equal vigor. The job is too big, too expensive, too demanding of management and employee time. Rushing to enact simultaneously all the principles we've discussed—to transform customer service overnight—is certain to end in failure. And the costs of this failure will be high, in terms of dollars, reputation, organizational disruption, and future opportunities. Few companies are as difficult to turn around as those whose employees have already weathered several failed drives to improve customer service.

Yet the record shows that companies caught in a service slump can recover, and even move to the fore. Remember American Express? In the 1970s, the quality of its service was headed for the cellar. Superheated growth, especially in Europe, had outstripped AMEX's service capacity. So the company revamped its service organization, beefed up its service factory, and installed first-rate systems for measuring customer expectations and satisfaction. Within a few years, AMEX had taken the lead in service quality, a position it has yet to relinquish. Recall Scandinavian Airlines System? Within eighteen months, chairman Jan Carlzon turned a whopping loss into a substantial profit by improving customer service. By redirecting service strategy, exercising leadership, and giving employees broad authority and responsibility for satisfying customers, Carlzon made SAS the businessman's favorite airline for travel within Europe. Colin Marshall, chief executive of British Airways, did much the same for his company. By launching a top-to-bottom training program and backing it up with new systems for evaluating and rewarding performance, Campbell transformed BA's culture. The payoff for his efforts—sharp upturns in customer satisfaction and demand—came in less than two years. Organizations as diverse as Cadillac, Beacon Hotels, Xerox, and National Car Rental have also achieved impressive turnarounds.

WHERE TO START

Planning and prioritizing are the keys to service improvement. What plan to adopt, and which elements and principles of customer service to implement first, depend on four factors: the basic health of your company's operations; your company's competitive position; the elements of service that are indispensable to kicking off a customer service program; and the appropriate mix of easy, short-term wins with more difficult, long-term improvements.

1. Is Your Company Strong Enough to Start?

We're convinced that outstanding customer service is the ultimate weapon in business battles. But we also see that basically unhealthy companies destroy themselves when they mount service offensives while ignoring underlying breakdowns in operations. True, if your core product or service is marginally inferior to the competition's in terms of features, price, and quality, you may be able to compensate with better service. That's exactly what IBM used to do in the 1970s, when its computer equipment cost more to make and offered lower performance than competitive equipment. Despite those disadvantages, customers remained remarkably loyal because they had come to trust Big Blue's service.[1]

But gross competitive inferiority makes a mockery of service. All of General Motors's efforts to improve repair service—its famous "Mr. Goodwrench" campaign—did nothing to raise customer satisfaction as long as GM remained scandalously uncompetitive. It's the same when core services break down. United Airlines gets no mileage from advertising that it's "rededicated to service" when it adds so many seats on its planes to Hawaii, and packs the aircraft with so many people, that passengers can't find room for their knees.

The fact is that sick companies can't afford to play the service game. They usually lack the time and money to train employees to produce outstanding service, and they don't have the continued growth and promotion opportunities needed to motivate those service providers. They can't find the cash to build a service infrastructure. If they somehow scrape together the time, effort, and money needed to improve service, they're simply diverting

[1]Even IBM couldn't use service forever to compensate for inferior products. By the early 1980s, chairman Frank Cary was well on the way to making his company a low-cost producer of leading-edge products.

resources uselessly. Customers are sure to see through the charade.

So, the first step in planning for superior service is to review your company's health. Are your core products and services competitive in features, price, and quality? How about marketing— does your company do a reasonably effective job of getting products into customers' hands? Is your firm doing well enough that it can invest substantial financial and human resources in service? Are employees so alienated by dismal corporate performance and poor treatment that they'll laugh at efforts to improve customer service? Or are they willing to give a chance to a new service program?

A surprisingly accurate thermometer of corporate health is word of mouth, as indicated by the attitudes and satisfaction levels of customers. If valid, independent surveys of customers show that your company is in the cellar, that it has a reputation for doing a much worse job than its competitors, you probably have some basic operational problems to fix before trying to upgrade service. And you certainly will have a long uphill fight, since word of mouth is so persistent and so hard to improve.[2]

If your diagnosis shows basic ill-health, stop now. Don't endanger your company by pushing for dramatic improvements in customer service; they'll only be a whitewash job that quickly flakes away, wasting resources and turning both employees and customers into hardened cynics. Concentrate instead on fixing the underlying problems and come back to customer service after you've succeeded.

But if the examination shows your company enjoys basically good health, read on.

2. Competitive Position and Implementation Strategy

Planning for customer service is largely a matter of prioritizing. Note that you can't choose which elements and principles of service to implement and which to ignore. They all hang together, and

---

[2]See chapter 2, p. 34–35.

achieving outstanding service means implementing them all. But since the task is so large, you have to decide which elements to stress first, where to place the heaviest bets. And that decision hinges on the evolutionary stage of competition in your industry and on the competitive position your company occupies.

As we explained in chapter 1, over time the competitive battleground in most industries tends to shift from the tangible and toward the intangible. In nascent markets, the fight concerns the features of a core product or service. As the market matures and customer requirements become clearer, competitors tend to offer similar sets of features. So they move onto the second battleground, that of price. In time, inefficient producers drop out, and the survivors achieve rough parity in price. Then the battleground shifts to quality. Competitors skirmishing over quality eventually sort themselves out into clearly defined tiers, ranging from low price/low quality to high price/high quality (think of the range of automobiles, from the Yugo to the Mercedes-Benz). Once again, the differences shrink, at least within tiers.

Ultimately, the battleground shifts to customer service. Though in theory the survivors of this conflict will all achieve roughly similar levels of service and lose their differentiation, we know of no market where that has happened. The fourth battleground is so new that most companies which have moved onto it don't yet realize the shift has occurred.

As you can tell, the contest during any one of the first three stages begins with high differentiation and ends in low differentiation, or commoditization. No matter whether the battleground is features, price, or quality, it's always possible to estimate where a market stands in its progress toward commoditization. And pinpointing that position is important to planning for customer service. Markets where differentiation still prevails are those where it's possible to realize prices well above cost. In commoditized markets, however, only slim premiums over cost are available. Thus a market's position on the continuum of differentiation helps determine the resources available to any company for investing in customer service.

Think of the market's degree of differentiation or commoditization as one side of a two-sided matrix. The other side is simpler. It refers to the competitive position of your company, where it stands on the continuum that runs from customer service leader to customer service laggard. The resulting matrix has four cells, and the cell your company occupies will indicate what elements of customer service to stress most.

The worst position is to be a *customer service laggard in a commoditized market.* It's equivalent to being miles behind in a marathon race without the cardiovascular capacity to catch up. In that circumstance, it's probably wisest to execute a fundamental shift in service strategy. By redefining the service segments your company targets and focusing on those whose expectations are closely related to your company's abilities, you effectively redefine the race course. That narrowing of focus may mean abandoning other segments and the revenue they produce. But taking this kind of shortcut may be the only way that service laggards in commoditized markets can hope to move to the front of the pack.

By contrast, companies that are *customer service leaders in differentiated markets* have many options. The biggest danger they confront is their own success. If you sell the most powerful personal computers at a competitive price and lead the industry in service, why worry? The answer is twofold: The market keeps trending toward commoditization, and competitors are scrambling to out-service your customers. To keep them at bay, it's smart to outspend them, often by making heavy investments in infrastructure. The rich are most certain of getting richer when they erect towering, costly barriers to keep out the poor.

By definition, *customer service leaders in commoditized markets* command only a slim price premium for superior service. If they raise prices very much above their competitors' levels, they lose market share. Thus their main reward for providing superior service isn't fatter profit margins, but a bigger slice of the market and larger total profits. To keep a lead, companies in this cell of the matrix probably need to stress elements of service that improve service efficiency and that incur one-time costs which can be spread across a large volume of products (or services). One of those amortizable elements is design for service, both the design of core products and services and the design of systems for delivering service. Another such element is investment in relatively inexpensive kinds of infrastructure, especially databases and information systems that link the company tightly with its customers.

Customer service laggards in differentiated markets often are complacent. Their performance tends to lag that of the service leaders, but it's seldom alarmingly weak unless the service laggard has failed to achieve differentiation through features, price, or quality. With no disaster looming on the horizon, why scramble to improve service? Again, the reason is that markets change, decreasing differentiation. And the service leaders are steadily picking up business from the laggards. Service followers usually have difficulty improving their standing by building infrastructures—economies of scale and scope are hard to combat. But followers often have the time and money to pursue most other elements of service. The elements of service with the most leverage for companies in this position tend to be those that attack myopia directly, mainly stronger leadership and better hiring, training, and motivating of employees.

3. Indispensable Elements

All companies, regardless of where they fall in the implementation matrix, have to pay attention to certain indispensable elements of service. These are sine qua nons, or prerequisites. Unless they are in place, your drive to improve service probably is doomed.

It's senseless to launch a major customer service program unless your company's leaders are deeply committed to it. No organization will make the sustained high effort needed to improve service without clear backing and constant prodding from the top. Besides, starting a service program, then losing interest, does more harm than good. It shows employees that senior management isn't serious. Front-line workers in particular won't pay much attention to future exhortations about the primacy of service if they have put a lot of effort into an earlier program only to see it fail. So the first rule is not to start unless you really mean it.

It's also folly to begin without some sort of service strategy. Beating the drum for service and throwing money at training and infrastructure do no good unless your company knows what segments it's addressing, what those segments expect, and how to set those expectations at levels the company can exceed. While a sharply focused strategy often highlights the need for new spending, it also reveals opportunities to save money and improve service at the same time. Actions such as eliminating marginal products, simplifying product lines, and reducing optional features cost little or nothing, but they can dramatically improve service quality.

4. Easy Wins and Long Campaigns

The best way to kick off a program for achieving service leadership is to show some early, easy, inexpensive wins that demonstrate the feasibility of change. Among these are putting in place systems for measuring service processes, service products, and customer satisfaction. You'll need such information anyway, both to create a service strategy and to use as a baseline for measuring progress. Getting the data, at least to begin with, needn't be a costly or lengthy effort—you can simply listen more closely to customers or hire outsiders to do quick and dirty studies. It's probably not a good idea to start off by closing the loop between service measures and reward systems, by tightly linking compensation and promotion to service performance and customer satisfaction. Until you have implemented a set of measurements, observed how employees react to them, and noted whether customers value those reactions, it's impossible to know if the measurements are appropriate.

Many other organizational actions, however, do qualify as easy wins. One of them is for leaders to begin fostering a service culture. When top managers start dramatizing their concern for customer satisfaction and world-beating service by changing their behavior—by giving customers their home phone numbers, by praising employees who give great service, and so forth—everybody takes notice and starts to feel that real progress has been made. Minor reorganizations and changes in policy—for instance, giving front-line employees more authority to solve customers' problems on the spot—can have a real effect on service quality as the customer sees it, as well as a stimulating effect on company morale. Such wins tend to be nearly free and relatively easy. You can give more power to front-line employees with the stroke of a pen, and most of them will jump at the chance to play a bigger role in delivering service (though middle-level managers may have trouble adjusting to their new roles as coaches instead of bosses).

At least in the early stages, your company may want to create a new executive position, perhaps a vice presidency, with an explicit charter for managing customer service. Whether to do so is a close call, for creating a service vice president carries real dangers. Everyone else in the company may assume they don't need to worry about satisfying customers since "that's Joe's job." Moreover, customer service groups often become corporate ghettos. So it's probably wiser to look for ways to improve customer service without creating a new bureaucracy. Perhaps service can be added to the responsibilities of an existing executive who's responsible for quality.

In some cases, though, there's no alternative. Customer service activities may be so scattered and ineffective that the only way to improve them is to hand that charter to a senior executive with high visibility. That action will show you're serious about service, and it forces at least one group within the company to make customer service its first priority. Over time, however, it's probably best to phase out the service bureaucracy.[3] Once a company fully accepts the service religion, it has scant need for a service ghetto. Satisfying customers has become everybody's job.

As for implementing the other elements of superior service, expect a long campaign. When leaders strive to make service

[3]Some companies will always need a well-defined service organization, especially firms with extensive field operations, like computer makers and car companies. Even for them, though, it's important to spread responsibility for service well beyond its formal home in the service department. One step in this direction, as NET demonstrates, can be to have service and quality assurance operations report to the same person.

everybody's business and to eliminate red tape and bureaucracy, they're pushing profound changes in corporate culture. But cultures, especially strong ones, take years to change. That's also a reason why you can't expect quick results from putting in place new, more service-oriented people policies. Changes in hiring, training, and motivational systems ultimately seek to modify employee behavior. It's an uphill fight against ingrained patterns, and just about the only way to accelerate the process is to fire everybody and start from scratch.

Redesigning core products and services to ease the production of customer service can't be done overnight. True, you can make some incremental improvements quickly—changing the layout of a bank lobby to help customers serve themselves, revising the operations manual that comes with a videocassette recorder. But unless you're willing to obsolete your products or services prematurely, to cut short their life cycles, redesigning them from the ground up usually means waiting until it's time for new models. It often requires two cycles, the first one to learn how to make the product more serviceable, and the second to perfect ease-of-service improvements.

Real-world constraints also set the pace at which your company can build infrastructures and implement full-blown measurement systems. Infrastructures are fixed investments. Their efficiency depends on how much they're used, but it's hard to vary their capacity to match demand. So the growth of infrastructures depends on the growth of demand. While it's wise to anticipate demand a little and to put infrastructures in place slightly before they're needed, only a company with unlimited funds could afford to hatch a complete service factory and have it sit idle until demand catches up.

Complexity controls the speed at which you can implement extensive systems for measuring service production and customer satisfaction. These computer-based systems call for painstaking design. They reach deep into the bowels of business operations and extend far beyond the business to embrace customers as well. Thus they have powerful effects on work patterns and customer relations. To ensure those effects are positive, and that they don't convulse your organization and alienate customers, it's best to implement new measurement systems as a series of small steps spread over many months. And it's necessary to wait even longer for the benefits of better measurement to show up in changed employee behavior and higher levels of customer satisfaction.

WHY TO START

Forging the ultimate weapon calls for near-heroic belief, dedication, and effort. The job takes years to accomplish and costs millions of dollars. Since the elements of customer service form an organic whole, you have to work on them simultaneously, a far more difficult task than attacking each one in sequence. And because a successful customer service program affects every person and every part of your business, driving to improve service means nothing less than driving to transform your corporation from top to bottom.

Is it worth it? Ask the managers of any company that has to compete with Nordstrom or American Express or Acura or Network Equipment Technologies. Ask any salesman who can't get in the door because customers don't believe his company provides good service, or any marketing director who watches in dismay as bad word of mouth shrivels his market share. Ask any chief financial officer as he totes up the costs of product recalls and warranty claims. Ask any chief executive forced to cut prices because his company's customer service is too shoddy to justify a premium. The benefits of producing superior customer service, we believe, far outweigh the costs, and so do the penalties of delivering shoddy service.

Besides, there's no choice. In the long term, service leaders destroy service followers. The only course for managers interested in survival is to forge and master the ultimate weapon.

Index